Engaging with Reality
Documentary & Globalization

Ib Bondebjerg

intellect Bristol, UK / Chicago, USA

First published in the UK in 2014 by
Intellect, The Mill, Parnall Road, Fishponds, Bristol, BS16 3JG, UK

First published in the USA in 2014 by
Intellect, The University of Chicago Press, 1427 E. 60th Street,
Chicago, IL 60637, USA

A catalogue record for this book is available from the British Library.

Upper left cover photo:
Still from *Blood in the Mobile* (2010). Photo: Mark Craemer.
Courtesy director: Frank Piasecki Poulsen.

Upper right cover photo:
Framegrab from *My Iranian Paradise* (2008). Directors: Katia Forbert
Petersen and Anette Mari Olsen. Courtesy: Katia Forbert Petersen.

Lower left cover photo:
Still from *Stealing Africa* (2012). Director: Christoffer Guldbrandsen.
Courtesy cinematographer: Lars Skree.

Lower right cover photo:
Still from *Burma VJ* (2008). Director: Anders Østergaard. Cinematographer:
Simon Plum. Courtesy head of production company Magic Hour Film: Lise
Lense Møller.

Cover designer: Stephanie Sarlos
Copy-editor: Richard Walsh
Book manager: Tim Mitchell
Typesetting: Contentra Technologies

Print ISBN: 978-1-78320-189-1
ePDF ISBN: 978-1-78320-240-9
ePUB ISBN: 978-1-78320-241-6

Printed and bound by Hobbs the Printers Ltd, UK

Engaging with Reality

Contents

Acknowledgements

The direct inspiration to write this book came in 2006 after having been to the cinema for the opening night of Danish director Christoffer Guldbrandsen's documentary film *The Secret War*. It is a documentary dealing with the Danish participation in the American led coalition against terror, in this case the war in Afghanistan. It is a very critical, investigative film, asking questions about the political background for the war and the way the military acts, especially in relation to prisoners and the Geneva Convention. It was not the film in itself that started the project, but the very heated discussions it raised in the Danish public, both on a more national level and in relation to more global issues and involvement. My interest in this incident was further fuelled by the heated debate on what a documentary film is, what a documentary film can and cannot be, in short what the role of documentary is in society.

The project started as an interest in documentary films dealing with war, in particular the kinds of wars Western countries have been involved in in Iraq and Afghanistan since the tragic 9/11 terror attack in New York. To frame the Danish case it became necessary to look into documentaries from other countries, and I decided to compare films from the USA and the UK on war and the War on Terror. However, while doing research on this topic in those countries it became more and more obvious that the broader issue of globalization and the way documentaries respond to, and engage in, global challenges would frame the case of war and terror more clearly.

Hence the book developed into a project on how documentaries engage in global challenges and what globalization means in our present situation. Besides the War on Terror, the issues that seemed the most obvious were the way the global dimensions of politics were described, the challenge of migration and multicultural developments and the environmental challenge. So it became a book about documentary and globalization seen through four different themes and cases and based on examples from three different countries. It is not a book about the global documentary scene as such, but a case study of how global themes are dealt with in selected countries and selected documentaries representing different genres. An important aspect of the book is furthermore to look into the ways in which documentary forms can influence our ways of thinking and feeling about the world, how documentaries as narratives of reality can shape and change social imaginaries of global problems and distant others.

Many of the chapters in this book were presented in very early form at MA level courses for students in my Department for Media, Cognition and Communication at the University of Copenhagen, and for colleagues at our regular research group meetings at this department. I would like collectively to thank my students and colleagues for valuable debates, comments and criticism. Special thanks to my philosophy colleague, Nils Holtug, for critical reading and comments on the philosophical and theoretical parts of the chapter on the multicultural challenge. Many of the chapters have also been presented at international seminars and conferences, for instance Visible Evidence Conferences, The Hong Kong International Documentary Conference, The ECREA conference in Barcelona, the DigiCult conference in Paris and a number of International Conferences in Copenhagen, conferences that have all helped to sharpen the arguments.

Parts of this book have been published in earlier versions, but are all revised and expanded in this book. Part II of the book is partly based on two articles: 'War on Terror – War on Democracy?' in *Northern Lights* (2009b) 7: 29–50; 'Behind the Headlines: Documentaries, the War on Terror and Everyday Life' in *Studies in Documentary Film* (2009c) 3(3): 219–31. An earlier version of Chapter 7 appeared as an article 'Politics Backstage: Television Documentaries, Politics and Politicians' in *Tidskriftet Politik* 9(2): 45–54.

Ib Bondebjerg, Copenhagen, 21 May 2013.

Introduction

Documentaries, contemporary society and media culture

In his book *The Cosmopolitan Vision* (2006), Ulrich Beck differentiates between 'globalization', which he argues is too often seen only as the neoliberal growth of the economy, the market, and the free flow of goods and capital; and 'cosmopolitanism', which he connects to a growing global public awareness of crisis, to a cosmopolitan empathy and a globalization of emotions (Beck 2006: 5ff). Globalization then, is not just taking place behind closed corporate doors or among global political elites, it is present in different forms and shapes in our media and thus our everyday life. The spectacular and horrifying images of the attack on The World Trade Center on September 11, 2001 are symbolic in the sense that those images were immediately circulated in a broad and diverse global public sphere through visual and other media. They were reported and reacted on in probably many different ways, but the incident and the mediation of it signals a new global media age that began in the 1960s but has now been developed further with a new digital speed.

The world as we know it today is still very much a world characterized by huge global divides. Even though the Internet represents a high point in the development of global connectivity, the whole world is far from being connected to the same degree to this emerging global media sphere. Globalization looks very different when seen from New York and from a remote, poor African village. But the media play an increasingly crucial role in letting audiences face and become aware of global problems, and as Beck has pointed out, media *can* play a role in creating a globalization of emotions, empathy and understanding of global issues and challenges. Creating a 'simultaneity of events and knowledge' globally will increase the cosmopolitan dimension of globalization (Beck 2006: 42). Documentary forms of film and television have a special role to play in this creation of both a cosmopolitan knowledge of global challenges and realities, and a stronger emotional understanding of our global others. Documentary film and television claim a special relation to our factual reality, and by circulating stories about aspects of our global reality and to a growing global audience they create new mental frameworks for understanding this reality. Even though the films and television programmes that are focused on in this book are made by directors from a few Western countries, they take us backstage not only in world politics, but also the lives of people in many parts of the world. They tell stories and reveal consequences of global politics and global challenges that have universal dimensions and affect us all.

This book is about documentary films and television in the US, UK and Denmark after 2001 dealing with some of the most central global themes and challenges of politics, conflicts of war and terrorism, the multicultural development in a world of migration and great social and economic divides, and the ecological challenge of climate change. Documentaries come in many forms and genres, but they all deal with contemporary realities, with ways of living, and social and cultural issues that can have strong critical and emotional effects. Media in general and documentary forms in particular thus have a special role in dealing with these global challenges, in making them visible and understandable to us. Often books about media and globalization deal with the news genre, because this genre, on a daily basis, frames our view of the world and the connections between our close and distant reality. But documentary film and television can go behind the scenes and tell human stories that bring identification, emotions and knowledge closer together.

Documentaries can give abstract dimensions of globalization a human and emotional character. The neoliberal discourse and reality behind globalization, the often destructive role of big global corporations, takes on a whole new form when Joshua Oppenheimer's documentary *The Globalization Tapes* (2003) allows us behind this neoliberal discourse and into the reality of Indonesian workers fighting this form of globalization. The everyday life of those experiencing the concrete realities of neoliberal globalization, and the way they try to counteract them, tell us a story that expands our social imaginary and brings distant others directly into our own public sphere and debate. The same effect can be seen in Michael Glawogger's *Megacities* (1998), where our image of life in some of the global megacities is expanded from the usual images of Western modernity and urban culture, so dominant in our mediated images of the global, to a much broader representation of life on the edge in Mumbai, Moscow and New York.

Documentaries can give us images and stories of close or distant global issues and 'others' that are often much stronger than news programmes. News is important as a constant and day-to-day framing of our sense of global issues, but documentaries to a larger degree combine actuality and a deeper background reality, that form global imaginaries and can create cosmopolitan emotions and empathy. This book deals with examples of documentaries, which are part of a growing global awareness of a need to act and think together, and reach towards a more global public sphere. Global dialogue, global solutions and even more so, a functioning global public sphere, is certainly more of a utopian idea than a reality. But even though we are far from living in a global political culture, media and politics have moved us far away from the traditional world of nation states. Globalization is a complex and contested issue, but compared to the world 50 years ago, both our everyday reality and our media culture is much more global, and a global mentality is more and more pervasive in all parts of our culture and society.

Cosmopolitan narratives: documentaries and the global agenda

From its historical beginning, and at least since the 1930s, documentary film, and later television, has been part of the project involving an engagement in reality based on both information, narrative, emotion and creativity. Documentary has also often had a role in developing public debate and democracy on social issues. When John Grierson founded the British documentary film movement in the 1930s and coined the notion of 'creative treatment of actuality' (Aitken 1990), he pointed to forms of engagement with reality in which documentary should expand the knowledge about, and the images of, social classes and cultures in the UK. Although these documentaries also occasionally dealt with aspects of the British Empire, it was to a large degree a national project. Documentaries today are still very much about aspects of a national reality, but the last decade has seen a rise in themes of globalization, and also projects with a broad global agenda and new forms of transnational cooperation.

In 2007, Danish public service broadcaster DR, in collaboration with The Danish Film Institute and the BBC, launched the first of a series of global documentary projects, *Why Democracy?* and in 2012 the second followed, *Why Poverty?* Behind the production of the many documentaries, short films and other media products launched through the two series is an international, non-profit organization, *Steps* (see www.steps.co.za) with a Danish and African branch. Their motto is 'Great stories can change the world' and even though they stress that they are not campaigning for specific solutions, they combine new media and old media in order to create a debate about global issues and reach out to a broad, global audience. In connection with the *Why Poverty?* project they defined their aims as (see www.whypoverty.net/en/about/):

1. To produce narratives that inspire people to think and be part of the solution
2. To involve the best filmmakers in the creation of bold and provocative factual films
3. To bring together broadcasters worldwide and engage with a wide and diverse audience through multiple media platforms
4. To create a global outreach campaign, supplementing the broadcasts with extra teaching materials
5. To engage with decision-makers and influencers to find solutions for change

This project is in many ways an advanced example of the power of documentaries to set a global agenda, to create a broader, cosmopolitan public and debate, and to combine old and new forms of technology and distribution between disconnected parts of an only virtual, global public.

The documentary films were made by, and with the help of, directors, producers and broadcasters from all over the world. The films were broadcast simultaneously by more than 50 broadcasters on all continents, in more than 180 countries – and were made available in many languages. They were also available online on a website immediately after having been broadcast, but since a large part of the world can neither be reached through broadcast or online, the organizers also developed multiple ways of bringing the films out to more remote areas, for instance by mobile cinemas. But this cosmopolitan documentary project is not just interesting because of its advanced collaborative, global and technological nature, or because of the way in which it combines several platforms and types of media. It is also interesting because of the kinds of narratives it creates, narratives that often go to the heart of global conflicts and heated emotional debates. In Karsten Kjær's Danish contribution *Bloody Cartoons* (2007), he follows protests against the Danish newspaper *Jyllands-Posten's* cartoons of Mohammed – with surprising results, almost a kind of cosmopolitan reconciliation (see page 172). In a film like Jehane Noujaim's *Egypt – We Are Watching You* (2007) we follow female activist characters behind the surface and deeper into the dilemmas of a young Arab democracy.

The films behind this truly global initiative represent an advanced form of cosmopolitan film production and agenda setting. A project like this indicates the power of documentaries on global issues in the context of a new digital media culture. They try to create a global public sphere, where formal political structures of a more global nature are often much too weak and haunted by conflicts of interests that are hard to resolve. But most of the films and television programmes dealt with in this book are not part of large-scale global initiatives. They are either programmes from broadcasters that have a reputation for producing critical documentaries with a strong social, political or cultural agenda and story, or they are films coming out of a more independent film culture, with support from both public and private institutions, or more recently forms of crowdsourcing on the Internet or social movements. This book thus deals with both independent documentary films and with large broadcasters like the American PBS series *Frontline*, HBO's *HBO documentaries*, the British BBC's *Panorama*, Channel 4's *Dispatches* or the Danish DR 2's *Documania*.

One very striking example of a single, documentary with a strong global impact is Davis Guggenheim's *An Inconvenient Truth* (2006), which certainly is one of those films that have helped create a global, public agenda around the problems arising from climate change. It was produced by two independents, Lawrence Bender Productions and Participants Productions, but winning an Oscar and getting both Paramount and UIP as distributor made *An Inconvenient Truth* a global success. One of the elements in the film's global success was no doubt Al Gore as the central character and presenter, but as we shall see later (see p. 224f) the film also combines a clear scientific, rational and very empirical rhetorical structure – almost like a classical lecture – with a rather strong emotional visual level and subjective storyline. *An Inconvenient Truth* underlines the concept going back to Grierson of 'creative treatment of actuality' and is an example of how reason and emotion, argument, narrative, word and visuality combine in documentary stories. Al Gore went on a world tour with the film and his book, based on the film, and the film was broadcast on numerous television stations around the world – again an example of the power that some documentaries have in setting a global agenda.

Social imaginaries – global imaginaries

The claim made in this book is that documentary film and television in itself is a very strong element in the forming of social imaginaries, the kind of mental framework formed by memory, everyday life experiences and mediated experiences and stories. Making the further claim that since globalization as a broad social and cultural process has increased in importance in our present day society, it has come to influence our everyday life in a much more direct and visible way than before, and this influences our media culture on several levels. We see it in our daily news coverage and the number of 24-hour channels both on an international and a national level, and, as this book demonstrates, we see it in documentaries that take up central issues with a strong, global dimension. There seems to be a growing awareness of the global dimension in many of the social, political and cultural issues taken up, and it seems easier and more common for documentary filmmakers to get access to places in the global sphere.

Fiction is an important form too, and often fictional films can direct our attention to real-life problems and react to reality in a very direct way. Some of the global issues taken up in documentary films analyzed here have a clear resonance in both Hollywood films and more independent American and European films. This is most certainly the case with war and terror (Prince 2009), for instance Kathryn Bigelow's Oscar winner and very realistic film *The Hurt Locker* (2008) about a bomb squad, or Paul Greengrass' *The Green Zone* (2010) about the absurdity of the political aspects of the Iraq War. Films like this repeat and expand on themes also taken up in numerous documentary films on the same subjects. Likewise we now see some of the popular Hollywood disaster movies dealing with global climate change, like Roland Emmerich's *The Day After Tomorrow* (2004). *The Day After Tomorrow* certainly has all the characteristics of the classical disaster movie, but the main character is a climatologist fighting for his son, his family and the survival of the human race. He tries in vain to warn the political system and urge them to act, but the system will not listen and the disaster unfolds without people being evacuated in time. There is, however, a happy ending finally against all odds.

So the post-2001 documentaries on global issues are not the only critical realist voice of contemporary cinema. A striking number of more independent Hollywood films and an increasing number of European film directors have started to develop global fiction film narratives, also on the multicultural challenge. American-Mexican director Alejandro Gonzáles Ináritu's *Babel* (2006) is a strong film about migration, multiculturalism and the global divides creating conflicts, oppressions and suspicion and misunderstanding among people. In European cinema, multiculturalism, migration and terror are also interwoven in the French Arab director Rachid Bouchareb's film *London River* (2009), about the unlikely meeting between an old black, Arab man and a typical middle-class British woman as they search for their son and daughter in the wake of the 2005 terror bomb in London. A similar film on migration and our multicultural reality is Austrian-born director Michael Haneke's moving *Code Unknown* (2000), about life in a modern European big city, Paris, the parallel hidden lives of immigrants and what it does to our society and the world we live in.

The happy end of Emmerich's global disaster movie is part of the mythology, wishful thinking and symbolic narratives always found in mainstream fiction films. In the real world the challenges of globalization can create an awful lot of talk and very little action. Global challenges very seldom have a happy end, instead they lead to war, terror and social, political, economic and cultural conflicts that cannot simply be solved by heroes and brave rescue teams. The documentary films analyzed in this book bear witness to that and they come up with a lot of questions and critical perspectives and can only very seldom tell stories from real life that strike a more optimistic and positive note. The few examples from both American and European cinema are examples of a much broader trend in which the theme of globalization has clearly entered not just documentary film but also mainstream cinema and the more independent and realistic forms of independent cinema. They indicate that the claim made in this book, that globalization is on our agenda and minds in a much more direct and pervasive way than before 2001, is substantiated not just by documentary films and the media news coverage, but by fiction on a large scale. The narrative of globalization has become part of our general 'social imaginary', which Charles Taylor has defined in his book *Modern Social Imaginaries*:

> By social imaginary, I mean something much broader and deeper than the intellectual schemes people may entertain when they think about social reality in a disengaged mode. I am thinking, rather, of the ways people imagine their social existence, how they fit together with others, how things go on between them and their fellows, the expectations that are normally met, and the deeper normative notions and images that underlie these expectations (Taylor 2004: 23).

Social imaginaries are thus deeply embedded mental frameworks of our social life and the way in which we perceive ourselves in relation to others, and social imaginaries are clearly addressed and can be influenced by media, whether it is the daily news, documentaries or fiction films and TV series. Social imaginaries are not easily changed from one minute to the next; it takes time to move and change ways of living and ways of looking at the reality we live in. But the fact that the globalization issue and narrative is beginning to develop not just in all sorts of media products and political discussions but also in our everyday lives is an indication of the beginning of transformations of social imaginaries in the modern world. Migration and the fact that we are living in a multicultural world is no longer a distant reality, but a fact to be seen in all major European and American cities. Global warming and climate change is no longer pure speculation and theory; we see the results in our own environment, and measures taken to prevent further problems affect our everyday life.

Documentary genres: realities, stories and emotions

We may not think about documentaries every day, but they play an important role in our contemporary society and media culture. They are present as background stories to the 24-hour global news format that is now a fact in most parts of the world both in national, regional and global formats (CNN, BBC World, Al-Jazeera etc). Documentaries furthermore often have their own scheduled place and format on television stations, just as more independent documentaries are produced by film companies and supported by national or transnational public film funds. Documentaries do not always attract blockbuster audiences around the globe, but as the films by, for instance, Michael Moore have shown, documentaries can become a global phenomenon.

The popularity of the documentary genre seems to be on the rise in modern media culture, but documentaries come in many forms and genres. Like fiction, documentaries tell stories of reality, but documentaries have a more direct and authentic relation to the reality they deal with. We expect documentaries to tell us about reality in a truthful way, but we also understand that *the* truth cannot be captured unedited, neither by the journalistic nor the documentary camera. Any documentary story of reality must make choices and select material, perspective and frame – the reality we see on the screen is always an edited reality. But the way the reality is edited follows very different patterns, partly determined by institutional norms, partly by the filmmaker's style and intentions and partly by the story the film wants to tell. Where fiction films can tell basically the same story as a romantic comedy or a romantic drama, documentary films can deal with the same theme in many forms and styles. Documentary films are not just based on factual information, not only journalistic stories of the reality behind the daily news. Documentaries are narratives of reality, powerful human and emotional stories with characters which we identify strongly with or distance ourselves from. Narrative, story, emotion, character, aesthetic and style are just as important for documentary films as they are for fiction films, but some of the same techniques and forms are used with a different purpose.

War is a strong theme in the post-9/11 documentary, and war has always been an important theme in both fiction film and documentary film. But documentary stories of war can have very different formats and focus, and they can call upon our cognitive and emotional responses in different ways. Let us briefly consider three films on the Iraq War: the PBS Frontline documentary *Bush's War* (2008, USA), Errol Morris' *Standard Operation Procedure* (2008, USA) and James Longley's *Iraq in Fragments* (2006, UK). *Bush's War* is produced by PBS and is part of their most prestigious, critical journalistic programme strand Frontline, and the reporter behind the programme, Michael Kirk, is one of the most senior and respected journalists of the Frontline team. The story and form of the programme is therefore clearly the investigative, authoritative documentary, based very much on journalistic ways of telling the story. We have the reporter as voiceover narrator, we have a heavy use of expert witnesses, we have on the ground and eyewitness reporting from battle, and from inside the political arena and military decision machine, we have a rather linear and causal kind of story that follows chronology or causal relations between parts of the chronology. The story gives us a dense, bird's eye view of the Iraq War, from the political decision to go to war, onto the battlefield and to the results of the 'victory' and its consequences on a number of levels.

Errol Morris on the other hand never tells straightforward, journalistic stories, he rarely uses linear storytelling and clear causal connections. He is interested in complexities, the psychological dimensions of the bizarre, the evil, the darker sides of society, politics and human life, and he uses a documentary form that underlines this. He includes uncanny images and music, repetitive montage and even though he insistently asks questions through his films and confront us with interviews, he is not authoritative or investigative in the same ways as the PBS programme. He leans towards a more poetic-reflexive strand of documentary filmmaking, in which the very form, style and montage is an important part of the story. *Standard Operation Procedure* is on the surface about the infamous Abu Ghraib incident, where American soldiers tortured Iraqi prisoners. Other films and television news have looked into this from other angles, but Morris take a deep dive into the soldier's psyche and the images they took of their torture. It becomes a film about human nature and how this plays into a concrete war incident, and by its form and way of addressing this incident, the films explores emotional dimensions behind war and politics.

With James Longley's film *Iraq in Fragments* we move into the more ethnographic, observational form of documentary. Based on two years of research and filming in different parts of Iraq, the film gives us three stories about everyday life in an Iraq split into ethnic and religious groups. The camera follows the life of a fatherless 11-year-old boy in Baghdad, Shiites and Sadr followers in two cities and a Kurdish farmer family. As a documentary this is a film that get us close to the lives of people that often in the global media flow just appear as terrorists, religious fanatics, or strange others from a distant culture and society. Here we get faces and stories, our social imaginary is expanded and we may be able to understand them, even though we may not sympathize with their views and actions. The film moves them a bit away from the distant and strange others and closer to universal dimensions of being human, no matter the social, cultural, ideological and religious background and persuasion.

Mediated reality encounters: documentaries and globalization

In Arjun Appadurai's book of cultural globalization (Appadurai 1996) he defines the term 'mediascapes' as an important part of globalization. Appadurai generally points to the way in which narratives, and social and cultural forms of imagination in modern, globalized societies, are set free from their traditional ritual and institutional forms and are now spreading through the media into our everyday lives. Local, national and transnational stories and images are mixed to a much larger degree, they form 'large and complex images, and ethnoscapes to viewers throughout the world'. They offer 'narrative-based accounts of strips of reality' that can take the form of 'imagined lives' (Appadurai 1996: 35).

Appadurai comes from an anthropological tradition, but also media sociologists like for instance Joshua Meyrowitz (1985) or Stig Hjarvard (2013) have talked about the 'mediatization' of society and culture. The main point of view here is that the media are such an integrated part of modern societies that we cannot understand these societies without understanding the pervasive presence and influence of the media in all parts of society, culture and politics. We use and rely on media when we are at work, when we do our banking, for research and teaching, and we use the media in our everyday life for both pleasure, communication and planning. Both the traditional mass media and the new more interactive forms of digital media are important platforms for, and dimensions in, the increased global connectivity and communication. Encountering distant parts of our globe, meeting others in far-away places, used to be dependent on physical acts and analogue communication. Today we can witness numerous dimensions of a global reality through electronic and digital images and forms of communication. Through various media we can almost instantly experience events and people through a global media sphere.

Mediated cultural and social encounters are thus an important part of the way we live our lives and experience others people and other parts of the world. Documentary film and television are an important part of these mediated, global encounters, because they tell stories of a more real and authentic nature than many fiction films. This book is about these forms of mediated, documentary encounters, about the way documentary film and television respond to and tell stories about some of the major global issues and conflicts that affect us, whether we are in the developed or less developed part of the world. It is at the same time a book about some major issues in globalization, and a book about the forms and functions of documentary in our present media culture. By analyzing how documentary forms have dealt with global issues in many different ways, the book offers a richer and more nuanced understanding of contemporary documentary genres, their expressive and thematic dimension, but it also offers a deeper insight into the ways in which global issues and challenges affect us and our lives.

Outline of the book

Engaging with Reality analyzes examples of documentary film and television from the US, UK and Denmark in the period after 2001 and discusses documentary genres from a cognitive, emotional, sociological and aesthetic perspective. The book combines concrete studies of different documentary genres dealing with a broader, sociological perspective on globalization and the role of media and documentary in shaping our social imaginary.

The book is divided into three main parts, each with three chapters, and a final conclusion of the whole book. In the first part of the book, *Globalization, documentary film and television,* focus is on the concept of globalization as such and the influence of globalization on the social, political and cultural dimensions of societies after 2001. But the focus is also on theories of documentary genres in a sociological, cognitive and aesthetic perspective and on the different forms of social and political documentaries. Chapter 1, *Globalization in a mediated world,* discusses major theories on globalization in general with special use of Appadurai (1996), David Held and Anthony McGrew (1999 and 2000), Ulrich Beck (1992 and 2006), Gerard Delanty (2009) and Joshua Meyrowitz (1985), and main trends in globalization processes after 2001. Globalization is not just about economy and transnational corporations and organization, although this dimension is of course very important. Globalization, to a large degree, also influences the media we watch, and our everyday life, national politics, finances and our environment are no longer just a matter for national decisions and debate. Whether we like it or not, we depend on the global contexts, and no matter how weak global institutions and networks may seem at times, they are very important. The discussion also includes reflections on the relation between documentaries, traditional news reporting and the Internet on issues related to the War on Terror, globalization, the multicultural challenge and questions of the global climate change.

The two other chapters in this first part of the book focus more specifically on documentary genres. In Chapter 2, *Sociology and aesthetics of documentary genres,* four basic modes of documentary are defined and the theoretical discussion of the relation between reality and documentary, between documentary and the viewer is analyzed with reference to the most important documentary theories in the works of Nichols (2001), Corner (1996), Plantinga (1997), Winston (1995) and Renov (2004) and others. In chapter three, *Engaging with and investigating reality: the social and political documentary,* the argument moves from general theory to documentary genres in a historical and contemporary perspective. The chapter traces the historical and development and institutional context of documentaries from flagship television programmes in America and Europe of the 1950s and onward (for instance CBS's *See it Now* or BBC's *Panorama*) and takes a deeper look at formats and tendencies after 2001. Special attention is also paid to the new, independent documentary movements and tendencies in the new digital media culture.

The second part of the book, *War, terror and democracy: the post-9/11 documentary,* deals with the national and global dimensions of war and in particular the so-called 'War on Terror' – a term coined by the American president George W. Bush – after 2001. The analysis compares the political and public debates on war in the US, UK and Denmark, the effects on concepts of democracy and security and compares documentary film dealing with all aspects of war. This part deals firstly with documentaries on politics and war, including aspects of corporate and political interests, secondly films dealing with war in itself and the effects and consequences of war and finally war behind the frontlines and headlines, the effects on everyday life and the population in countries at war.

Chapter 4, *Into the dark side: the politics of war,* analyzes those documentaries that focus on the political dimension and political debates behind the decisions to go to war in Afghanistan and Iraq in the US, UK and Denmark. It also deals with the relation between critical documentaries and the political system in a situation where the War on Terror put strains on public debate and democracy according to several analysts (see for instance Mayer 2008 and Priest and Arkin 2011). Chapter 5, *On the battleground: reporting and representing war,* looks at the many different ways in which documentaries and news reporting has dealt with combat and soldiers in action. But it also shows that documentaries have gone much further than simply documenting combat and war, by focusing on the relation between the battle front and the home front, and the deep psychological consequences of war. Chapter 6, *Behind the headlines: documentaries, war, terror and everyday life,* is about life in war zones and how the image of 'the other', or even the enemy and the potential terrorists, are portrayed. Also here, documentaries show a large variety of approaches, going deep into women's life for instance, or the life and culture of the younger generations growing up in a war zone.

In the third and last part of the book, *A new global order: political, social and cultural challenges*, we shift focus from war and terror as a global challenge to other important themes of globalization. Globalization does not just influence our communication and the way we think and live; it also raises broader questions of global matters in relation to politics, financial markets, social inequalities and cultural differences. Establishing a sort of global order and debate is certainly not an easy task, but documentary filmmakers all over the world have taken up that challenge and their films have become part of a global dialogue. Chapter 7, *Politics and spin in a mediated world*, analyzes documentaries dealing with politicians, political institutions and political processes in a national and transnational context and with examples of documentary projects that use the digital media culture to create a global dialogue. In Chapter 8, *A multicultural world: migration, culture and everyday life*, the focus is on one of the main themes of globalization: migration, and the cultural and social tensions arising from living in an increasingly multicultural world. In Chapter 9, *Risk society: the environmental challenge*, the last major global challenge is taken up and discussed, both in relation to theories of the risk society and climate politics (Beck and Giddens) and through documentaries from all three countries, where this theme has been dealt with in numerous and often very creative ways.

The concluding part of the book, *Cosmopolitan narratives: documentary in the new digital media culture*, raises the broader question of the development and role of the new digital media culture for global communication and understanding. The new digital media sphere makes us part of a communication network that also has elements of a very individual and interactive expansion of earlier forms of mass communication. Social and communicative networks like Facebook or Twitter on mobile platforms have indeed changed the way we communicate with our networks on a personal level. They have also proven to be efficient in some forms of political and other citizen actions. In the last part of the book this global digital revolution is described, and there is discussion of what impact and new possibilities it gives to documentaries dealing with global matters and problems. The conclusion also discusses the documentary and its role in creating a new cosmopolitan dialogue and understanding.

PART I

Globalization, documentary film and television

Chapter 1

Globalization in a mediated world

Globalization is not just about economy and transnational corporations and organizations, although this dimension is of course very important. Globalization, to a large degree, also influences the media we watch, the culture we live in and our everyday life. In a more and more global world our national politics, finances and our environment are no longer just a matter for national decisions and debate. Whether we like it or not, we depend on the global contexts, and no matter how weak global institutions and networks may seem at times, they are very important. The global networks are both formal and informal networks, they can be democratic and public or just private. The period pre- and post-9/11 has seen a huge increase in terror networks, just as these terror networks have been met with counter-measures that some researchers and journalists have characterized as 'top secret institutions' beneath the surface and between intelligence agencies globally (Svendsen 2010 and Priest and Arkin 2011). Global threats and challenges tend to create counter-responses of an equally global nature, at least in some areas, and sometimes these responses can challenge our very notions of democracy, the independence of the media and basic human rights. But global networks are not related only to war and terror, and in the world after 2001 many other challenges on a global level have given already existing global institutions and networks new importance. At the same time the whole development of a global network society has reshaped the way we interact and communicate, and the relationship between old and new media.

The challenge of the global realities has also created a strong development of, and change in, the major theories on globalization in general, and within specific areas of globalization in particular. Globalization has, of course, in some form or other, always been part of both ancient and modern societies through trade, migration, war, conquest, travel, communication etc. But the rise of global communication technologies – first telegraph, cable, radio and later visual and digital communication, are important for the speed and intensity of globalization. The degree to which global processes of a global economy and global politics go hand in hand with global communication indicate the stages of modern globalization and the way we experience it. Just as the basic human rights of freedom of expression and access to information and communication have been central to the development of national democracies and national media cultures, they have also been a central dimension of the debate on global democracy and global governance. In the early stages of modernization and globalization, news and communication travelled slowly and mainly just between the financial and political elites in the highly developed countries. Today, history is broadcast almost instantly when it happens, and even in not so developed countries new mobile technologies can make a difference.

This discussion is connected to issues of global inequalities and the question of hegemony and diversity. The fall of communism in 1989 and the end of the Cold War created a new situation for the 'free flow of information' on a global level. The global reach of satellite television, and digital and mobile communication, further developed the technological infrastructure on a global scale. But technological infrastructures are of course still more developed in some parts of the world than others. On a more transnational political level these kinds of questions and problems have been dealt with in, for instance, the UN, UNESCO and the international commission for a New World Order (NWICO) since the 1970s (see Thussu 2006: 33f). The so-called MacBride Commission Report from 1980 reflected very critical positions to the present state of globalization and to the dominance of superpowers on a global level and in global communication. But although the global dominance of big companies and big communication corporations is an empirical fact, the conclusion that the world is dominated by a political, economic and cultural hegemony is also contested in modern globalization theory.

Critical theory and globalization

One of the strongest and most influential theories of globalization is the critical theory based on studies of the global economy and the global media systems. In many ways, this theory expands the theory of imperialism to modern societies and to the role of global media in a new cultural and communicative imperialism. Typical representatives of this theory are Edward S. Herman and Robert W. McChesney's *The Global Media: The New Missionaries of Corporate Capitalism* (1997), where they argue for a dramatic structural change in the global media culture since the 1980s, from a classical, nationally controlled and defined media system, to a global, commercial system dominated by a group of 30–50 big global corporations. What they argue is that this development undermines a democratic, public sphere, and national and global democracy and citizenship, and brings the media outside democratic and political control. Globalization thus means concentration, commercialization, unbalanced global competition and is seen as a serious threat to political and democratic standards and control. The US–UK case against Rupert Murdoch's News Corporation and the scandal around and closing down of *News of the World* in 2011 based on illegal phone tapping of politicians, celebrities and ordinary people, certainly represents a clear example of the relevance of the arguments put forward by Herman and McChesney. The argument put forward here could furthermore be expanded to the global financial sector as such, where global finance, despite global political initiatives such as the World Bank, The International Monetary Fund or the trade regulation organization GATT, in numerous cases has created instability. As we have seen in the worldwide financial crisis in 2010–2011 there is a huge fight going on between transnational political institutions and the global financial sector. Globalization is challenging our national frameworks, media and politics to a very large degree.

In critical theory the global media are American, and this global dominance is, of course, nowhere so symbolic as in the notion of 'Global Hollywood', which is actually the title of Toby Miller et al.'s book from 2005. Large, global companies have a strong base in the US, and the US has some of the leading software and content industries among the creative media industries (television, film, computer, smart phones etc.). But global companies are dominated by transnational company structures and ownerships and they integrate very different sectors. The strong growth of globalization in the media sector broadly speaking was also a result of the deregulation of this market in both the US and the EU. The European single market, the US Telecommunications Act in 1996 and the WTO Telecommunications Agreement in 1997 (see Herman and McChesney 1997: 110f) clearly paved the way for transnational media corporations and the merging of sectors. The fact that digital production and distribution around 2000 became 'the global communication highway' furthermore increased the merging of global players and sectors in different parts of the corporate media and communication system.

The focus on dominance of the US in the global media and communication sector in critical globalization theory is not just based on financial strength and quantitative dominance in many sectors. Herman and McChesney also talk about the dominance and export of the 'American model' (Herman and McChesney 1997: 137f), that is, the deregulated, market-oriented model. Toby Miller combines the statistics on the world dominance of Hollywood movies with a more qualitative, cultural argument: Hollywood has found a way to speak to the universal, cultural mind of the whole world, accepted by a world mass audience, although sometimes rejected by European intellectuals as a kind of 'colonization of our subconscious' (Miller 2005: 3f). As Miller points out in his book, Hollywood is not, in terms of production of films globally, the largest market. Both Europe and Asia produce more films, but nevertheless the average market share of Hollywood films in 2004 was around 70 per cent in most regions of the world, in some places a little less and in other places more (Miller 2005: 11ff).

The global cultural language of globalization is probably American, although Hollywood and the American creative industries in general today are heavily influenced by Japanese and Chinese money – a sign of changing patterns in the global finance system. But, if we look at the world's global media and communication companies they are not completely American, and they stretch across regions, continents and sectors. Changes occur all the time, but by 2005 the six largest companies were the US-based Time Warner, Disney and Viacom, the Japan-based Sony and the Europe-based Bertelsmann and News Corporation (Rupert Murdoch). Most of these companies own both TV industries and TV channels, radio, film, print media and internet software and also in some instances hardware (Thussu 2006: 98f). They are thus able, at least in principle, to control production and distribution of all types of media and media content in large parts of the world. But as many observers have pointed out (Thussu 2006, Katz and Liebes 1990, Tomlinson 1999 and Appadurai 1996), globalization is not just a one-way street: the global is used and interpreted in a local context. Furthermore, there is clear evidence that new patterns of consumption in the global media context may arise in the digital age where availability becomes more individualized and decentralized.

A cognitive, socio-cultural approach to globalization

In Held et al.'s book *Global Transformations: Politics, Economics and Culture* (1999) they define globalization as part of a continuum from local to global:

> Globalization can be located on a continuum with the local, national and regional. At the one end of the continuum lie social and economic relations and networks which are organized on a local and/or national basis; at the other end lie social and economic relations and networks which crystallize on the wider scale of regional and global interactions. Globalization can be taken to refer to those spatio-temporal processes of change which underpin a transformation in the organization of human affairs by linking together and expanding human activity across regions and continents. Without expansive spatial connections, there can be no clear and coherent formulation of this term (Held et al. 1999: 15).

In this definition of globalization we stay clear of normative, critical-pessimistic or utopian optimistic notions of globalization (Tomlinson 1999: 71 ff). Globalization is a sociological phenomenon in the modern world, but it does not in one fell swoop take away the importance of local and national levels in which we all live at the same time, even though we also live in a more and more globalized world. What Held et al. are discussing and analyzing in their book are concrete, historical and sociological transformations and the intensity, extent and speed of these transformations in areas of national politics, trade, finances, migration patterns, culture and climate.

This sociology of globalization, which points to the fact that we all inhabit different 'life worlds' in any historical junction of modernization and globalization, connects well with the kind of cognitive sociology of the mind that the American sociologist Eviatar Zerubavel has formulated in *Social Mindscapes: An Invitation to Cognitive Sociology* (1997). In his book, he argues for a sociology of the mind that avoids both extreme subjectivism, in which we are all seen as very different in the way we think and live, and extreme universalism, in which we are all very much alike, because modern biology and cognitive neuroscience has found out how much genes and biology mean for us. When studying the mind and the way we live, act, think and communicate it is therefore important to think in a continuum of 'mindscapes' from the individual to the more universal, and to acknowledge the fact that people today live in a 'modern society characterized by its cognitive pluralism (…) that most people nowadays belong to multiple thought communities' (Zerubavel 1997: 17). The foundation of this cognitive, sociological concept of the mind is expressed in Table 1.

Table 1: Scope and agenda of cognitive sociology (Zerubavel 1997: 20)

Cognitive individualism	Cognitive sociology	Cognitive universalism
Thinking as individuals	Thinking as members of thought communities	Thinking as human beings
Subjectivity Personal experience	Intersubjectivity Conventional cognitive traditions	Objectivity Natural or logical inevitability
Personal cognitive idiosyncrasies	Cultural, historical and subcultural cognitive differences	Universal cognitive commonalities

A cognitive, sociological theory like this clearly questions aspects of the critical theory on globalization and the underlying thesis of homogenization and cultural dominance. But at the same time it gives another explanation for the universal reach of many media products, because this kind of cognitive sociology underlines the fact that basically all human beings have the same kind of cognitive, emotional and experiental framework. The cognitive sociology points to social and cultural patterns as a kind of 'unity in diversity': there is both a cognitive universalism and a diversity created by individual and collective experiences and life stories. In recent cognitive film and media research this has been underlined by studies of how narrative structures and basic generic patterns cut across cultures (Grodal 1997, 2009; Anderson 1996; Anderson and Anderson 2005). This theory rejects primitive constructivist theories that have dominated parts of both humanities and social sciences and have been the basis of much critical theory. As Grodal has pointed out, this paradigm has a much too short historical sense of man, and it does not take the biological architecture into consideration: 'For extreme constructivists, minds have only a short history: the product of socialization from birth onward combined with recent cultural history, but not with the long foregoing history of evolution' (Grodal 2009: 3).

But when we look at modern, global societies it is important to remember that globalization is not developed and does not influence individuals and groups of people without entering into dialogue with universal human elements with a very long history, and social and cultural experiences with a much shorter history. It is not difficult to point to differences between a man born and brought up in a primitive rural society in Mali, a man from Berlin who has lived through the fall of the Wall and experienced both a totalitarian communist state and a modern European democracy, and a man from New York, Manhattan, living in Little Italy and with an Italian background. We are bound to find different 'mindscapes' here, but they also share very basic human elements, and they can all in some way understand and relate to a Disney movie or a documentary film on nature and climate. As Grodal points out, 'Within a given culture, many agents interact on the basis of capacities that are human universals, as well as culture-specific or agent-specific schemes, concepts and habitus' (Grodal 2009: 11).

As 'narratives of reality', documentary genres are particularly suited for creating emotional and cognitive connections between individual, group-based and more universal dimensions of reality. If we take the area of migration and multiculturalism in today's more global reality, many images of people with different ethnic, cultural and religious background are generated by the news. Many people may have little or no personal contact and knowledge of people from other ethnic groups or cultures, because our individual and group experience by nature must be limited to those we encounter in our everyday life. Some may live in mixed neighbourhoods, and certainly at work or other institutions an ethnic and cultural mix may exist. But documentaries dealing with this issue, for instance, the Danish *My Denmark* (see p. 199f), can show us the life of others in such a way that we become aware of how much 'strangers' are also 'like us' in many ways, how they have the same dreams, problems and concerns. The universal dimension of global diversity is an important part of a documentary narrative, a dimension where individual or group differences are not removed but put into perspective, and where information and knowledge link cognitive and emotional dimensions.

Complexities of global interactions and media experiences

Unlike the more structural and economy-based theories of globalization that take a more general, critical stance on globalization, theories dealing with media and audiences in a more qualitative perspective have focused on cultural exchange. In Katz and Liebes' book *The Export of Meaning: Cross-cultural Readings of Dallas*, a famous and comprehensive study of the American TV serial *Dallas*, the central argument is that a universal dimension in this serial meets with social and cultural-specific readings in different world audiences. Contrary to theories of homogenization and the 'Hollywoodization and Americanization' of the mind of global audiences, this study of several receiving communities of the serial stresses the negotiation between the local dimension and the global.

Katz and Liebes point to three different explanations for the tremendous global success of this serial:

(…) the *universality, or primordality*, of some of its themes and formulae, which makes programmes psychologically accessible; *the polyvalent or open potential* of many of the stories, and thus their value as projective mechanisms and as material for negotiation and play in the family of man; and the *sheer availability* of American programmes in a marketplace where national producers – however zealous – cannot fill more than a fraction of the hours they feel they must provide' (Katz and Liebes 1990: 5, my italics).

The critique of certain aspects of corporate dominance in the global media culture and societies as such is, of course, not made irrelevant by studies of global meetings between media and audiences. But, they seem to question the cultural homogenization thesis and to underline the kind of argument for the complexities of globalization that can be found in theories combining a cognitive and a socio-cultural dimension. Humans around the globe are not simply brainwashed by globalization and global media; there is an interaction and negotiation going on in global cultural encounters. People can continue living in their local and national context and network, and yet be part of globalization.

The complexity of globalization is also underlined at the more structural level and the level of corporate strategies. 'Think globally, act locally' is the slogan of one of the global channels, MTV, that has managed to reach and sustain a global youth audience (Thussu 2006: 149). In 2006 they had a worldwide audience of 419 million in 164 countries, but the interesting thing is that MTV reached this audience through a strategy where all their channels had certain features in common, but were broadcast in 22 different languages by 122 locally operated stations all over the world, along with a similar broad spectrum of locally anchored websites. As a global player MTV thus adapted to local/national tastes, traditions and cultural trends while at the same time maintaining a universal brand and product.

The complexity of globalization is also sustained by what Thussu (Thussu 2006: 180f) calls 'contraflow in global media'. Although American-Western European dominance is strong in the global media culture, we see both a diversification of global channels and a development of new regional cultures into the global public sphere. Al-Jazeera's 24-hour news channel is perhaps the strongest indication of this development, a development recently boosted by this channel's ability to report from within the 'Arab Spring'. But the pan-Arabic Middle East Broadcasting Centre (MBC) or the Chinese channel Phoenix directed towards the worldwide communities of Chinese speakers point in the same direction. This development has caused both CNN and BBC World to focus even more on regionalization of their new channels, in order to compete with the new regional players – although not always successfully, as the abandoning of BBC Arabic after just two years in 1996 shows.

Global social imaginaries

Just as Zerubavel talks about our multiple social mindscapes, social scientists like Appadurai (1996) and Charles Taylor (2004) have talked about 'social imaginaries'. As Taylor explicitly points out, his concept is directly inspired by Benedict Anderson's concept of 'imagined communities' (Anderson 1983), and his analysis of the rise of the modern nation state and the kind of 'collective identity' created historically as part of this. Like Anderson, Taylor is searching for social imaginaries of modern societies in images, stories and collective social mentalities in areas of both the private and the public. He deals with different social rituals and institutional and communicative forms.

Taylor's attempt to create a mental sociology of the modern world has no broad reference to the role of global media, although images and narratives are seen as important elements in the creation of social imaginaries. But, this is compensated for by Arjun Appadurai's media-centred, though similar, analysis of the processes of global imaginaries in *Modernity at Large: Cultural Dimensions of Globalization* (1996). Appadurai focuses on what he calls the two major ruptures in the 'global now', media and migration, which he defines as clearly interconnected. His project is defined as exploring their joint effect on the *work of the imagination* as a constitutive feature of modern subjectivity (Appadurai 1996: 3). Instead of raising the critical voice towards the global media, and their homogenizing effect on a global population, he focuses on how everyday discourses can be transformed in a rather different perspective:

'(…) they are resources for experiments with self-making in all sorts of societies, for all sorts of persons. They allow scripts for possible lives to be imbricated with the glamour of film stars and fantastic film plots and yet also to be tied to the plausibility of news shows, documentaries (…) electronic media provide resources for self-imagining as an everyday social project' (Appadurai 1996: 3–4).

Appadurai looks at the conjunction of mass migration and the fact that global media have created 'global diasporic public spheres'. People are creating images of possible future lives in other parts of the world, partly inspired by global images and stories, while those already migrated look back on their homeland with narratives combining their old and new homelands. In Appadurai's perspective, globalization is not creating a more homogenized world but a world where social imaginaries are not 'easily bound within local, national or regional spaces' (Appadurai 1996: 4). Furthermore, he is directing our attention to the fact that the same global-American media products can be used very differently by people in different parts of the world, even by 'enemies' of America, like Islamic terrorists using the Rambo figure in their own, social imaginative way (Appadurai 1996: 7). If one master narrative of globalization has been growth, technology and modernization, Appadurai also wants us to focus on global micronarratives in the social and cultural dynamics of the more complex processes of globalization in the 'diasporic public spheres' arising from globalization (Appadurai 1996: 10).

Social and cultural landscapes of globalization

Theories and debates on the social and cultural dimensions of globalization often tend to lack a broader historical dimension and often seem to focus too narrowly on the tensions between national cultures and globalization. But as Held et al. have pointed out, globalization is a constant historical process with different phases stretching back to before 1500, in fact they describe four major periods of globalization: Premodern (–1500), Early modern (1500–1850), Modern (1850–1945) and Contemporary (1945–) (Held et al. 1999: 363 f). In this mapping of the historical periods of globalization it is only in the modern period that nation states become important frameworks for the processes of globalization. An interesting aspect of the historical development of nation states is that in Western Europe and the US, many of the ideologies for the forming of these were based on cosmopolitan and rather universal ideas of culture, politics and social and communicative rights (Held et al. 1999: 328).

But as pointed out by other researchers dealing with the rise of modern nation states (Anderson 1983, Gellner 1983 and Smith 1998), there was also a historical need for the nation state to create a feeling of community and identity around the physical space and within the borders of nation states. This imagined, national community was based on both political, social and cultural institutions and it was a communicative space formed by national media, literature and a whole range of symbols, signs and rituals. National culture became a 'banal nationalism' in the sense that national citizens were part of an everyday culture reflecting social and cultural forms embedded in the national culture (Billig 1995). We also know for a fact however, that national cultures and societies can be extremely heterogenous and that more thick and not so banal forms of nationalism can erupt from time to time and create tensions either internally (towards social and cultural minorities) or externally (against other nations).

In a very simple definition, globalization can be seen 'as the movement of objects, signs and peoples across regions and intercontinental space' (Held et al. 1999: 329). According to Held et al. these processes have always taken place. After the rise of nation states approximately 200 years ago, nation states became important players in, and regulators of, globalization. In the contemporary phase of globalization however, it is exactly this role of the nation states and the national cultures that is challenged in a new way. The intensity and speed of globalization is changing, the global, communicative structures and frameworks are changing, and following this we see institutional transformations on a global level changing the context of interaction between nation states and regions. Appadurai along with Held et al. put strong emphasis on the communicative and cultural dimension of globalization: '(…) the centrality of national cultures, national identities and their institutions is challenged (…) this challenge comes, in part, from the products and meanings of popular cultures and the diffuse and ambiguous cultural field of consumerism and materialism' (Held et al. 1999: 328).

In Appadurai's theory of cultural globalization he clearly rejects both the understanding of globalization as homogenization and Americanization, and the dominating role of the nation states in the cultural processes taking place at the level of media and audiences. In fact, he talks of 'the terminal crisis' of the nation state, the birth of a new type of imagined community called 'the post national imaginary' in which migration and media help create different spaces in a 'diasporic public sphere' (Appadurai 1996: 21). Even though it is probably exaggerated to dismiss the nation states there is certainly reason to look at the new spaces that global media and communication are opening up.

Appadurai talks about six global cultural and communicative spaces through which what he calls 'imagined worlds' are made visible to world audiences: (1) *ethnoscapes*, referring to the representation and communication of tourists, immigrants, refugees, exiles, guest workers and other migrating groups and peoples on the move; (2) *technoscapes*, representing the modern world, not just communication technology but a whole set of things symbolizing progress and modern life; (3) *financescapes*, representing the whole world of global trade, banking and finance; (4) *mediascapes*, representing the very core of global communication and cultural exchange and which are the carriers of many of the symbols and images of globalization; (5) *ideoscapes*, making up the fuzzy world of the Western ideologies and values, the universal set of human rights and all the clashes of ideologies and values between different regions of the world. These different social and cultural spaces in the modern, mediated global culture are all part of a cultural globalization, the creation of an at least fragmented form of global imaginary. This global imaginary is not strong in all parts of the world, and of course is mediated and formed in different ways. But, it is no doubt a sign of what Beck is also talking about when he points to a rise in a cosmopolitan mentality and emotions.

Cosmopolitanism and globalization

Appadurai's notion of cultural globalization incorporates a certain increase in universal imaginary worlds where cultural imaginaries with different backgrounds meet and negotiate. In fact he sees this imaginary world as a kind of global work and social practice: '(…) the imagination has become an organized field of social practices, a form of work (in the sense of both labor and culturally organized practice) and a form of negotiation between sites of agency (individuals) and globally defined fields of possibility' (Appadurai 1996: 31). We are rather far away from critical theories of global, corporate capitalism and dominant media giants using and suppressing the masses. Appadurai takes an ethnographic or anthropological look at global media and cultural globalization, and he is mainly interested in what audiences and individuals do with the mediated, global world they increasingly have open access to. We are closer to a cognitive sociology in which culture is based on active processes related to both individuals, groups and to more universal dimensions of culture.

The discussion on cosmopolitanism raised by, for instance, Ulrich Beck in *Cosmopolitan Vision* (2006) and Gerard Delanty in *The Cosmopolitan Imagination* (2009) takes Appadurai's analysis of globalization into new and more political and social domains. For Beck, the discussion of cosmopolitanism – a historic term with deep roots in Western philosophy and political thinking – is connected to the transformation from the first to the second modernity, a transformation having to do with the fact that 'national borders and differences are dissolving and must be renegotiated' (Beck 2006: 2). This second modernity creates the need for a new cosmopolitan outlook and politics, which he defines through five interconnected and constitutive principles (Beck 2006: 7):

1. the principle of an experience of a global crisis in society resulting in the need for a civilizational community of fate on a global, transnational level
2. the principle of the recognition of cosmopolitan differences and the cosmopolitan character of many global conflicts
3. the principle of cosmopolitan empathy and the ability of cosmopolitan perspective-taking

4. the principle of the impossibility of living in a world society without borders, meaning basically that a united world is a utopia
5. the principle of mélange and the acceptance of the fact that local, national, ethnic and cosmopolitan cultures and traditions interpenetrate, interconnect and intermingle.

Although Beck's definition and analysis of cosmopolitanism may seem to rest on a cultural and social relativism undermining universal norms and principles, he actually makes a strong argument against a radical cultural relativism in a global world. There is both an empirical realism involved in Beck's notion of cosmopolitanism in contemporary society and a more utopian, normative concept which he at one point connects to a notion of 'contextualist universalism' (Beck 2006: 55). What Beck seems to suggest is that cosmopolitanism is the universalism of a globalized world: we have to accept that we are different, that borders, cultures and values can divide us, but also that politics and actions based on universal norms and principles, including respect for others, can form the basis of social, cultural and political collaboration in this global world. Those parts of the book where he becomes very concrete in his fleshing out of cosmopolitanism are, for instance, principles for solving the ecological crisis, the ways in which we regulate global flows of communication, the way in which we deal with citizenship in a global world of multiple identities, how we solve and report on war and conflicts, and how we solve and negotiate problems of mobility and migration.

Media, globalization and the digital revolution

Globalization means faster and more extensive communication between people and regions, but it doesn't necessarily mean a more cosmopolitan understanding on a global scale. In 2005, when the Danish newspaper Jyllands-Posten decided to have a number of drawings of Mohammed on the front page, this was meant to be a national, local communication act, a provocative defence of freedom of speech. The newspaper had no doubt expected some turbulence and criticism, but not the kind of global media event and crisis it became. Within hours the case had spread to global media and escalated into a global crisis, with strong clashes between the Muslim and Western worlds. A local, national event was catapulted to a global public sphere through the Internet and global media networks.

When two planes hit the World Trade Center's twin towers on 9/11 this was within seconds turned into a global event with an immense symbolic power. This was not just a specific attack on two buildings in New York, it was intended, interpreted and received as an attack on Western civilization and, although condemned in most parts of the world, it was also rejoiced at in other parts. This highly mediated event in a globalized world had profound consequences, with the period after 2000 in world politics being very much shaped by the US-defined War on Terror, which also set the agenda in large

Figures 1a and b: Franny Armstrong's *The Age of Stupid* (2009). Pete Postlethwaite as curator of The Global Archive in 2055 – after a global climate disaster. Frame grab. Cinematography: Lawrence Gardner.

parts of Europe, expressed in Bush's words: 'you are either with us or against us'. Dozens of news programmes, films and documentaries have subsequently dealt with this symbolic event and its aftermath. The 9/11 terror attack has become a symbol of the more destructive dimensions of globalization and the role of the media in relation to divisions and conflicts in our globalized world.

But the role of media in globalization and the consequences of a more digital, global media culture also have other consequences. In terms of documentary production and distribution, globalization has certainly changed the landscape. Although documentaries are still anchored in national and regional spaces, they are also increasingly dealing with global matters and spreading along lines that are not just following traditional national lines. When Franny Armstrong made *The Age of Stupid* in 2009 – a film about the global climate crisis – she did so through crowd funding, involving thousands of people on the Internet, and she also used a method of so-called 'indie screenings' for the film, where groups of people acquired the right to screenings of the film. She dealt with a global issue with production and distribution techniques that went beyond the traditional channels and used the global Internet as a platform. As already pointed out, projects like *Why Democracy?* (2008, see http://whydemocracy.net/) and *Why Poverty?* (2012, see www.whypoverty.net) created a global media event on many platforms, and used a documentary format to redefine a global agenda. Very different directors from ten very different countries tried to illustrate why democracy matters and why it is important for all of us that we fight poverty.

The role of the media has been a central part of most theories of globalization, and the rise of the Internet has been equally well covered. When Manuel Castells published his three volumes on the 'network society' (Castells 1996, 1997 and 2000) and subsequently *The Internet Galaxy: Reflections on the Internet, Business and Society* (2001) the discourse on the Internet and how deeply it affected our contemporary society became almost too much. The central argument in Castells' writings was that the new networks of global communication created by the digital revolution transformed the world of capitalist nation states into a potentially dynamic, open, innovative and much more decentralized and interactive global system. In the three volumes on the network society Castells followed the consequences of this basic observation into such different areas as the emergence of new forms of regional or collective identity constructions, socio-political movements, the environmental movements, family politics, a new economy and work culture, and also the area of media and communication. Generally speaking he predicted the end of the industrialized mass society and culture, and potentially the rise of network structures both beneath and beyond the traditional nation states.

Castells is well aware that this transformation is not erasing all power differences and inequalities in the world – far from it – and in Chapter 5 'The culture of real virtuality' in volume one of the trilogy (Castells 1996/2000, 2nd edn: 355 ff) he maps the global development of the Internet. The US, European and Asian dominance is striking, based on late 1990 data. More recent data on the global use of the Internet, broadband and mobile phone communication (Thussu 2006: 208 ff) confirms these global differences, but also indicates a rapid closing of some of the gaps, particularly in mobile phone use. But even though the digital revolution has not yet resulted in a truly global network, Castells' main point is that the new system of communication is different because it integrates all sorts of communication on one, converging platform:

> What characterizes the new system of communications, based in the digitized, networked integration of multiple communications modes, is its inclusiveness and comprehensiveness of all cultural expressions. Because of its existence, all kinds of messages in the new type of society work in a binary mode: presence/absence in the multimedia communication system. Only presence in this integrated system permits communicability and socialization of the message (Castells 1996/2000, 2nd edn: 405).

Googling the world: the power of social networks

Social networks were not created by modern technology, they are simply cognitive and social mainframes of human communication and interaction. But where social networks and communication in pre-modern and early modern societies were often rather local and regionally restricted, and more advanced forms of networking and communication were linked to elites, digital communication facilitates global and more general networks. In Christakis and Fowler's *Connected: The Amazing Power of Social Networks and How They Shape our Lives* (2010) this linking of our universal, cognitive framework with the development of modern, global technologies is the key argument, and also one of the reasons they warn against hyper-techno-optimism:

> Human sociability and social networks have ancient genetic roots (…) but humans take these traits to a whole new level. The tendency to form social unions beyond reproductive ones is biologically encoded in humans: we seek out friends not just mates (…) In short the human brain seems to be built for social networks. Over time, evolutionary selection has favored larger brains and greater cognitive capacity to respond to the demands of a more complicated social environment. Individuals living in social networks confront a set of cognitive challenges not faced by solitary individuals or by those in disconnected groups. These challenges arise from the need to understand others and to cooperate with them, as well as to occasionally act altruistically for the benefit of the group (Christakis and Fowler 2010: 215).

Social networks in most people's everyday life reflect social structures connected to usually smaller circles: our family, our friends and our work place. Our social network is likely to have a core of connected dots with connections often activated and dots a little further away, not so often activated. But the reach and scope of an individual's social and communicative network may vary according to, for instance, social status and position. We usually network and communicate with people we share a lifestyle with, not complete strangers. The same mechanisms can of course be found in digital and global networks, but the sheer scale and magnitude globally of digital networks and the number of connections for an individual on a site like, for instance, Facebook is quite amazing. The concept of personal networks certainly seems to have expanded – maybe because connecting is easy and without real demand for intense interaction with all your friends.

According to data on Facebook (2011, see www.checkfacebook.com) the total amount of active users is almost 800 million, with the US and EU as the regions with most active users, but also with an incredibly wide spread in Asia and India. There is no doubt that even though the core of Facebook uses and communications are tied to people's social networks in everyday life, there are also a lot of other communication issues and discussions on the agenda. Political parties, media, grassroots organizations, artists and cultural organizations are also present on Facebook, just as transnational links and communications feed into the system, sometimes becoming part of the political agenda with the circulation of news. Documentary filmmakers and political activists have found ways of using this network that expands the concept of network far beyond that of personal social networks. As Christakis and Fowler point out, all networks have a life of their own that no one in the network can control (Christakis and Fowler 2010: 24f), the global network of Facebook has become a phenomenon that is hard to control and oversee.

Facebook is just one example of the new digital, online, global networks that have boosted and intensified our connections and forms of communication. The new digital media culture has already transformed the everyday life of our communicative culture. The different services of Google, another major player, have become so integrated that we use the phrase 'just google it', indicating that this is a service that democratizes access to information through global digital archives and services that makes world information seem very close at hand. It has become a tool not just for ordinary people, but also for professionals, with the development of Wikipedia being another example of the power of online communities for creating and distributing information and knowledge. Digital networks are boosting instant global communication and network functions, lowering costs and possibilities of production and distribution for both professional and user-driven products, and they are enhancing contextualization of products and programmes, because single products are linked to others, and to contextual and additional information and experience.

The new, more intense and widespread forms of digitally enhanced social networks and other forms of communication have taken the basic cognitive and emotional needs of humans for social bonding and group coordination to a whole new level. But it is important to understand that we are talking about a new technology meeting very basic human patterns of networking and communication: the facilitation of interpersonal bonds, the synchronizing and aligning of behaviour and attitudes and the communication of professional and personal information. What takes place in these new social and communicative networks is a technological revolution in the sense that it facilitates activities on a completely new global scale, and in a way that connects individuals, groups, institutions and regions and places in the world much more directly and with potentially interactive dimensions not seen before. But this techonology is not fundamentally changing human nature, and most of the well known actors and problems of 'the old world' can be found also in 'the new world'.

Pragmatics of the new, global media culture

There is no doubt that the development of a global, digital network culture is a revolution that can probably only be compared to the invention of the alphabet and the printing technology. It is a technology that has already changed the world. But there is no reason for hyper-techno-optimism saluting the birth of a global democracy and the death of social, cultural and political divides, nor for a just as unfounded techno-pessimism where concentration of power by the elites and the global corporate companies will be even greater. All historical experience tell us that revolutions and technological changes are important, but also that new media like all media can be used for different purposes. New media do not replace old media, old media and new media interact and form new alliances, old media adopt new strategies and form new platforms, and much of the activities and content is simply moved to new platforms, perhaps with new features and formats.

On many of the popular, new, global platforms this convergence of old and new media is very visible. Google is a characteristic example, because it is in fact a conglomerate structure of services combining old and new media and services. Google Books is a gigantic project turning the world's libraries into an online library, Google News links 4000–5000 news sources around the world, Google mail is a personal webmail system, Froogle provides online shopping and Google Talk is an internet telephone service. We are talking about a combination of very old traditional media and functions, and a new digital platform, not all of which are successful.

YouTube is another interesting example. It was created in 2005 by three former PayPal employees as a means of removing barriers for sharing videos online. The technology is simple and user-friendly: you can upload, publish, view, embed and share your videos with other users in a closed or completely open public space. YouTube was bought by Google in 2006 and is by now far the most used visual network globally, with more than 100 million videos posted. But if you take a deeper look at the content and content providers on YouTube (Burgess and Green 2009:38f), you find that although 50 per cent seem to be user-driven low-key and private videos, 42 per cent come from professional media and corporate groups. YouTube is a revolution for user-driven content, no doubt about that, but you also find all the big players there: BBC, CNN, Al Jazeera, The Guardian, CBS and all the major film companies in the world, and you also find major political parties and organizations, like Greenpeace, the Democrats, the Republicans, the British Labour Party etc. But YouTube is also one of the major platforms for globalization of documentaries.

YouTube is user-driven content, but it is also an arena for exchange between the professionals and the amateurs, and it is a window for big corporations, organizations etc. Burgess and Green therefore also dismiss the more romantic notion to be found in, for instance, Yochai Benkler's almost romantic notion of a new popular culture in *The Wealth of Networks* (2006):

> In the light of the convergence between commercial popular culture and community participation that YouTube represents, this claim that the emergence of peer-produced culture represents a renaissance of folk culture reproduces too simplistic a divide between the culture of the people and the culture of the mass media industries (Burgess and Green 2009: 13–14).

Documentaries and globalization

There is no doubt that the general trends of globalization have already influenced the ways in which journalism, news, documentary films and television are produced and distributed. We have already seen a number of examples of co-production between user-communities and directors or film companies and television stations around the world, which indicates the potential power of the new social networks. We can see that documentaries are already much more visible and accessible through the new, digital global networks, both on sites dedicated only to documentary film and on sites where they become part of professional, institutional websites or websites belonging to social and political activist groups. We even find documentaries made completely through funding via social networks.

In many ways documentary formats have a possibility to find an audience or even funding outside the dominant and established film and media companies, and in principle anyone can become a documentary directory and upload directly. The traditional gatekeepers are not completely dominant any more. But in reality the chance of someone making it alone and just via the digital platforms that are open and available, is very small, and in fact the traditional film and media companies still completely set the standard and dominate the new media culture.

The democratization effect is indeed there, but it is perhaps most visible in the distribution of the films and programmes made, perhaps most importantly in terms of making the viewing of films much more independent of time and place than in the old media culture. In that sense the documentary film, although still very much made by the same people and media companies, is getting out there much more. The documentary films since 2001 have thus has both an increased global agenda and, at the same time, been much more visible as part of an emerging global, online documentary culture.

Chapter 2

Sociology and aesthetics of documentary genres

The distinction between fiction and non-fiction is a very crucial cognitive distinction in human communication. Just as children very early on become familiar with the difference between the world of playing and the real world, the difference between a fictional and a non-fictional relation to reality is embedded in both our everyday communication and the cultural and institutional production of these to basic types of communicative genres. Even though fiction is based on the reality we all share and can also come very close to actual, historical events and characters, fiction in principle suspends any demands of a direct link to a factual reality. In many cases audiences react to some forms of fiction with expectations of realism and plausible characters and plots, but those expectations are not of the same nature as the expectations towards non-fiction. In his book, *Narrative Comprehension and Film* (1992), Edward Brannigan defines the fictional reference to reality by its open and more indeterminate nature.

> (…) fictional terms denote real things, though not determinate ones (…) A fiction does not determine exactly which object or objects it represents, and this openness is what distinguishes fictional references from other sorts of references (…) to interpret a symbol fictionally is to operate in a precarious, intermediate zone between sets of possible references (…) and a specific reference (…) Considered as a cognitive activity, fiction is a complex way of comprehending the world in which one is first required to hold open sets of variables while searching for a reasonable fit between language and live experience, between a set of symbols and acts of the body (Brannigan 1992: 194).

Brannigan's way of defining fiction has clear implications for the definition of non-fiction. If the distinction is primarily in the cognitive activity of audiences and the type of the reference to reality, this takes us away from a primarily aesthetic way of making a distinction. It also takes us away from more normative expectations of objectivity and truth as the *par excellence* definition of the relation of non-fiction to reality. Non-fiction is instead characterized by a more determinate and direct reference to a factual historical or contemporary reality, and cognitively the audience of non-fiction or documentary film performs a different kind of interpretation of the story, the scenes, the characters or the arguments put forward in the film. Since we are made to believe that the non-fiction film is about reality and real people in some form, depending on the actual non-fiction genre used, the activity is much less about the metaphorical translation of the universe we are presented with into some kind of reality, than with the represented reality in itself.

In Carl Plantinga's book on non-fiction film, *Rhetoric and Representation in Nonfiction Film* (1997) we find a similar line of thought. Referring to pragmatic theories of communication, to speech act theory and to cognitive film theories he talks about the importance of *not primarily* basing the distinction between fiction and non-fiction on 'intrinsic textual properties, but also on the extrinsic context of production, distribution and reception' (Plantinga 1997: 16). He furthermore makes a reference to Noël Carroll's theory of *indexing* (Carroll 1983) and the fact that the indexing of films as either fiction or non-fiction encourage different types of spectator activity.

Following Wolterstorff's theory (Wolterstorff 1980) of both fictional and non-fictional works as world projections and systems of reality representation, Plantinga furthermore points to two different forms of stances we can take to projected worlds (Plantinga 1997: 17). *The fictive stance* is characterized by a spectator activity that is functioning within the projected world and which is not primarily occupied with whether the projected world is true and represents things that have actually occurred. In the fictive stance we may well compare the projected world with experiences in our own real world, but epistemically the fictive stance is not defined by that. *The assertive stance*, on the other hand, is characterized by exactly the opposite kind of primary spectator activity, because the film is based on the epistemic and defining assertion that the projected world is about things that have happened in the actual world. This, on the other hand, does not exclude documentary formats with a more complex structure and ways of playing with the assertive stance and the relation to reality. But basically non-fiction films and the assertive stance establish a direct cognitive link and mental activity between the films projected world and the projected and represented world. As we shall see, this does not, however, exclude the viewer of a documentary film from getting involved with the characters and the real-world-related events in ways that have the same qualities of identification, and emotional and narrative pleasure as fiction.

The social and cognitive roots and development of documentaries

The distinction between fiction and non-fiction is, as already indicated, connected to deep, cognitive structures, and is fundamental for our society, culture and the ways we communicate. The two basic modes have existed and been described since the dawn of civilization, and in the history of communication they also developed side by side. This has also been the case in the history of film and television, where non-fiction and documentary genres from the beginning were just as important as fiction. The explosion of media and media platforms has of course increased the role of all types of media, and especially the rise of television after 1945 has given documentary and non-fiction forms an extremely central role. But why have documentary forms been important historically, and why has the role of documentary increased in modern societies?

Both fiction and non-fiction genres expand and challenge our imagination, and they do so by interacting with the 'scripts' or 'schemata' that are the building blocks of our mind and our social experiences (Rumelhart 1980; Fiske and Taylor 1991; Bordwell 1985). Scripts and schemata are built into our cognitive frameworks, but they are also changed and developed in social interaction and communication. Scripts and schemata are very active in the interpretation of media products and can also be developed and changed by media products. But even though this kind of basic cognitive and social activity is common to both fiction and non-fiction, the two basic modes represent different ways of working with our imagination through the different ways in which they refer to reality.

Cognitive theories on narration generally point to narrative structures as a very basic form of cognitive schemata in all human beings. In Jonathan Gottschall's *The Storytelling Animal: How Stories Make Us Human* (2012) the basic argument for the evolutionary development of narrative schemata goes like this:

> Evolution has given us an 'inner Holmes' because the world is really full of stories (intrigues, plots, alliances, relationships of cause and effect) and it pays to detect them. The storytelling mind is a crucial evolutionary adaptation. It allows us to experience our lives as coherent, orderly and meaningful. It is what makes life more than a blooming, buzzing confusion (…) The storytelling mind is allergic to uncertainty, randomness and coincidence. If the storytelling mind cannot find meaningful patterns in the world, it will try to impose them. In short the storytelling mind is a factory that churns out true stories when it can, but will manufacture lies when it can't (Gottschall 2012: 103).

So even though narrative structures may be especially strong in fiction films, where the plot is more decisive than in many documentary films, neither the creator of documentary films nor the audience will be able to avoid narrative structures and schemata. They impose themselves on our perception of reality and the way we read and experience visual works. Gottschall suggests that documentary films with a weak narrative structure may be more open to our critical inquiry, because we are more absorbed by and emotionally engaged in narratives and stories, whether fictional or non-fictional. But even though this may be true, documentary films often tell stories that make us react strongly with emotional identification.

Documentary film and television is perhaps particularly strong in the activation of the *social and psychological dimension of imagination* in the sense that they activate scripts and schemata directly linking us with a part of a factual reality that we may have little prior knowledge of. Fictions can also take us to quite unexpected worlds and places, but they are fictions and not representations of an actual, projected world. One of the major developments in modern documentaries is precisely the expansion of reality coverage, the fact that we get closer and closer to parts of reality that have not previously been shown in a documentary form.

Science documentaries have gone deeper and deeper into our bodies and have changed our perception of our body and biology fundamentally, just as they have discovered and visually represented the physical universe on a macro and micro level. Nature documentaries have in an equally revolutionary way changed our images of the planet and its many different worlds, places and species, and they have in doing so been an important part of the development of a new, global, ecological mentality (see p. 221f). But most important of all, at least in connection with the theme of this book, modern documentaries have developed the global, social imagination of 'the other'. Let us consider a pretty basic, schematic representation of the kind of social relations and networks people typically have in their everyday life, based on both the intensity and regularity of actual physical contact and on the basis of mental attitude (Table 2).

Table 2: Typology of social types schemata of others. Inspired by Alfred Schutz (1932) and Fiske and Taylor (1991)

The close other: family, friends, working partners and people in our close everyday life	**The close stranger:** professional relations and distant persons in everyday life
The mediated other: Mass media & network media	
The imagined close other: Organized groups and communities Communicative communities Imaginary communities	**The imagined distant other:** People of different culture, ethnic and ideological persuasion, social losers, criminals etc.

Schutz' work *Phenomenology of the Social World* (1932/1967) is a very early sociological study of how humans create images of others through social interaction, and his categories and observations were made long before the modern media became so central for extended social networks and social interaction. But his theory is based on the observation that distance and forms of contact play an important role. So those that are near us and who we interact with on a regular basis become our 'close other' whereas the more 'distant other' is perceived in ways influenced by distance and our lack of direct experience of them. The 'imagined close other' could – before the massive development of electronic media – be somebody we had communicated with by letter, but never met. The distant and threatening other, the complete stranger, would just be people we had heard or read about.

In modern theories of social cognition this role of distance and contact in images of others is confirmed. In Fiske and Taylor's standard book *Social Cognition*, the basic mechanism is related to social perceptions and schemata that make us form ingroups and outgroups (Fiske and Taylor 1991: 122f). Empirical research clearly supports the fact already pointed out by Schutz, that we do believe groups of people we belong to to be different from others, and we have 'less complex conceptualizations of them' (1991: 123). So the more we perceive others to be a near group, the more we tend to see them as 'us'. The less we are in contact and have relations with others, the less we are inclined to see others as having social or cultural elements that are like us.

Media play a large role in giving us access to the images of others, and in three ways at least they feed directly into the model presented above. First of all, the media today can work in relation to all four boxes, because they can create images that confirm social groups and identities that we feel close to already from our everyday life. Second, they can make it much easier to belong to social networks of a distant, imagined kind; this is exactly what social networks are doing and why social media have become such a strong factor in modern social life. Third, and certainly not least, they bring the 'distant other' closer to us: we can see and experience in our own national reality the lives of others that are very distant and seem very different from us, and they can bring social and cultural stories of a more global nature closer to us as well. This is the power of documentary film and television: that the distant and stereotyped other can come very close to you, that people and ways of life that seem very strange and maybe even threatening can become more familiar. As already pointed out, the mediatization of culture and society in our modern globalized world has increased the role of mediated encounters. Documentary genres and forms have a privileged and central role in mediatized, global encounters, because their special reality status bring us closer to parts of the global world that we cannot possible experience ourselves.

Documentaries and emotions

In her book *The Documentary: Politics, Emotion, Culture* (2010) Belinda Smaill points to what she calls a tendency to downplay the role of emotion, desire and pleasure in theories of documentary genres (Smaill 2010: 4f). In trying to offer an explanation for this, she points to a tendency in documentary theory, represented by among others Bill Nichols, to see documentary as representing a 'discourse of sobriety' (Nichols 1991: 3f), that is, the voice of science, politics, education, information etc. Documentary is primarily defined in relation to what is seen as the rational discourse of the public sphere. There are certainly both historical and contemporary reasons for pointing to this dimension in documentary, and as one of the main genres of non-fiction, many documentaries have a clear connection to news and journalism, just as documentary genres and filmmakers have been part of a project that combines enlightenment, criticism, and social reform and action. But as Smaill's book clearly demonstrates, affects, emotion and desire are a powerful and fundamental part of many types of documentaries, also those engaged in social critique and reform.

Belinda Smaill takes a Freudian, psychoanalytic point of view in her analysis of forms of contemporary documentaries, dealing with both public and private issues, and her book is an important contribution to the understanding of emotions in documentary formats in general. In Bill Nichol's seminal theories of documentary genres, emotions and psychology may not play a major role, but he has certainly also contributed to the understanding of the role of emotions in documentary, for instance when he talks about psychological and emotional realism (Nichols 2001: 93 f). In Elisabeth Cowie's book *Recording Reality, Desiring the Real* (2011) the dimension of emotions and desire is of central concern, and she argues convincingly for the link between

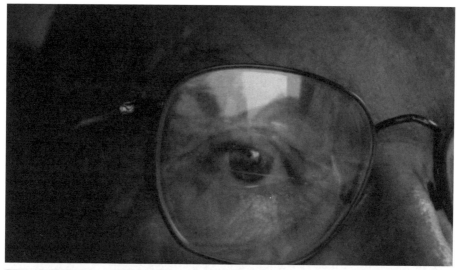

Figures 2a and b: Errol Morris' *The Fog of War* (2003). A portrait of Robert McNamara and global politics close up – very alone and with President Lyndon Johnson. Frame grab. Cinematography: Peter Donahue and Robert Chappell.

knowledge and fascination of reality, and for the role of emotional identification. This is even more the case with Michael Renov, who deals quite a lot with affect and emotions in his book *The Subject of Documentary* (2004). He analyzes different forms of subjective documentaries, and in doing so clearly shows how emotional patterns of relation to both self and other are an integral part of the modern, documentary project. But even though Renov's and Smaill's books represent important contributions to the establishing of emotions as part of documentary film and film reception, it is important to further develop theories of emotions in all types of documentaries. Smaill in fact contributes to this, because she deals with rather different documentaries, and in the chapter on what she calls 'dissent documentaries' – exemplified by, for instance, Spurlock's *Super Size Me* (2004) and Achbar and Abbott's *The Corporation* (2003) – she shows how these modern social documentaries with a clear, public agenda are actually dominated by emotional, affective rhetorical and narrative strategies.

Documentary filmmakers have probably always been aware of the fact that even when presenting stories from a factual reality and wanting to make an argument or state factual information based on rationality, emotional dimensions are integrated. Emotional dimensions will always in some form and to a certain degree be part of the way things are presented and perhaps even more so in the viewer response to documentary. Even when we watch and listen to public characters or experts, we see people, and we make judgments and react to what they say both on a personal, emotional level and on a more discursive, rational level. Visual communication always brings the human and personal dimension to the front, and we read facial expressions and body language. A documentary filmmaker like Erroll Morris is famous for using long takes and close-ups of his main characters, for instance in the portrait of Robert MacNamara in *The Fog of War* (2003), and thereby priming our focus towards both the public political figure and the human being MacNamara. Many researchers have pointed to the blurring of boundaries in public life and communication through this personification of visual communication (Meyrowitz 1985; Bennett and Entman 2001; Corner and Pels 2003; van Zoonen 2005).

The fact that some researchers see this as a potential danger for the quality of mediated, public communication, through a more sensational, populist media discourse, is perhaps in itself a sign of the precarious status of emotions in our way of thinking about and understanding factual communication and the documentary genre. Just as there may be a tendency to define documentary as 'a discourse of sobriety', our culture seems to regard emotions as something with a much lower esteem than rationality. At least that is what a number of researchers working with emotions in the new cognitive tradition in both neuroscience, linguistics and film and media studies are claiming. One of the leading neuroscientists, Antonio Damasio, called one of his first books on emotion *Descartes' Error: Emotion, Reasoning and the Human Brain* (1994), and with the title and his arguments he wanted to argue against a deep split in Western philosophy and culture between emotion and rationality. His argument is not that emotion cannot cause problems for debates and for reasoning, the fact that we can all – as the saying goes – get too emotional or get carried away by emotions. Rather, his main argument, based on what we now know about the brain and the links between brain and body, is that emotion and rationality are biologically and directly linked to each other in such a way that we cannot be rational if for some reason the link between emotion and rationality is cut. Clinical examples of this exist in patients with different forms of brain damage, and those data and general studies of the brain makes Damasio claim:

(…) certain aspects of the process of emotion and feelings are indispensable for rationality. At their best, feelings point us in the proper direction, take us to the appropriate place in a decision-making space, where we may put the instrument of logic to good use (p. xiii) (…) Feelings, along with the emotions they come from, are no luxury. They serve as internal guides, and they help us communicate to others signals that can also guide them. And feelings are neither intangible nor elusive. Contrary to traditional scientific opinion, feelings are just as cognitive as other precepts (p. xv).'

This very basic cognitive understanding and explanation of the role of emotion in our life, and in human interaction and communication, has lead to a new development in both linguistics, literary studies and film and media studies. George Lakoff and Mark Johnson's seminal book *Metaphors We Live By* (1980) was a very early attempt to show how our basic use and construction of language was influenced by our body-brain connections. Lakoff's work on different aspects of thinking, language and communication, based on this fundamental notion of the embodied mind, has recently also taken him into a study of political communication, with US politics as the main example. In his book *The Political Mind* (2008) he looks at political language and communication from a cognitive and emotional point of view. His main argument is that we do not understand politics if we do not understand the role images, metaphors, narratives and emotions play here:

According to Enlightenment reason was assumed to be conscious, universal, disembodied, logical, unemotional, value neutral, interest based and literal (…) but voters don't behave like that (…) language gets its power because it is defined relative to frames, prototypes, metaphors, narratives, images and emotions. Part of its power comes from its unconscious aspects (Lakoff 2008).

What we can conclude based on Damasio and Lakoff is that communication cannot be seen just as the result of rationality and discourses based on meaning in a more abstract sense. All meaning and communication is embodied, and embodied communication is based just as much on rational arguments as on images, metaphors, and narratives that carry with them emotional dimensions and experiences. Not all documentaries use narratives and visual strategies in the same way, in fact many types of documentary differ in their communicative strategy. But there is no doubt that we always as spectators infer some elements of metaphor, image and narrative when we watch documentaries. Our way of thinking is in fact very much based on images stored in our brain, images of earlier experiences and memories. Images are also very much in use when we try to plan future actions and events, when we try to imagine how things will develop, and thus images are also an important part of the way we perceive and evaluate characters, arguments and events in documentaries.

Images and metaphors are one way of linking body and brain, emotion and cognition, but narrative structures are just as important. Narrative structures are not just social, cultural and aesthetic constructions, they are an embodied structure in all human beings that is quickly developed with age. As Lakoff points out, the sort of 'complex narratives' we find in novels, films and television are made up of more simple structures of smaller narratives that he calls 'frames or scripts'. Frames and scripts are simple but very powerful structures in our brain that store vital information for social interaction, communication and social and cultural knowledge. Frames and scripts play a role for our social cognition of others and resemble what cognitive sociologists often call 'schemas' (Fiske and Taylor 1991: 96ff). The main point here is that such frames, scripts and schemas are heavily involved when we watch all types of films, and they bring real-life emotions and experiences into our understanding and reactions to what we see:

> (…) frames tend to structure a huge amount of our thought (…) dramatic event structures are carried out by brain circuitry. The same event structure circuitry can be used to live out an action or narrative, or to understand the actions of others or the structure of the story. In addition, neural binding can create emotional experiences (…) narratives and frames are not just brain structures with intellectual content, but rather with integrated intellectual-emotional content (Lakoff 2008: 27–8).

As Carl Plantinga has also demonstrated in his study of emotions and other structures of reception in relation to fiction films, *Moving Viewers* (2009), 'emotions are intimately tied to our cognition, inferences, evaluations and all other mental activities that accompany the viewing experience. Emotions have implications for ideas (…) they play a role in the creation of both cultural and individual memory' (Plantinga 2009: 5–6). It is not just modern cognitive studies of media and communication that know about the important role of emotions and the persona, it is a key dimension of classical rhetorical theories, theories that do not deal with fiction and storytelling, but with how to argue and persuade. The three main dimensions of rhetoric – *logos* (logic, rationality and arguments), *ethos* (personality and credibility of the speaker) and *pathos* (emotions, the use of metaphorical expressions, the style) – in fact point to an understanding in pre-modern times of the connection between emotion and rationality.

Since the link between emotion and rationality is so central to our whole way of experiencing reality and other people, and for language and all forms of mediated communication, there is reason to assume that the emotions elicited in real experiences are basically the same as in both experiences of fiction and non-fiction. Emotions in fiction films and in documentaries are of the same nature as real-life emotions, even though they can be orchestrated and lived out in different forms and with a different intensity. But we know that people cry, laugh, identify with and live through the characters and stories or cases they are presented with in a film, that different stories, different genres and different characters elicit feelings that resemble emotions in real life. These emotions are experienced and felt in our minds and bodies, whether we are watching a fictional story or a documentary story based on real-life material.

We do not have clear empirical evidence of the potential differences between fiction and non-fiction reception. One hypothesis might be that the fictional experience allows a more free emotional experience because the direct link to reality is suspended, whereas the non-fiction experience balances the emotional and rational reception because we know this is about reality. However, many documentaries do tell very strong human stories with an often very emotional core. In one of the very few empirical studies of reception of fiction and non-fiction, based on cognitive theory, Birgitta Höijer (1992a, 1992b) actually shows that very similar emotional responses can be found in television fiction and factual programmes, even though the reception follows slightly different paths.

As will be demonstrated in the following analysis of different documentary films and television programmes, the emotional dimensions in such genres are just as important as the more rational arguments and the factual documentation put forward. If for instance we look at climate change documentaries, it becomes quite obvious that some of the same rhetorical, visual, narrative and thus also emotional elements that we find in fiction films like Roland Emmerich's *The Day After Tomorrow* are present and widely used. In Davis Guggenheim's *An Inconvenient Truth* (2006) or Leila and Nadia Connor's *The 11th Hour* (2007), there is a strong, rational and argumentative structure in the film and its often very heavy scientific documentation of facts to prove the climate change problematic. But in both films this rhetoric of fact is embedded in an immanent catastrophe narrative that gives the film a very dramatic drive and visual dimension, bringing global images of change in nature and the environment to the front. In both films, but most clearly in *An Inconvenient Truth*, the use of a personality with ethos and iconic, symbolic value is dominant. Former Vice President Al Gore is the key figure and narrator, and we see him lecture on stage, but we are also presented with memories and images from his personal life and his childhood and family experiences. Leonardo DiCaprio has a similar, although weaker, role in *The 11th Hour*.

Documentaries and social imagination

Humans are genetically, biologically and socially created as storytelling animals; narrative structures are a fundamental way of experiencing, exploring and thinking about reality. Stories come to us with an invitation to both cognitive and emotional responses and those two dimensions are linked intimately to each other in both real life, fiction and documentary forms. As Damasio points out in his book *The Feeling of What Happens: Body, Emotion and the Making of Consciousness* (1999): 'emotions probably assist reasoning, especially when it comes to personal and social matters involving risk and conflict' (Damasio 1999: 41–2). Documentaries deal with all sorts of social, cultural and human problems and conflicts, and looking into the history of the development of the notion of documentary and documentary genres it is pretty obvious that the creative dimension of documentary has to do with precisely the balance between rationality and more emotional, expressive dimensions. There is a strong dimension of social engagement in documentary as a genre, it is a form clearly aiming at influencing and developing our social imagination, the schemas, scripts and frames that influence the way we perceive society, culture and our fellow human beings in all shapes and forms. But to reach that goal, a creative strategy involving both the rational and the emotional is needed, also stories of reality must take the form of images and narratives that appeal to us.

The classical documentary developed among others by John Grierson in the UK in the 1930s (Aitken 1990, 1998) had a social vision, a vision of changing the public concept of the nation so that it included the working classes and the new industrial working places that were beginning to form and lay the foundation for the modern welfare state. In his book *The Art of Record* (1996), John Corner describes it in such a way that Grierson's position and vision seem to be a foundation for most documentaries:

> Documentary is *authorial* in that it is about *creativity* and transformation based on vision. In being this it is also emphatically *dramatic,* as part of its bid for *public imagination* (…) 'the *raw material*' for the creative endeavour is provided by '*reality*' (…) it also provides Grierson with the basis for his social democratic theory about film as *agency of citizenship and reform* (…) As a practice and a form, documentary is strongly *informationalist* (and therefore requires a level of accuracy) but it is also an exercise in creativity, an art form drawing on *interpretative imagination* both in perceiving and using the sounds and images of '*the living scene*' to *communicate the real* (Corner 1996: 14–15).

In giving voice to this new social reality, and to new social groups and representing parts of reality never really represented before in the public sphere, Grierson and his collaborators worked under constraints. First of all, technology did not allow for a mobile and free representation of sound, voice and image, and second, they made their films for private and public organizations that set limits. But despite these historical limits to what they could do, they managed to transform the early documentary movement from a dominant kind of informational lecture or actuality film to a much broader and creative kind of documentary. Grierson from very early on expressed the belief that documentary film could be a strong factor in forming social concept:

> (films have) a practical monopoly over the dramatic strata of the common mind in which preferences, sympathies, affections and loyalties, if not actually created, are at least crystallised and coloured (…) cinema is recognised as having a peculiar influence on the ideological centres (…) what people want more than anything of cinema is practical example and a renewal of vitality (Grierson, EMB-memo (1927), in Swann (1989: 27).
>
> We believe that the cinema's capacity for getting around, for observing and selecting from life itself can be exploited in a new and vital art form (…) We believe that the original actor and the original scene are better guides to a screen interpretation of the modern world (…) They give it a power of interpretation over more complex and astonishing happenings in

the real world than the studio mind can conjure up or the studio technician recreate (…)
(Grierson *First Principles of Documentary* (1932), reprinted in Aitken 1998: 81f).

In the late 1950s and 1960s the role of documentaries for social imagination was increased globally by the new lightweight cameras with sync sound and by the fact that television stations worldwide took up documentaries as an important part of their schedule. The American direct cinema was important here, and Frederick Wiseman can be seen as one of the modern documentary directors continuing Grierson's work and vision with new means. The new Free Cinema in the UK, however, also became important. Despite the role of television in this process, documentary film in many ways also became more independent and free in the selection of topics and form. In the Free Cinema Manifesto (1956) they said: 'a belief in freedom, in the importance of people and in the significance of the everyday (…) We believe that 1) no film can be too personal 2) the image speaks, sound amplifies and comments, size is irrelevant, perfection is not an aim. An attitude means a style. A style means an attitude'.

Wiseman in his work, starting with the trendsetting *Titticut Follies* (1967) – filmed at a Massachusetts correctional institution – described his whole oeuvre as a kind of continued drama on American everyday life, about ordinary American life and institutions, and he states that they are often about 'a gap between the formal ideology and actual practice, between the rules and how they are applied' (Wiseman in Westin 1974: 60). But what his films do is exactly to show us social life as it is lived, not only in those institutions all of us have been in contact with (schools, hospitals) but also in those where all 'the others' are (jails, mental institutions, the homeless and poor). They show us American life in all its aspects, front stage and back stage, and by bringing us closer to aspects of the lives of others.

Wiseman is the epitome of observational documentary film, his camera is an anthropological camera searching reality, and he never speaks or lets any other authoritative voice speak and interpret what is happening. Reality in his films is a montage of voices and images, but it is of course an edited reality, a dramatized reality, a concentrated reality, not the objective truth. In this sense he continues in the creative footsteps of Grierson. He has explained his strategy in the following way:

For me, the making of a documentary film is in some ways the reverse of making a fiction film. With fiction, the idea for the film is transformed into a script by the imagination and work of the writer and/or director, which obviously precedes the shooting of the film. In my documentaries the reverse is true: The film is finished when, after editing, I have found its 'script'. If a film of mine works, it does so because the verbal and pictorial elements have been fused into a dramatic structure. This is the result of the compression, condensation, reduction and analysis that constitute the editing process for me. Nothing in my films is staged for the camera (…) I generally use about 3% of the material shot (…) There has to be a rhythm that implies that the final film represents the only possible form of the material. The structure must create the illusion (…) that the events seen in the film occurred in the order in which they are seen on the screen. In this way the form of documentaries can be called fictional, because their structure is imagined and therefore may resemble plays or novels, the more traditional dramatic forms' (Wiseman in Grant (2006: i).

The creative tradition of documentary genres has been taken further in the modern documentaries dealt with in this book. But the role of documentaries for the forming of social and cultural imaginaries remain the same. Just like the classical documentary tradition, the modern tradition comes in many shapes and forms, and the rhetorical, visual and narrative techniques used represent a creative diversity. Focus in many of the documentaries after 2000 seems to have shifted towards a more global perspective, and the issues raised are loaded with drama, conflict and risk. These documentaries deal with issues that cause serious problems in a broader social and political sense, because they are issues that cannot be solved on a national, local level, but demand a new global mentality. But even though they seem to deal with global issues that can be difficult to grasp and react to, they also touch upon something that may affect us deeply in our personal and everyday life. Problems like that call upon the creativity of documentaries to tell stories dealing with all levels of globalization, stories that can relate to and challenge both our hearts and minds, our ability to act and reflect rationally and emotionally.

The creative treatment of reality: a typology of documentary genres

For some it may seem contradictory to connect creativity with documentary formats. But this connection is a cornerstone in most new theories on documentary, whether based on more general sociological and aesthetic theories (Corner 1996) or cognitive theories (Plantinga 1997). The theoretical and analytical contributions to the understanding of the creative diversity of documentary forms and genres are many, and in, for instance, Bill Nichols' influential typology of documentary genres (Nichols 2001) he outlines a very useful categorization of basic modes (poetic, expository, observational, participatory and reflexive) with a rich variety of historical and contemporary examples. Other important contributions to the understanding of basic documentary genres can be found in the works of Michael Renov (2004), Stella Bruzzi's study of especially the modern observational formats (Bruzzi 2000) or Roscoe and Hight's (2001) useful study of the dramatized forms of documentary.

Like all other forms of communication, documentary is first and foremost an expressive genre in the sense that it speaks in certain ways about reality and uses special rhetorical and aesthetic forms in doing so. As Carl Plantinga points out:

A nonfiction film doesn't first and foremost 'catch' reality (...) Nonfiction film makes no claim to *reproduce* the real, but rather makes claims *about* the 'real' (...) Nonfiction films encompass a limitless variety of discourses about the world. Thinking of nonfiction as expressive (…) allows us to initiate our discussion of nonfiction without descending into the confusions raised by notions of objectivity and realism. Nonfictions are rhetorical, not primarily re-presentations. We can also see that nonfiction assertions and implications can be housed in the most subjective, stylistically expressive nonfiction films (Plantinga 1997: 38).

To state this about documentary formats doesn't mean rejecting the need for factual and true representations of reality or the fact that many aspects of documentary have to do with trying to find out what is true and false about a particular aspect of this reality. It is not about rejecting that we try to get as close to 'objectivity' as we can, when dealing with controversial public matters, and when we research material for the documentary we want to make. But we have to accept that 'objectivity' is very difficult to obtain, and that many documentaries do not deal with reality in only one way and one form. You cannot deal with matters in social reality in the same controlled way you can in a chemical laboratory. So objectivity in documentary is a relative term, but especially in the more journalistic, investigative or informational formats we may think of documentary objectivity the way Plantinga suggests:

We might think of objectivity not as a representation free of point of view, but as one that takes conflicting positions into account in a balanced fashion, to be fair to 'both sides' of an issue (…) uses patterns of reasoning, routines for assessing evidence (…) objectivity in whatever sense has no *necessary* connection to the nonfiction film' (Plantinga 1997: 30).

Documentary film and television programmes cannot just be considered journalistic forms. Journalism and documentary belong to the same macro genre, the factual or non-fiction genre, but they are clearly embedded in partly different institutions and different levels of expressive freedom. But then again, journalism also comes in many forms. The most regulated form of journalism is the news article or programme, and here the kind of objective strategies and ways of dealing with reality are central. News cannot be objective in the fullest and most philosophical meaning of that word, but we do expect news journalism to try to be impartial and neutral, we do not expect news to use too creative, expressive means. But not even the most neutral piece of news can be completely objective: editing and selection of material always take place, a piece of news is a special kind of framing and forming of a factual reality. This is even more true for background news or reporting, where a greater freedom of expression and ways of reporting reality are at work, because the reality of factual content reported is much more complex. Finally, when it comes to editorials other rules apply.

If we look at the basic modes or genres of documentary (see Table 3), the many ways of relating to reality become obvious. Basically, when we watch documentary film and television we are already influenced by institutional cues: the products are indexed by the producer or broadcaster, and we will often experience a documentary based on these institutional cues.

Table 3: Cognitive pragmatic model of documentary prototypes

Cognitive pragmatic model of documentary prototypes	
Basic cognitive schema: reality status check– direct/indirect reference to factual reality	Pragmatic-institutional context: cues directing attention to genre status

Basic documentary prototypes	
Authoritative: Epistemic authoritative Observational: epistemic open	Dramatized: epistemic hypothetic Poetic reflexive: epistemic aesthetic

Documentary Exemplars: Historical variations, mixing of elements from different prototypes	
Authoritative voice: journalistic, informative Observational voice: ethnographic, explorative	Dramatized voice: staging, testing, provoking Poetic voice: formal, experimental

Institutional cues merge with our basic cognitive schemata of different forms of genres, the experiences we already have from earlier situations. These cognitive schemata and experiences help us determine the reality status of what we are watching, the kind of reference to reality that is claimed by the particular documentary. As argued by both Bill Nichols (2001), Carl Plantinga (1997) and others, documentary film and television come in different basic modes or prototypes with a specific form of reference to reality. Inspired by both Nichols and Plantinga, this book argues for four such basic modes or prototypes: authoritative, observational, dramatized and poetic-reflexive. Although they all claim a more direct reference to a factual reality than most fiction formats, they have different ways of positioning the viewer towards this reality and they typically have a different rhetorical strategy or voice. These basic prototypes appear as exemplars in any given historical context, with variations, and it is quite common that elements from one prototype are mixed with elements from another prototype.

So the four basic genres, described in their most prototypical form, simply have a different epistemic entering point to reality and a very different way of claiming and representing reality (see Table 4). *The authoritative genre* makes claims and statements about reality based on a premise where it wants to inform or report on an investigation into a clearly identified theme or problem in the world. The use of authoritative rhetorics (voiceover, experts, witnesses, empirical data etc.) serves to establish the epistemic authority of the film. The maker of the film claims that this theme/problem needs to be explained and understood, and the intention is education, information or critique, which again can lead to political action or other forms of intervention in reality. *The observational genre* in its purest form is a series of sequences documenting a part of reality, very much based on visual observations of and statements from the people representing or defining this reality. There is no authoritative voiceover and no experts or witnesses outside the slice of life portrayed, and the intention is much more open and indefinite. Often the director simply wants us to

Table 4: Four basic documentary genres, translated from Bondebjerg 2008a, with reference to Plantinga 1997

Authoritative	Observational	Dramatized	Poetic-reflexive
Epistemic authority	Epistemic openness	Epistemic-hypothetical	Epistemic-aesthetic
Explanation-analysis	Observation-identification	Dramatization of factual reality	Reality seen through aesthetic form
Linearity, causality, rhetorical structure	Episodic, mosaic structure, everyday life	Reconstruction, narration, staging (drama-doc, doc-drama, mockumentary)	Symbolic montage, meta-levels, expressive, subjective form
Q and A, interview, witnesses, experts, Authoritative VO	Actor-driven, human-institutional life world	Testing borders between reality and fiction	Form-driven reality experience, the poetics of reality, framing reality
Information, critique, propaganda	Documentation of lived reality, social ethnology	Narrative drive, reality-driven narrative. Media-reflexivity	Challenging reality concepts and traditional doc-forms

experience life in a particular part of reality, wants us to learn about others. Epistemically the relation to reality is very open, what is portrayed is not explained, but represented as slices of lived experience, and voices from within this represented reality.

The two documentary genres mentioned above are probably the two genres most often accepted by the broad audience as the core documentary genres. If we look at the history of documentary, and especially the history after 1960, these are two of the main genres in the film and television documentary. But the two last genres – although maybe more controversial – also have an important place in modern documentary history. *The dramatized documentary* has a special relation to reality, here called epistemic-hypothetic. This is a complex genre which often tests and challenges our concept of reality and the borderline between fiction and non-fiction. One way of doing this is simply to recreate a historical, factual reality in a fictional form, another is to create a story that is claimed to be real, looks like a documentary, but which in fact is a fake. Yet another form is to stage reality in order to create a sociological experiment, like for instance letting people change lives for a time. The last main documentary *the poetic-reflexive documentary*, is also a rather complex genre, but basically its epistemic-aesthetic perspective on reality has to do with the fact that there is a special focus on form and style. The factual world is seen through a formal principle or filter which is part of reality itself, but is given a special priority by being the main principle of the film.

The tendencies in the four main genres defined here are often mixed in actual documentaries, and besides, the four main genres also have different sub-genres. The four main genres defined are therefore prototypes with fuzzy edges and soft boundaries rather than strict and separate entities. Plantinga in his book (Plantinga 1997) talks about the three basic voices of documentary (formal, open and poetic) in a way that clearly overlaps with the categories mentioned in Tables 3 and 4, and he also points more towards the drama documentaries. But he also points to the ways in which documentaries use structuring and rhetorical principles that we know from other types of film and television to organize the projected real world: narrative forms, rhetorical forms, associative forms, categorical forms and abstract forms. His main point is the same as already underlined: a documentary can use and combine different voices, stylistic features and narrative and rhetorical structures without losing its status as a documentary and its claim on reality.

A similar useful, pragmatic and non-normative model of elements that are typically used by documentary filmmakers is John Corner's five building stones of documentary genres in *Television Form and Public Address* (1995: 85ff): exposition, interview, observation, dramatization and mise-en-scène. Corner's main purpose is to point to the very flexible ways in which many documentaries combine these elements and give them a different weight that makes the particular film or television programme speak with a voice that has lots in common with other documentaries but also allows for large variations. Dramatization, for instance, can be very low-key and just related to the necessary organization and selection of a chronological narrative or a sequence of arguments and the documentation connected with it. But it can also be more extensive use of dramatic and narrative structures or forms of staging and reenactment. Mise-en-scène can, by the same token, simply be the way experts and witnesses are framed and the setting, or it can be a much more expressive use of camera positions, movements, light etc. or even more abstract symbolic uses of associative images.

The multiple voices of documentaries

If we start looking into historical and contemporary examples of documentary films representing the four main genres indicated, it becomes clear that although mainstream exemplars fitting the different categories are easy to find, the variation is huge. The authoritative documentary, for instance, can be found in very traditional informative formats, such as the America-based History Channel's four-part documentary *The Iraq War* (2007). It is a classical war documentary with authoritative voiceover narration, dramatic visual footage and documentation, and experts and witnesses. But the authoritative documentary also comes in more critical-satirical forms with a much more creative and varied use of stylistic effects, such as Michael Moore's *Fahrenheit 9/11*. Moore's film is a subjective audiovisual missile against those in power who took the US to war, with some very well founded forms of documentations, but also with strong performative elements of pure satire and provocation.

But perhaps one of the best examples of how refined a strategy a basically authoritative and critical investigative documentary can use is Erroll Morris' *The Thin Blue Line* (1988), a film Carl Plantinga (1997: 71) calls both 'evocative and expressive'. Despite the fact that this film documented the innocence of a man condemned for police murder and pointed the police to the real murderer – it is also a surreal and poetic thriller, dense with arguments, testimonies and documentation that utilise all the powers, multiple voices and styles of documentary. From the very beginning of the film, Philip Glass' slow, repetitive and hypnotic background music, the use of shots of the Dallas, Texas skyline with visual effects, the special colour and lighting in the main character interview sequences, Morris creates an uncanny film noir feeling. This feeling is sustained in the many different reconstructed versions of the murder event on the Dallas freeway, illustrating and documenting the versions of the events by the suspect and the authorities. It is also further developed in the sequences at the police station during the interrogation.

The stylistic elements used in this documentary have clear references to narrative and aesthetic structures also to be found in fiction thrillers, crime stories and the film noir tradition, but this does not undermine the film's strong, investigative, documentary intentions and status. The use of this particular style is to a large degree legitimized by the fact that the film actually documents that this is in fact an uncanny story of reality, a story where everything was not as it seemed to be. The mystery and style of the film is founded in and reflects the reality depicted, and this makes the factual evidence presented in detail almost appear like a symbolic retrial of the man accused. The documentary style and narrative structure and montage used in the film also adds a more general, symbolic dimension to the film. Dallas, Texas is not just an ordinary place in America, it is an icon of both richness and progress and of sombre events that have spurred conspiracy theories in connection with the assassination of President Kennedy in 1963. Morris' film is also a piece of symbolic Americana, a way of seeking the heart of what America is: the dream, but also the uncanny feeling of something rotten and wrong. As Plantinga says: 'A documentary is more that the sum of its documents' (Plantinga 1997: 72).

Everyday life and the many layers of observational documentary

Morris' film has one foot in the traditional journalistic camp of the authoritative, investigative documentary, but he uses elements from dramatized documentaries and from the poetic-reflexive documentary. His work illustrates how actual documentaries often combine genres and styles in order to tell exactly the story they want to tell. This is also the case with the very dominant observational documentary that we have already discussed with Frederick Wiseman as the example. But an example of just how creatively and expressively one can use the observational format is British Michael Grigsby's films. His early works date back to the break through of Free Cinema in the 1960s, and he has through most of his career made films that also in many ways continue the Grierson tradition. His films are about the life of ordinary people, about the British working class, and he often deals with the distance between their hopes and dreams and the longer historical and political perspective of British history.

This is the case with his film *Living On The Edge* (1986), which John Corner has analyzed in some detail (Corner 1996: 108ff) as a clear example of an observational documentary with a very strong symbolic dimension. It is based on the story of four groups of people in Thatcher's UK, told in their own words and by following them in their everyday life. But, at the same time, the film uses a wide variety of symbolic elements and very contrasting montage that connects those observational stories to the conditions of contemporary society and broader British history. Grigsby himself has characterized the film as being about the betrayal of the postwar visions for a new society:

> Right from the start I wanted to make a film about the betrayal of the post-war dream. For all its impressionistic structure, there is a sense in which *Living on the Edge* is more direct than my other films, and perhaps that is because I personally feel a very deep sense of betrayal (…) Right through the class structure there is a deep sense of unease, cynicism, isolation and betrayal – betrayals of the ideals of the compassionate, caring society promised in 1945 when everyone dreamed of a real change and a new era (Grigsby in Corner, 1996: 123–4).

The same structure, but not with the same kind of political anger and criticism, can be found in Grigsby's *Time of Our Lives* (1993). It is a documentary about five generations of a British family from East London with the focus on an 85th birthday with all generations present. The film has a complex structure, moving between past and present, memories and historical realities and as an observational documentary it stands out as an interesting and quite unique kind of memory- and history-building through the voices of five generations commenting on their lives and dreams. At the same time, the film has a very complex and expressive style. The film creates a network of subjective, historical memories and actual clips from and representations of history, a web of public and private, of social and cultural history and everyday life history.

The testimonial statements from the five generations of the family are both filmed at the birthday party or in their homes, which gives us insights into the life and different places of the family. But also throughout the film there appear very expressive images of cityscapes or landscapes, situating the stories in the North East context and combining them with other more iconic places in the UK. The film uses radio clips representing different historical periods during the whole film, and thus anchors the private stories of the family in historical events of a national and more monumental, historical character. The film also uses clips from film, television and commercials from different historical periods with the same function as radio clips. In a classical authoritative documentary this historical dimension would have been inserted differently and it would have been accompanied by a clear voice indicating the nature of the clips and the context. But by doing it indirectly and without comments, and by creating a montage that combines private narratives along with public and symbolic narratives and images, the film creates another position for the spectator. The interpretation of reality happens through interpreting of emotional and social experiences that are more open than the authoritative documentary would allow.

Poetic and dramatized realities

There is no doubt that the authoritative and the observational documentaries are the formats dominating modern film and television culture, and also that the socially engaged documentary mostly uses those two genres. But within those two genres we find many stylistic and creative variations. At the same time, much more experimental and sometimes also controversial uses of documentary formats can be found in documentaries dealing with global issues. In 2003, two of the most experimental directors in the European art cinema tradition, Jørgen Leth and Lars von Trier, sat down to challenge each other through the film *The Five Obstructions*. The starting point was to remake five times and under very different circumstances Jørgen Leth's classical, poetic-reflexive documentary *The Perfect Human* (1968), and for Lars von Trier the main challenge was to try to get the cool, cosmopolitan Leth to confront the harsh realities of the global world. The film becomes a kind of metafilm about the aesthetic attitude towards life and a more engaged, moral attitude. This becomes especially clear in the Bombay film, where Leth is forced to repeat a very sumptuous meal in his original film, but this time set in one of the poorest districts of Bombay. The visual setting of the scene, with the poor locals just visible behind a veil, becomes a strong symbol of global inequalities and very different lifestyles and conditions. A very aesthetic-oriented and highly stylized poetic documentary can thus in fact be used to create debate and confront ways of relating to global issues.

Other examples of documentaries using more dramatic and poetic forms and strategies include the dramatized documentary, a documentary genre of a rather complex nature. One more simple form is reenactment documentaries, like for instance Nick Broomfield's film *Battle For Haditha* (2007), where he uses a documentary style to recreate and investigate the happenings in the Iraqi town Haditha in 2005, where 24 civilians were killed. But other dramatized documentaries can go further down the mixing of fictional story elements with documentary form. This is the case with Danish director Morten Hartz Kapler's *AFR* (2007), in which a completely fictional story around the then Danish Prime Minister, Anders Fogh Rasmussen, is told in an almost news reportage style, including actual news footage used out of context to support the documentary look of the film. Yet another example could be Franny Armstrong's environmental documentary *The Age of Stupid* (2009), in which a fictional curator of a human archive in a devastated 2055 world is looking back on what led to the catastrophe. The fictional sequences are mixed with documentary footage from news programmes and with portraits of real people. The socially engaged documentary can thus, like all documentaries, take many different, aesthetic and narrative forms.

Chapter 3

Engaging with and investigating reality: the social and political documentary

D ocumentaries, especially in the classical period before 1960, were forced to make films that were commissioned by private companies or public institutions. There was no free and independent position for a documentary film, and there was no economy for the production of films that came without strings attached. In many countries the commissioned film and the theme of it did leave some creative freedom to the filmmaker, but there were limits. But as both US and European documentary history shows, with Grierson as a key figure, it was possible to make very different documentary films despite the institutional and thematic constraints. Apart from the films commissioned by private companies or public institutions for mostly informational or educational purposes, there were also, from early on, documentaries made for political movements – not just parties, but also movements with a more general political agenda. This is a tendency and type of film that has continued in the contemporary documentary film culture with the rise of transnational social networks on issues related to ecology, human rights, democracy etc.

Since documentary filmmaking is naturally linked to the actual world and reflects themes, problems and conflicts in this world, it seems only natural that documentary films, more than fiction films, feel inclined to take up issues of a controversial, social and political nature. US filmmaker Emilio Antonio was concerned with the Vietnam war when he made *In the Year of the Pig* (1968), a film that was not just a compilation film about the war, but also a critical and engaged attack on the US for going to war (McEnteer 2006: 11ff). A respected journalist and documentary filmmaker like John Pilger was just as concerned and critical when he made his *Vietnam – The Quiet Mutiny* (1970) by reporting from the frontline and showing the internal collapse of the war on the American side. He has since continued with a long series of films focusing on the suppression of democracy, freedom of speech and social groups around the globe. He has become the critical voice and watchdog of the dark sides of political and social globalization. The Vietnam war and issues related to democracy and globalization are just some of the themes that the issue-oriented documentary has taken up. Other historical issues could be class-related struggles and conflicts, the feminist issue, the race equality issue, just to mention a few. Many documentary filmmakers have made independent films on these issues but many have also been part of movements and organizations promoting the agenda of such social and political movements.

A typically contemporary and engaged documentary filmmaker with a clear social and political agenda, and at the same time using and connecting to a social network, is the American director Robert Greenwald. As Christian Christensen has pointed out in his article 'Political documentary, online organization and activist synergies' (Christensen 2009),

Greenwald's films illustrate a 'coalition model' of documentary filmmaking, in which both the connection to a powerful political grassroots movement (Brave New Foundation or moveon.org.) and the use of a digital platform are merged. Robert Greenwald's films are part of a well organized independent social and political movement building a platform outside the established media production and distribution system and securing not just independent production, but also distribution through Brave New Theatres. The presentation of Brave New Films on their website (www.bravenewfilms.org) stresses the engaged, activist nature of the project and the intention of breaking the traditional media dominance of television: 'A pioneer in twenty-first century activism, Brave New Films are the centrepieces of guerrilla campaigns designed to break through noisy news cycles (…) we are producing entertaining and engaging films, blogs, television shows (…) while building the essential distribution infrastructure needed for long term social change' (quoted from Christensen 2009: 78).

Using words like 'guerrilla', 'activism' and 'engaging' links Brave New Films to a long tradition of critical, issue-oriented films, but this doesn't mean that they produce films with unbalanced propaganda. The films are mostly traditional, investigative documentary films dealing with central social and political issues that are also present on the agenda in the mainstream media. But the films represent a different, critical angle on contemporary issues, and Brave New Films produce and distribute film in ways that clearly connect to political and activist grassroots movements and seek to create and sustain an alternative public sphere that may hopefully somehow influence the dominant public sphere and media. The coalition model in this form of documentary film production means both using existing social networks and also creating a digital platform and network. These networks in some cases also contribute to the financing of films, but mostly the site creates synergy between different activities and partners in a much larger network.

The rise and crisis of critical, investigative documentaries

In the classical period of documentary film between 1930–1950, independent documentary filmmaking was rare. However, the rise of television to the centre of the public sphere in the 1960s created a stronger and more independent variety of journalism and documentary format. In the two leading television cultures, the American and the British, this gave room for famous formats like CBS's *See it now* (1951–1958) or *60 minutes* (1968–) and, in the UK, the BBC's *Panorama* (1953–), ITV's *World in Action* (1963–1998; see Goddard et al. 2007) or *This Week* (1956–1992; see Holland 2006) were early flagships. These formats gave a boost to independent, critical reporting and to television documentaries that were a popular and widespread supplement to the independent documentary film production. But, even though some of the programme formats still exist today, major changes occurred in the 1980s and 1990s as commercial competition got fiercer and public service cultures in Europe were severely challenged. In the US the television documentary production almost disappeared from the major networks and moved to cable stations like HBO, History Channel or National Geographic Channel, and to a certain degree also to CNN. But the older networks like NBC and ABC no longer had a strong, independent, documentary profile and production. Fortunately, the public service channel PBS increased documentary production, despite being faced with opposition from the government (see Bullert 1997).

In Scandinavia, the history of the television documentary and documentary in general is rather different (see Bondebjerg 2008a and 2012; Furuhammer 1995; Diesen 2005) because of the strong public service culture. Until around 2000 public service television stations kept a high documentary profile and the combination of a strong television culture and a strong, more independent film culture (supported by public funding) created a very strong and varied documentary film culture. After 2000, however, a decline in public service television and documentary output took place. The same development, but earlier, happened in the UK, but despite the crisis for many of the classical programme formats, the UK situation is now somewhat stabilized.

Basically, this type of documentary has been characterized by a critical agenda aimed at those in power, in the social, economic, political and cultural spheres, and some of the more independent films may also have an affiliation directly or indirectly with alternative institutions or movements. But they have also carried a broad programme load of observational documentaries on social and everyday life issues. They can have affiliations with or leanings towards specific political or social ideologies, but they can also represent what we might call universal claims for human rights, global ethics and democratic values and principles generally expressed and embedded in global institutions and networks. A film like Danish Frank Piasecki Poulsen's *Blood in the Mobile* (2009) certainly has a very strong critical edge towards the global, corporate mobile industry, but the core argument of the film is a universal claim for ethics in the way the developed West uses labour from the underdeveloped parts of the world. The American Morgan Spurlock's *Super Size Me* (2005) is definitely a very direct attack at the American fast food industry, but with personal courage it is also a film arguing the case for universal food and health standards.

Critical documentaries and the American reality

The American direct cinema movement was the first to move away from the kind of more issue-oriented and information propaganda-dominated documentary of the classical period. In the 1950s and 1960s, when American television developed into the dominant communicative centre, documentary filmmaking was developed along two strands: the observational documentary on contemporary life and the more critical, investigative form dealing with social and political issues. But, at times, the two strands would touch each other, as was the case with Robert Drew's production company Drew Associates and the films they made called *Primary* (1960) and *Crisis: Behind a Presidential Commitment* (1963). Robert Drew was a photo editor at Time's magazine *Life* and began to feel the competition from television in the 1950s. He developed a concept of getting closer to all aspects of American life, without the journalistic interference dominant in most film and television documentaries at that time (see Saunders 2007: 8ff). In 1962 he basically defines the ideology of the new observational documentary:

> What I found out was that real life never got out of the film, never came through the television set. If we could do that we could have a whole new basis for a whole new journalism (…) It would be theatre without actors; it would be plays without playwrights; it would be reporting without summary and opinion; it would be the ability to look in on people's lives at crucial times from which you could deduce certain things, and see a kind of truth, that can only be gotten from personal experience (quoted from Saunders 2007: 9)

Robert Drew and his co-directors first made *Primary* – a groundbreaking *political* documentary in the sense that the American audience for the first time experienced close and, as it seemed, almost direct access to the political campaign of John F. Kennedy and Hubert Humphrey during the Wisconsin primary. The film doesn't just signal a change in the political documentary, but also the historical turning point in the relationship between the media and politics which Joshua Meyorwitz, in his book *No Sense of Place: The Impact of Electronic Media on Social Behavior* has called 'the lowering of the political hero to our level' (1985: 268ff). It was a turning point for the media in getting closer and closer to the political persona and going backstage in the political system, but also a sign of how important it would be for politicians in the future to command the stage of broadcasting and visual media.

The main networks did not broadcast *Primary*, which only aired on Time Corporation's few channels, but the following couple of years Drew Associates produced a number of documentaries that were broadcast by ABC, and it was also ABC that broadcast *Crisis*, which caused a broad debate, because it combined the focus on a controversial and debated issue (in this case Kennedy's policy on racial policy) with the observational style. In *Crisis* we go behind the walls of the White House during a political crisis and confrontation. The dramatic quality of the film is that we witness two very different worlds: the east coast liberal Kennedy family, and the southern racial segregation supporter, Governor Wallace in Alabama. It is a piece of close-up, observational, political drama, that was hugely debated for showing life in the White House so directly, and also the private life of the Kennedys and Wallace, and of course also for the racial policy issue involved.

The debate created by programmes like this was, however, nothing compared with the kind of controversy raised by CBS's investigative magazine *See it now*, edited by Edward R. Murrow. The series represented the birth of independent, critical journalism and investigative documentary on American television, and the programme's way of taking up the most touchy and controversial issues at that time was legendary. The critical attack on Joseph McCarthy and the hunt for communists in America is historic and has now also been portrayed in George Clooney's film *Good Night, and Good Luck* (2005). The kind of documentaries made on CBS's *See it now* programme critically followed the development of the US engagement in Korea and in Vietnam, and they also intensively covered the fight against racial segregation in American schools and racism in American culture in general. Programmes could be studio-based with clips and critical commentaries, like the famous programme on McCarthy on 9 March 1954, that perhaps led to the later closure of the programme in 1958. But programmes could also take the form of documentary reports from Korea, Vietnam or from parts of the US, observing reality, talking to ordinary soldiers or people, or to experts and people in power. The programme represents the breakthrough of critical, investigative documentaries in the US, and it corresponded to the birth of the same genre in the UK in the same period with *Panorama* and *This Week*.

Murrow appeared on the front cover of *Time* on 30 September 1957, and was saluted as the most outstanding television journalist for his outstanding social conscience, his focus on serious matters and as the editor of the only continuing issue-oriented television series in America (McEnteer 2006: 8). Less than a year later CBS closed the programme. The tradition for this kind of critical documentary programme was, however, continued with *CBS Reports*, but Murrow only occasionally made programmes for this series. *CBS Reports* (1959–1992) did, however, just like *60 Minutes* (1968–), become one of the more stable platforms for critical investigative documentaries in the US. Both programmes have won numerous Emmy and Peabody awards over the years. Besides the permanent documentary slots, American television also carries a number of special programmes and reports that give room for deeper investigation and documentaries going behind the daily news.

CBS was the pioneering network in developing critical documentaries for television, but in the 1960s the other networks followed. NBC introduced *NBC White Paper* in 1960 as a series of specials and ABC started the documentary series *Close Up*. In the 1960s all networks started documentary series and organized special production units inside their news departments for documentary specials, and the 1960s and part of the 1970s became a golden period in television documentaries called 'the Camelot moment' by television historian Eric Barnouw (Barnouw 1992: 281f). From time to time programmes on American television would touch upon not just controversial, national problems and policies, but also the global dimension. This was the case with one of the first openly critical programmes on the Vietnam war, ABC's *The Agony of Vietnam* (1965), which began to see the war not only from an American perspective, but by bringing in international voices and protests – a highly controversial move back then. An interesting follow-up to this came in 1967 when CBS commissioned Felix Green to make a documentary which was entitled *Inside North Vietnam*, inspired by his book *A Curtain of Ignorance* (1964). Green's criticism concerned the appalling lack of knowledge about countries they considered enemies. The film was never shown on CBS, only on National Educational Television, but CBS did show clips of it in a CBS special news programme with a panel discussion (Barnouw 1992: 393f). Globalization and global knowledge in those days had a limited place on American network television.

The decline of American network documentaries

CBS and other television networks did promote critical documentaries in the 1960s and 1970s, and CBS in particular can be credited for making documentaries that stand out even today. In 1965 they recruited Peter Davis, and over the next ten years he made at least three films that carry the stamp of an almost independent film production. He was the writer behind the interesting *The Berkeley Rebels* (1965), which gave voice to the student movement and thus changed the general image of the average news broadcast. However, he also wrote and directed *The Selling of Pentagon* (1971), one of the first critical, investigative documentaries to take up the growing power of the military-industrial-political complex. It is a film that points ahead to the films made in the period after 2000 in connection with the wars in Iraq and Afghanistan, and the War on Terror in general. He also made the best and most influential film on the American failure in Vietnam, *Hearts and Minds* (1974). The film combines a critical, investigative unravelling of the whole military and political failure with observations from the frontline, among the disillusioned American soldiers and the frustrated and angry Vietnamese people.

All of Davis' films caused public debate, but none more than *The Selling of Pentagon*, which was called both 'un-American' and 'propagandistic manipulation' by Vice President Spiro Agnew, who attacked CBS directly (McEnteer 2006: 15). This attack was a warning about the changing climate in the 1980s for network television documentaries with a critical agenda, and the scandal of a *CBS Reports* programme in January 1983, *The Uncounted Enemy: A Vietnam Deception*, where the director Mike Wallace presented undermining statements on General Westmoreland and the suppressing of vital intelligence information during the Vietnam war. The problem with this highly critical documentary was, as a later investigation and a PBS programme showed, that the programme was very biased and based on false premises and information (McEnteer 2006: 21ff). In 1984, following many critical network programmes and this incident, FCC changed the public service guidelines which had been in place since 1960. Even though the documentary strands of network television continued, they were changed and downgraded, and many of the critical functions were left to the much weaker Public Broadcasting System (PBS), a system that republican presidents in particular were not eager to support.

Both McEnteer (2006) and Bullert (1997) point to the early 1980s as the watershed in the decline of critical and more independent documentaries, and they see this historical moment as a starting point for both alternative independent filmmaking and PBS. In this period there was in the US a general conservative attack on public support for culture and especially artists that were seen as liberal, biased or downright against American values (Bullert 1997: 10), which also damaged public support for independent documentary production and for PBS as an independent broadcaster. In McEnteer's words:

> Emboldened by the Vietnam credibility gap, documentary filmmakers of the 1960s and 1970s produced narratives contradicting the official stories about war. Through control

of broadcasting licenses and legislation, government pressured the television networks to limit criticism and ban more radical attack on its version of events. By the 1980s, as filmmakers explored the lingering physical, emotional, moral and political damage from Vietnam, the Reagan and Bush administration limited media appraisals of their policies by stonewalling, restricting access, and scripting photo opportunities and stories of the day. As media became less critical, independent films became an important means of circumventing the veils of fantasy and disinformation (McEnteer 2006: 20).

The independent and public American documentary sector

PBS was founded in 1969 as a private non-profit organization funded by viewers connected to its rather decentralized network, but also by the Corporation for Public Broadcasting (CPB) and a number of educational and cultural institutions and funds. The main difference in funding is that, unlike the networks, PBS is not funded by commercials and thus it is independent of commercial interests – it is the closest the US comes to the European public service stations. PBS has a very broad and diverse production and broadcasting of documentaries in series representing both different formats and different communicative purposes. *Frontline* (1983–) is the flagship of contemporary, investigative and critical documentaries, filling the gap after the decline of this type of programming on the commercial networks. Around 25 programmes are made a year (each one hour) and they are seen by approximately 6 million viewers and very often reviewed by national newspapers, causing public debate.

P.O.V. (1986–) is much more experimental and a series where independent documentary filmmakers can get support for and distribution of their work. The name, referring to 'point of view', indicates that more opinionated, subjective types of documentaries are given a space here, but the PBS generally receive many more suggestions than they can take in. According to Bullert (1997: 32), almost 98 per cent of the more than 500 entries they receive are rejected. Two other important PBS series are *American Experience* (1988–), dedicated to national, historical documentaries about both recent and older historical events, and *American Masters* (1986–), a series of portrait documentaries dedicated to stories about important American artists. All documentary series have since the mid-1990s been supported by programme websites with extensive possibilities for viewing and additional information.

Frontline is basically a series for in-house produced, investigative documentaries that live up to the best traditions of journalistic documentaries. As such, *Frontline* is almost unique in the American television documentary landscape and, as we shall see in the following chapters, *Frontline* and PBS are strongly represented in the post-9/11 critical documentary tradition. They have often been the first to raise criticism and they are the ones to systematically follow up on cases when they tend to disappear from the mainstream media agenda. *P.O.V.*, on the other hand, is the only continued free space for independently produced documentaries on American television, with the exception of HBO, who occasionally decide to broadcast already-produced documentaries, for instance, Charles Ferguson's *No End in Sight* (2007) and Alex Gibney's *Taxi to the Dark Side* (2007) (see. p. 83f). *P.O.V.* is thus a major contribution to the maintaining of diversity in a highly commercial and competitive film and television culture, but the independent documentary film culture also exists outside PBS.

'It's not television – it's HBO': the birth of a documentary giant

HBO had its first rather humble start as a local New York cable service in 1972, but the channel was soon boosted to national prominence and reach in the late 1970s after investment from, among others, Time-Life. The channel is now owned by Time-Warner and reaches around 30 million American viewers and the same number abroad. Regional streaming services were created around 2011, for instance HBO Nordic, launched in 2012. HBO made its first success on sports and film, but in the 1990s developed a remarkable quality production of television series and documentaries. HBO shows documentaries made by independent directors not just from the US, but also internationally, for example they broadcast the Danish director Anders Østergaard's prize-winning documentary *Burma VJ* (2008) in 2009. HBO's documentary profile in general is rather global in content and themes, and they do take up issues that can be quite controversial in the US, for instance the problems of global warming rejected by many republicans, but taken up in a film like Maryann DeLeo and Ellen Goosenberg Kent's *Too Hot Not to Handle* (2006) in a very authoritative and investigative way.

However, HBO is not very strong in critical investigative journalism, although they do take up important social and political themes. HBO often take the human story approach to the social and political problems they address, whether it is a national or a more global agenda. Dealing with the catastrophic gulf oil spill, Irene Taylor Brodsky in *Saving Pelican 895* (2011) puts the endangered pelicans in focus and with this perspective perhaps catches a bigger audience for the themes that the film actually address. Another example of this human approach to global issues is Tanaz Eshagian's *Love Crimes Of Kabul* (2011), an observational documentary from inside a Kabul prison, following the lives of women in Kabul accused of illegitimate sexual behaviour. There is a strong attention on globalization in many of HBO's documentaries, focusing on parts of the world not often dealt with in mainstream media. HBO's Alexandra Pelosi has also investigated the multicultural dimensions of the USA in her *Citizen USA: A 50 State Road Trip* (2011), an observational documentary following a large group of new Americans just about to become citizens.

Even though HBO cannot be seen as quite as strong in critical, investigative documentaries as PBS, HBO has a strong global and social profile that is complementary to PBS, and they do occasionally make documentaries that really enter contested, political areas and issues. With their human issue-oriented documentary stories they probably reach a broader and different American and global audience than PBS, which may be preaching to the already informed and critical audience. At the same time, HBO has an important role together

Figures 3a and b: Michael Moore's *Fahrenheit 9/11* (2004). Moore in action as activist and provocateur on the streets. Frame grab. Cinematography: Andrew Black, Mike Desjarlais, Urban Hamid.

with PBS in creating a space for independent directors. One of the later, most successful, independent and critical film directors in the US, Michael Moore, actually made his first film, *Roger & Me* (1989), in collaboration with PBS, and even though the film also got a wide theatrical release, the case shows the importance of stations like PBS and HBO, since commercial broadcasters rejected the film in the first instance (Bullert 1997: 161).

The British documentary movement and television

Europe is the heartland of both public service television and public funding for films, and in this respect the whole film and television culture of Europe is very different from that in America. But in terms of the start of documentaries and the kind of genre developed from the early days of television in the 1950s and onward, and the relation between the television sector and the independent film sector, the story and structural development has many similarities. In the UK both the BBC and the regional commercial broadcaster ITV (1955) quickly developed documentary strands of programmes for both current affairs with a social and critical edge, and programmes with more of a human issue orientation. The BBC series *Panorama* (1953–), in particular, became the origin of a completely new, more independent and critical form of journalism and documentary, which Goldie in his book *Facing the Nation: Television and Politics 1937–1976* (1977) has described as a new concept of journalism and factual reporting: 'It was not always necessary to be respectful; experts were not invariably right; the opinion of those in high places did not have to be respected (…) a manifestation of a broader democratization (…) an effect of the familiarizing, demystifying effects of television itself' (Goldie 1977: 216).

Current affairs magazines like *Panorama* soon became the backbone of this new television documentary, where journalistic reports on a broad number of issues developed along with critical investigative documentaries. ITV and Associated-Rediffusion Television launched *This Week* in 1956, later carried on by Thames Television (1978–1986 under the name *TV Eye*) until 1992 (see Holland 2006). Almost as influential and important as BBC's *Panorama* was ITV/Granada's *World in Action* (1963–1998) which, despite being launched on a commercial channel, proved to be independent and critical. The first really trendsetting British television documentary is often identified as the BBC programme *Report from Germany* (1948), with a quite unusual on-the-spot look into postwar Germany, but a BBC *Special Inquiry* programme from 1955, *Has Britain a Colour Bar?*, is also groundbreaking because of its focus on the hidden racism in everyday life around Birmingham and for including different voices of ordinary people.

As Corner (1996) and Goddard et al. (2007) have pointed out, the development of the British television documentary was a clear continuation in both the form and vision of Grierson and the film documentary movement and the radio documentary. Here, more authoritative ways of reporting on social life and problems meet with an anthropological attempt to show or give voice to the lives of ordinary people. ITV already in 1956 ran another extraordinary and innovative documentary series, *Look in on London*, which simply focused on different people's work and life in London through interview and reporting on location (Corner 1996: 72ff). Early tendencies like this were later further developed by documentary filmmaker Denis Mitchell, for instance in his feature-length documentary *Morning in the Street* (1959) or *Soho Story* (1959), or in the series he directed for ITV called *This England* (1965–1967 and 1977–1980), where other important documentary directors like Mike Newell and Michael Grigsby made films.

The British development is characteristic for a big European nation with a firm basis in a national and regionalized public service culture, but with a dual structure of commercial and public service. The competition in the 1950s and 1960s was met in 1964 with a strengthening of the BBC public service remit (Pilkington Report 1962) and a second channel BBC2. Much of the early radio and television documentary can, according to Scannel (Scannel, 1996), be seen as mostly a projection and panoramic representation of national life and actualities. But an early series like Norman Swallow's *Special Enquiry* (BBC 1952–1959) did in fact raise serious social and political questions in its close-up investigation of British realities, never before seen in that way on national television. In Swinson's book *Writing for Television* (1955) the early forms of television documentaries are interestingly enough described as: *dramatized documentary* based on actual events and problems but shot and recreated in a studio with actuality films inserted; *the actuality documentary* where current affairs approaches are mixed with more creative film documentary strategies; *the magazine documentary* combining actuality and more entertaining formats.

The more and more creative and critical development of the television documentary in the UK runs parallel with developments in the more independent sector. As Corner has pointed out (Corner 1996: 38f), realist, documentary traditions developed outside the journalism or documentary departments, for instance the BBC strand of Wednesday Plays in the 1960s and 1970s, where drama-documentaries by writers such as Peter Watkins or Ken Loach paved the way for other kinds of critical representations of reality. Such drama-documentaries were not uncontroversial, as the case of Peter Watkins' *The War Game* (1965) or Ken Loach's historical series *Days of Hope* (1975) show. Peter Watkins' recreation of the potential effects of a nuclear attack on London and how official institutions might handle the situation was never shown at the time, officially because it might scarc the population. *Days of Hope* about a famous mining strike and the general development for the working class in Britain from 1914–1926 was shown, but met with criticism for being leftist propaganda.

The breakthrough of the British investigative documentary

The 1970s were crucial for the development of a more critical, investigative documentary tradition, and the UK was a leading country in the shaping of this. The critical, investigative method was combined with a strong development of the social, observational documentary tradition. The developments of the 1970s had roots both in earlier television forms and in the independent documentary cinema of the late 1950s and early 1960s. Out of this grew, as already pointed out, a new observational and critical documentary both inside and outside television, with early television representatives such as Paul Watson and Dennis Mitchell and with later examples such as Michael Apted, Molly Dineen or Michael Grigsby or the many producers and directors on formats like *World in Action* (ITV), *Panorama* (BBC), *This Week* (ITV/Thames Television), *Modern Times* (BBC2) or *Dispatches* (Channel 4).

This development of much more independent and critical forms of documentary on television, where television suddenly became a sharp watchdog of political and social life, did not pass unnoticed. One programme in particular, *Death on the Rock* (1988, This Week), dealing with the shooting of an alleged Northern Irish terrorist in Gibraltar by the British counter-terror force, led to a direct attack from the Thatcher government on ITV and the independence of television journalism (Holland 2006: 190f). The Broadcasting Act of 1990 meant stronger privatization, deregulation and competition in television, but also attempts at stronger control on balance and objectivity. However, this attempt at political control by and large did not have a lasting effect, although for a period in the 1990s critical and independent programming seemed to suffer.

The period from 1970–1990 was in many ways a golden age for documentaries and critical journalism. Contributing to this was the establishment of Channel 4 in 1984 and the fact that they commissioned independently produced documentary programmes, and thus helped develop an independent sector outside television – though dependent financially on television. In her analysis of *This Week*, Patricia Holland clearly shows how this programme both followed and set the agenda on a number of highly controversial issues and themes in this period: the youth revolt, working class culture, sexuality and gender roles, race and oppression, the Vietnam War, global issues (Middle East, South Africa) and the conflict in Northern Ireland, to mention a few. But, she also points to the fact that perhaps the reporting and the documentaries on Northern Ireland created especially strong tensions between journalists on the ground making the controversial programmes, the management of the channel and the political system. *Death on the Rock* (1988) was therefore really just the culmination of a long critical period from the mid-1970s to the end of the 1980s, where the new conservative government finally struck back.

This Week both made critical, investigative documentaries and more observational documentaries, and when they reported from the national front lines of Northern Ireland they actually tried to portray both the conditions and lives of British soldiers on duty, the locals, the IRA people and to go behind the conflict in more authoritative forms. But the increased anti-terror laws of that time were just as problematic for a free and democratic press as the post-9/11 laws became. The 1974 Prevention of Terror Act (PTA) had specific implications for the media (Holland 2006: 139f) and eventually this led to the death of the series, first for a shorter period in 1986, and then finally in 1992, when Thames Television lost its franchise after the new 1990 Television Act came into force.

The oldest and most consistent of the television formats, *Panorama* (BBC), has survived since the 1950s and has been able to be innovative and follow new trends in journalism and documentary. The same goes for the third dominant programme, *World in Action* (ITV), which turned the format into a kind of umbrella for all sorts of new documentary experiments: they made drama-documentaries in collaboration with Granada Television's drama-doc department, they did of course develop critical, investigative documentaries, but they also developed various forms of observational documentaries, for instance in direct collaboration with the icons of the American cinema verité movement, the Maysles

Brothers (Goddard et al. 2007: 31). Just as is the case with *This Week* and *Panorama*, the mid-1970s seem to be the heyday of the development of critical, investigative documentaries. The executive producer and later head of current affairs and features in that period, Gus MacDonald, estimates that one-third of the programmes at that time were investigative, despite the problems they gave the channel on several levels: 'Investigative journalism has always been the most difficult area of current affairs programme making (…) It costs a great deal of money; one programme can wipe out experienced team members for most of a series; there are formidable legal problems; it strains relations with the IBA (…) powerful interest groups fight back; viewers protest; civil servants put on pressure' (MacDonald in Goddard et al. 2007: 65).

The contemporary British documentary culture

The period after 2000 for documentary film and television in the UK has dramatically changed for two reasons: first of all, the major commercial strands for documentaries of the kind we saw in the period 1970–2000 have almost disappeared, leaving only BBC and Channel 4 on the scene – both of them, however, with a huge diversity in documentary programming; second, the swift move to a digital culture has changed the game and the ways documentaries are made and distributed. At least to a certain degree, this has put pressure on the classic, critical, investigative documentary in particular, both on BBC's *Panorama* and also on Channel 4's *Dispatches*. *Panorama* for a longer period disappeared from its historic primetime position as a current affairs programme, and as it came back in 2011 it was reduced from 60 to 30 minutes. BBC also developed a strand for more international documentaries, *Storyville*, and outside the strands a number of other single and series documentaries were sent. So despite the disappearance of some of the classical strands, the period after 2000 does seem to develop a new growth in very diverse forms of documentary. Channel 4's *Dispatches* is a real quality strand with documentaries dealing with important global and political issues, as is a strand like *Unreported World*, with a systematic focus on parts of the world that normally never enter news reporting. Like the BBC, Channel 4 also makes room for international documentaries on *True Stories*, and a strand like *Cutting Edge* is the main avenue for national documentaries, just as *First Cut* is a space for new and upcoming talents.

There is no doubt that the Thatcher years and the 1990 Television Act were a setback for the television sector and creative independence. There is no doubt either that the digital development and explosion in types of channels has been a challenge to all the major channels. Potentially the digital development has great possibilities both for production and distribution, but the new media culture has yet to develop forms and functions that work. But despite all the challenges, the development in the UK after 2000 is characterized by a strong and diverse development of documentary strands and formats, especially on the BBC and Channel 4. In the Pact Report in 2009, the percentage of the programming dedicated to 'factual' is 9 per cent (a decline from around 13–15 per cent in the two previous years), but at the same time the report documents that documentary is by far the most successful genre as far as international sales are concerned; 58 per cent of the channels report this, followed by entertainment/comedy at 45 per cent. So in general both nationally and internationally, documentary seems to be on the rise again.

The Danish documentary way

Compared to the system in the UK, Denmark actually represents a different European model, although Danish documentaries developed along with the early British documentary movement in the 1930's, and were directly inspired by the UK model. As in the UK, the Danish documentary movement was from the beginning financed either by private companies or by public sector film units and film funding. In the UK it was the Empire Marketing Board, the General Post Office and later the Crown Film Unit under the Ministry of Information that represented the public side. In Denmark it was the public National Film Board, the private organization Danish Culture Film, and during the war the Ministry of Employment as well, and occasionally other ministries. But unlike the UK development, where the more independent film documentary soon became a rather small part of the documentary production and television became the main producer of documentary, the Danish system continued to be a dual system, with both strong film funding through the national film institute and a strong television system.

In 1964, and even more so in 1972, film became part of the new cultural policy of the welfare state and public funding was set aside to support both documentary films and feature films through the Danish Film Institute (DFI). From around 1975 Danish public service television (DR) – with a monopoly until 1988 – increased and developed new, more critical and independent television documentaries as well. This created a strong and very diverse documentary tradition where the two forms of documentary to a large degree supplemented each other, and where co-production also gradually developed. The early television documentaries on Danish television were mostly characterized by portraits and social reportage from around the country, and a more critical tradition was slow to develop. None of the formats known from the UK or the US model were created until 1975 with *TV-Aktuelt/TV-actuality*, which became a space for critical documentaries and current affairs (Bondebjerg 2008a: 319f). Controversial programmes on politics, private business, organized crime, corruption and problems in the public sector for health, between the political system and the industrial complex etc., changed the documentary television language dramatically and often created huge debates in public. Also, more global issues were taken up and, together with critical and experimental documentaries from the youth department (Bondebjerg 2008a: 243f) – for a very long time an experimental platform on Danish television – Danish television documentary definitely set a new agenda.

Documentary became a very popular genre on Danish television in this period and when a new Danish channel, TV2 – inspired by the British Channel 4 model – was established on 1 October 1988 it paved the way for other more commercial channels in the following decades, and documentary became an important genre in the competition. DR created *DR-Dokumentargruppen/DR-documentary group* and gave them creative autonomy and rather big budgets, and TV2 created both *Fak2eren* and *Reportageholdet* (Bondebjerg 2008a: 373 f). The result was a clearly golden age for critical, investigative documentaries and social, observational documentaries on both channels until around 2000, where a change in programming towards more factual light programmes and reality television took place (Bondebjerg 2008a: 487 f).

After 2000 the two platforms for documentary production, the independent film sector and the television sector, seem to have changed position and roles, but also developed a more direct co-production, despite some internal fighting and conflict (Bondebjerg 2012: 73ff). The commercial television channels, but also to a certain degree the public service channels of DR – now multiplied into DR1, DR2, DR3, and DRK – have lowered the in-house production of serious, documentary production, and the number of formatted factual light programmes have increased. But when they do produce and broadcast serious documentaries, they often do so in co-production with the film sector. At the same time, the DR channels in particular have increased the number of international documentary productions (mainly on DR2 and the programme called *Documania*), but also reruns of modern or classic documentaries on other channels.

Just as in the UK and US, a new, strong and independent documentary tradition seems to develop again after the crisis around 2000. Part of the reason for this development is a doubling of the funding for film production from 1997 at the Danish Film Institute, and another explanation is probably that the famous Danish Film School in 1996 started a formal education in documentary film and television production. Important Danish documentary filmmakers with international reach like Janus Metz and his *Armadillo* (2010) or Anders Østergaard and his *Burma VJ* (2008) and more recently Mads Brügger with *The Ambassador* (2011) are not a product of television, but of the independent sector. The innovative dynamic seems to have changed from television to the more independent film sector, although in collaboration with television.

PART II

War, terror and democracy: the post-9/11 documentary

Chapter 4

Into the dark side: the politics of war

When the terrorists hit the Twin Towers on the fatal day of 9/11 it was not just a human tragedy, but also a political and symbolic media event with far-reaching consequences for American and global politics. In war, truth is always the first victim an old saying goes. Subsequent investigations into the political events leading to the war in Afghanistan and, in particular, the war in Iraq, indicate that many of the basic assumptions that led to the War on Terror, especially the war against Iraq that divided the European allies, were fabricated or false intelligence information. According to many later news reports and documentary films, the media were used, as Danny Schechter has called it, as 'Weapons of mass deception' (Schechter 2006a, 2006 b). When deception becomes the mainstream and events lead to widespread bending of fundamental human rights, as critics and many documentary films and books now indicate (see for instance, Mayer 2008), then the War on Terror is in danger of becoming also a war on democracy.

In Jane Mayer's remarkable and detailed account of American post-9/11 politics, *The Dark Side* (2008), she quotes both the Columbia Law professor Scott Horton, and the republican legal activist, Bruce Fein, for saying that the Bush administration extended the executive powers of the presidency in a way that was unprecedented in earlier history and even went beyond the normal extension of that power in earlier war periods: 'His war powers allow him to declare anyone an illegal combatant. All the world is a battlefield […] he could kill someone in Lafayette Park if he wants! It's got the sense of Louis XIV: "I am the State"' (Mayer 2008: 70–71). Jane Mayer is a very respected journalist with a background as reporter for *The Wall Street Journal* and as author of several books. When a journalist with such a reputation writes a book where the subtitle is 'The Inside Story of How the War on Terror Turned into a War on American Ideals' there is reason to be concerned. But her book was not the only critical book on this development. Dana Priest – also the author of *The Mission: Waging War and Keeping Peace With America's Military* (2003) – together with William Arkin published a book with a similar, critical agenda, *Top Secret America: The Rise of the New Security State* (2011), in which the authors point out how the intelligence system has grown like a cancer cell and become a state within the state that nobody seems able to control or even get a clear picture of. The message in both books is that something that started as a protection of democracy has become a threat to that democracy.

From patriotism to a critical agenda: US media and the War on Terror

The independent journalist and filmmaker Danny Schechter has argued that there was a real and understandable sense of national unity after 9/11, which the media had a natural, active part in shaping. However, he also claims that the media in the time after did not see just how far the Bush administration and the Pentagon were taking advantage of that situation (interview with Danny Schechter in New York, October 2008). They hired Hollywood people to plan the campaign and the launching of the concept of the 'War on Terror'. This is obvious in, for instance, a classic government propaganda film like Chuck Workman's five minute rapid film montage *The Spirit of America* (Faludi 2007: 6–7) that efficiently and metaphorically connects the War on Terror with classical Hollywood scenes of patriotic unity and the tough lonely cowboy seeking revenge, directly quoting Fords' *The Searchers* (1956). Another example is *Operation Enduring Freedom: America Fights Back* (Richard Dekmejian and Robert Kline 2002), a modern version of patriotic WW2 propaganda films. In Schechter's words the media were in a situation where you were either for or against: 'If you dissent, if you offer a counter-narrative, you are soft on terrorism. If you ask questions, you are sending the wrong message to the enemy (Schechter 2006b)'.

From around 2006, however, the war in Iraq climbed up the agenda in the American mainstream media, mainly because the war was not easily finished, many soldiers and civilians were killed, and because the presidential election campaign of 2007 became a platform for an open critique of that part of American foreign policy. The American public was highly divided on the issue, but a majority became more and more critical. With Obama as the new president, the agenda on the War on Terror and Iraq finally seems to have changed. The public, political discourse on these matters has moved towards a critical discourse so far in the periphery of public media discourse and debate.

But until 2006 the critical agenda on the War on Terror was rather restricted in the US mainstream media, except for quality newspapers like *New York Times* and *Washington Post* and on PBS news programmes and documentaries. The background for going to war in Iraq erupted as a theme in 2003 and 2004 when the *New York Times* reported that the intelligence on weapons of mass destruction was not correct, and this did to a certain degree hit the television news on a broad scale, particularly in a series of CNN news specials. The theme of the War on Terror was also clearly an issue in the 2004 presidential election between Gore and Bush. But before 2003–2004 this theme and any deeper critical agenda towards the politics against terror can only be found on television via PBS. For instance, in a Frontline programme on PBS from 2002, *Target America*, the theme is the split and conflict inside the US security apparatus, security system and the political system. PBS is thus one of the first audiovisual media to deal with the theme taken up later by both Mayer, and Priest and Arkin in critical perspective and detail. But even in the case of PBS the more sharp and outspoken criticism of the War on Terror and especially the Iraq War doesn't take real form until late 2002–2003. The patriotic feeling and unity was very strong the first couple of years after 9/11.

Sharp light on the dark side of politics and war

'We also have to work, though, sort of on the dark side, if you will. We've got to spend time in the shadows in the intelligence world. A lot of what needs to be done here will have to be done quietly, without any discussion' (Vice President Dick Cheney on *Meet the Press*, 16 September 2001). This statement, five days after 9/11 and shortly after it had also been publicly announced that there were plans to invade Iraq as a consequence of 9/11, on the one hand just confirms what we have always known, that the secret intelligence work has sides that operate outside the public awareness. But it is also a statement revealing the strategy behind one of the most debated elements in the War on Terror, the quite extraordinary powers given to the executive branches of the US government, outside public control, and the use of extreme torture methods, most famously waterboarding. In fact, fictional narratives can sometimes have direct political influence. In *The Dark Side* Mayer (2008: 196ff) refers to the role the TV series *24* (Fox Networks 2001–2010) had in military and political circles, when the new strategy for getting terrorists to talk was planned. *24* shows an agent who always gets answers using extreme violence and torture, and the series was, according to Mayers, a direct inspiration for those in the US government arguing for the need and efficiency of torture. In late 2012 and early 2013 a similar debate broke out after the premiere of Kathryn Bigelow's film *Zero Dark Thirty* based on the actual history of the killing of Osama Bin Laden. The film's very realistic depiction of torture again raised an ethical debate in the American public, and whether this was fiction or the real story.

Many experienced field personnel knew that torture was not very efficient: evidence given under torture is often false, because people say what they think the torturer wants to hear. The statement also explains the title of Alex Gibney's film *Taxi to the Dark Side* (2007), a documentary film that won the Oscar for Best Documentary, and in October 2008 was shown on HBO. Like Danish Christoffer Guldbrandsen's film, *The Secret War* (2006), Errol Morris' *Standard Operation Procedure* (2008) and the HBO documentary by Rory Kennedy *Ghosts of Abu Ghraib* (2007), Gibney's film is about the use of torture as part of the whole American post-9/11 policy and mentality. Gibney's film is one of the first American films systematically documenting the uses of terror way beyond international conventions and one of the first films to show that this is not just the result of a few rotten apples among the soldiers, but something that goes to the very top in military ranks and the political sphere.

Gibney's argument in the film is that the top brass may not have orchestrated that kind of torture specifically, but they have created the framework, the policy and the mentality that made it grow. As Gibney has stated in several interviews (see for instance *Wall Street Journal Online*, 28 April 2007), nobody in the beginning would talk to him or appear in the film on camera. A wall of silence and denial met him. They got permission to film in Guantanamo in early 2006, but they were not allowed to talk to or interview anybody: they got the standard tour of the camp and were allowed to film in designated areas. Eventually they got in contact with people with real insight and knowledge willing to talk and they also managed to get highly disturbing live footage.

The film focuses on one very strong human story about the Afghan taxi driver Dilawar, who was arrested by the Americans and tortured to death at the now infamous Bagram Air Base, where other cases of severe torture and death took place and eventually lead to a public investigation. The film starts with this story, taking us back to the Afghan village where the family of the completely innocent Dilawar is interviewed. But from there Gibney takes us directly into the heart of the dark side of American policy and the memo of special presidential adviser John Yoo, which should legalize the new political decision to torture suspected terrorists in ways not legalized by the Geneva Convention. We hear opponents and experts talking about the 'fog of ambiguity' created by the Pentagon and Cheney, Rumsfeld and Bush and the urge for results that was transmitted down the ranks and created this atmosphere.

Gibney uses footage from already published media material to give an impression of how these people in the top thought, because none of them wanted to be interviewed for the film, and he combines this footage with interviews featuring experts and people with a former affiliation to the Bush-Cheney-Rumsfeld administration. But the link and the connection is very clear and many of the things brought forward in the film have – both before and after – been confirmed in book publications (Mayer 2008; Power 2002) and have also been taken up by other TV documentaries such as, for instance, the PBS programme *The Dark Side* (2006). We also hear public statements pretending that international conventions will be met, but interviews with people on the floor tell another story and not even those public statements by Rumsfeld, Cheney and Bush are very clear statements.

Apart from the Bagram Air Base, the film also deals with Abu Ghraib in Iraq and Guantanamo in Cuba. It takes a detailed look into both the actual torture and the interrogation techniques there and puts them in context with commands and techniques described in public military papers. In this way the film clearly demonstrates that this torture is part of a *politically defined* culture and framework, and it also traces the history of these methods in science. The film uses both reconstructions and very disturbing authentic pictures never shown before on US television from Abu Ghraib. Using experts, the film shows that Abu Ghraib was seen as a kind of torture laboratory where Rumsfeld gave wide-ranging freedom that went beyond the military field manual. Gibney says, in the already-mentioned interview, that he does not consider himself to be a leftist political filmmaker. Instead his work is trying to get 'inside the thinking perspective' behind the War on Terror and those involved in forming the policy in this area. To Gibney this is not just a political, but also a universal moral issue.

As an Oscar winner, one would think that *Taxi to the Dark Side* would be secured wide distribution in the United States, but in 2008 Gibney accused the distribution company Think Film of not having done enough for the film. It did not really get theatrical success and never made it to TV. Discovery Channel originally bought the film but dropped it again as too controversial, but finally HBO took over and screened it (October 2008). But what is obvious is that this is not just a case of mismanagement by the distributor, it is simply the basic story of independent, critical documentaries. Even the HBO premiere did not result in reviews and public debate in many mainstream media (especially not on television), and the theatrical premiere of this film did not get newspaper reviews in any great number. Independent documentaries travel in another alternative and partly online community of the critical elite and are shown in local organizations and communities. The mainstream media outside HBO and PBS are silent.

Gibney's film is clearly an important contribution to the contextualization of mainstream media images of soldiers performing torture. The film links this incident to a broader political context pointing the camera towards the Pentagon and the political power elite. But, one year earlier, Rory Kennedy's HBO documentary *Ghosts of Abu Ghraib* (Kennedy 2007) already went in that direction and furthermore managed to get deep interviews not just with the soldiers in charge of the torture, but also some of their surviving victims. Interviews with suspected terrorists in American films, like interviews with Arab and Muslim people in general, are very rare in American mainstream media. So for this reason alone, Kennedy's film is unique. The film has an even stronger psychological depth than Gibney's film and does not lose sight of the political agenda either.

But the most interesting and disturbing film about torture and the War on Terror so far is *Standing Operation Procedure* (Morris 2008), also based on the Abu Ghraib case. Unlike the two other directors, Errol Morris takes away the general footage from TV and focuses intensely on the photos from Abu Ghraib and the soldiers doing the torture. He makes a really deep analysis of both the pictures as media icons and symbols and the characters involved. He does not follow the more political context in any detailed way, although the film clearly states that the incidents were orchestrated from the highest level, but he restores the humanity of those demonized and condemned. Furthermore, he creates his own style and documentary universe with an intense sense of mystery and new angles and perspectives on an already well-known and documented reality and media event.

Morris' approach – as in all of his films – is more psychological than political: he wants to understand the nature of torture and how ordinary people can do the things that were done in Abu Ghraib. He does not buy the official political excuse about 'a few rotten apples'; instead he digs into the human mind and takes a systemic view that involves a critical look at both the military as an institution and the political mentality behind the War on Terror that created this. Morris' technique is to focus especially on the public scapegoat, the female MP Lynndie England, and to let her own narration expand. He does not want to acquit or whitewash anybody, but he wants to understand. So the film becomes a visual and narrative trip into a darker mental space that is 'normalized' in the sense that we are witnesses to a story about the actions of completely normal, everyday people. Like a slow thriller or mystery, the film keeps returning to the same situations and actions, the same feelings and states of mind both in the pictures of those tortured and in the mentality of those performing the torture.

Even though the film does not use a lot of time to point to the political context and background, it is clearly there. We see Rumsfeld visiting the prison early on in the film and his eagerness to get away without seeing too much, and the title in itself indicates that what we witness in the film is not a perverted, individual vendetta, a case of a few people going way beyond their limits. It is indeed just part of 'a standing operation procedure' orchestrated directly or indirectly from the highest office of the United States. *Standing Operation Procedure* could be called a psychological, documentary thriller about the dark side of the American mentality, and it has been criticized for turning politics into psychology and epistemology (Arthur 2008). But even though the political agenda is subdued in the film and the aesthetic form of the film differs very much from a journalistic, critical investigative form, the film is a powerful tale of the consequences, and the mentality, of a politics undermining democracy and very basic human rights and moral norms. The horror is with the dark side of American politics in the War on Terror.

The military-industrial complex: the global American Empire

One of the greatest fabricated lies in recent American history is the political story (backed by false intelligence) that Iraq had weapons of mass destruction and that Iraq had close connections with and supported Al Qaeda. In the inner circles of the CIA there is a joke: 'If Iraq had weapons of mass destruction we would know, because we would have the receipt.' The joke, quoted by an ex-CIA agent in Eugene Jarecki's *Why We Fight* (2005) points to the role of the military-industrial complex in American foreign policy after WW2. Jarecki's film is perhaps one of the most penetrating and sharp analytical films about the Iraq War and its connection with the historical development of foreign policy and its deep influence on media and public debate on critical issues. It is also a film with a very dense and diverse style and documentation, going behind the stage of high politics, into the military zone of war and peace and also giving ordinary people in both the United States and Iraq a clear and strong voice.

The film has a complex but very efficient intellectual, and emotional, narrative and rhetorical structure. The initial sequences of the film illustrate this. The first images are of a stealth fighter airplane filmed on the first day of the Iraq War, 19 March 2003. But from that the film takes a giant historical leap back to Eisenhower's abdication speech on 19 January 1961, the famous speech where he warned against the growing military-industrial complex and its worrying influence on politics and the potential dangerous consequences for democracy. Then we see American soldiers as liberators of Europe in WW2, a shot of the Statue of Liberty, and then – as a contrast – American forces in a chaotic and violent Iraq. A line of presidents and their decision to go to war somewhere in the world is shown, and finally the opening sequences show a mixture of statements from ordinary people and experts and politicians trying to answer the film's basic question 'Why we fight'. These layers of the story structure the whole film and the same type of sequences keep coming back.

One of the more powerful stories in the film is the story of a retired NYPD officer who loses his son in the World Trade Center on 9/11 and whose hate and desire for revenge reflects both the political establishment and many ordinary Americans. We learn how he managed to get his son's name on one of the bombs falling in Iraq. But in the final part of the film he loses faith in both Bush and the war, because it becomes clear to him that the reasons

Figures 4a and b: Eugene Jarecki's *Why We Fight* (2005). Donald Rumsfeld and Dick Cheney spreading war propaganda. Frame grab. Cinematography: May Ying Welsh.

for going to war in Iraq were fabricated and had nothing to do with 9/11: 'The government used my patriotic feelings to do something that was not right.' The strength of the film is not least the combination of a deep historical perspective, and a critical contemporary analysis of a broader, institutional political perspective, with an added focus on the feelings, reactions and opinions of ordinary Americans, and ordinary people in Iraq.

Where many other films on the post-9/11 situation and the War on Terror tend to see everything in the light of the policy of the Bush administration and the present generation of neo-conservatives around him, this film takes a closer look at the American global policy doctrines since Eisenhower. In many ways this defines Eisenhower as one of the last presidents with a democratic, global vision that did not include a single superpower concept and who, because of his strong military background, could control the military-industrial complex. A fundamental perspective in the film, illustrated among other experts and witnesses by Gore Vidal, the author behind *Imperial America: Reflections on the United States of Amnesia* (2004), is that from the Cold War onwards the United States developed a mentality of an imperial superpower with the capacity and legitimate right to intervene everywhere on the globe in defence of freedom and democracy. But part of this historical development is also, as a former CIA witness expresses it, that the fight for freedom and democracy often is a disguise for other more economic and political imperial interests. What the film is trying to show is thus that the Bush-Cheney-Rumsfeld doctrines are part of a much longer history, but also that this power group has taken the imperial superpower concept to a much higher level than earlier.

The film elegantly combines a historical explanation of the United States' military-industrial complex development with footage from US military history and politics since WW2, including a look at Frank Capra's WW2 propaganda films in the series *Why We Fight*. But the film makes a detailed analysis of how the situation since then has changed and how the influence of the military-industrial complex has grown dramatically. There is a special focus on the post-9/11 development, where contracts for companies – some of them very close to government people at the top – rose to staggering figures, and where half the jobs and contracts did not fulfil the job. The historical background for the Iraq War, and all the US mistakes in that connection back to the 1950s, is discussed, and it is clearly indicated that the war had nothing to do with 9/11 but was most likely tied to oil interests and the power balance in the Middle East. The film never sticks to just the historical and contemporary analysis but also keeps coming back to human stories in both the United States and Iraq, and some of the stories from the United States are with originally-strong supporters of the war having now changed their minds. A very impressive part of the film is also the lyrical montage sequences showing images of life in the United States from different angles, also the patriotic feelings, and life in Iraq from both the positive and the negative side. A strong story at the end of the film is about a young guy who joins the army, a story about those that clearly have strong patriotic feelings and believe in the importance of the military. Even though the film is very critical it also tries to show other opinions and views of the situation.

The military-industrial complex is also clearly in focus in Robert Greenwald's *Iraq for Sale: The War Profiteers* (2006). The film looks into how large a role private companies have played in the Iraq War, both in Iraq and US. Experts clearly define this war as the first privatized war in US history, although private companies have always played a certain role. The film combines the perspective of the families to employees of some of these people killed in Iraq with a larger, analytical perspective. The film uses a number of experts to draw up the network of politics and the military-industrial complex with special focus on the important Blackwater and Haliburton companies that were given a very big slice of the cake in Iraq. Greenwald is a clear example of what some have called guerrilla film-making in the United States. He creates films with a very strong actuality and political agenda on very small budgets and gets them financed and distributed through an online community of political activists and grass root movements. He is often able to get access to very unusual footage and experts.

The ambush artist: satire as journalistic weapon

Documentaries like PBS's *Truth, War and Consequences* (2003) or *The Dark Side* (2006), both written and directed by the main journalist and director Richard Kirk, are classical, journalistic documentaries in the critical investigative genre. They never get the same kind of audience and attention that the independent director Michael Moore has managed to get. If we look at the arguments, main points and documentation in the PBS films, and Moore's film on the War on Terror, there are big similarities – but the voice, tone and attitude is different. The PBS documentaries clearly demonstrate the network of powers behind the War on Terror, the political mistakes and the dubious developments of a secret state outside public awareness or even the role of the military-industrial complex. But they just state the documented facts and put the puzzle together with arguments.

Seen in a public debate perspective it is clearly Michael Moore's film *Fahrenheit 9/11* that has managed to reach a broad mainstream audience, but also to divide the audience and create very diverse reactions. Nevertheless, Moore's film is the largest grossing US documentary ever, based on theatrical income alone (McEnteer 2006: 98). Brent Toplin has written a whole book on *Fahrenheit 9/11* (Toplin 2006) dealing with the production, content and reception of the film. His main point in the book is that much of the critique and debate on Moore's films was masked as attacks on his journalistic form for being partisan, when in fact the disagreement was about the interpretation of the facts and arguments presented in the film. Toplin very carefully runs through all the facts and arguments presented in *Fahrenheit 9/11*. He also points out and criticizes a few sequences for not being fair and accurate but he finds most of the film journalistically corroborated although it sometimes uses the facts in a very satirical way. In his conclusion he compares the main arguments of the film with the arguments put forward in two contemporary books: *War and the American Presidency* (Schlesinger Jr 2004) and *Losing America* (Byrd 2004). Both books confirm the analysis of the Bush administration put forward in Moore's film.

But looking at *Fahrenheit 9/11* in retrospective, it becomes very obvious that McEnteer's characteristic of Moore as an 'ambush artist' is very true: he uses his own persona and his films to go on the attack by any means, with a strong visual language that is both serious and funny. The facts presented in Moore's films are almost always convincing and well substantiated by experts and visual and written documentation, but Moore knows his film language and how to send a clear message. The opening sequences of the film about the election scandal in Florida represent a stunning piece of rhetorical and filmic montage, and when it finally shows the president going on vacation, the satire becomes very clear. This is the kind of film strategy that makes Moore's films popular and, at the same time, controversial with mainstream America. He has an eye for the comical details even in connection with the most serious political issues and problems. Another example is those small clips during the introduction of the film where we see leading figures off-screen preparing to go on television: it is political satire with a sharp edge.

Even though the film clearly deals with the post-9/11 situation, the beginning of the film shows that Moore sees 9/11 as just one element in a longer political trauma in the United States starting with the Bush era and particularly his second term of office. But the images from the 9/11 tragedy are not commented on by Moore, the images of human sorrow and tragedy are just backed with music. When his commentary starts it's with the now-famous minutes in the Missouri school where Bush just sat and waited. With rhetorical elegance he continues the listing of the things *not* done by Bush and his administration in connection with the fight against terrorism. When a report about a potential Bin Laden attack inside the United States was presented, 'Bush went fishing' is the commentary. The sequences showing how the Bin Laden family was helped out of the country after 9/11 adds to the confusion about what is really going on inside the hearts and minds of this government.

Another reason Moore gets to the hearts and minds of the big audience is his very heavy use of popular music to underscore his points and the satirical or symbolic use of popular visual culture: television, film and advertising etc. The TV series *Dragnet* (Webb, 1954–2004), for instance, comes in handy when he questions the way Bin Laden's family get out of the country without anybody ever asking them one question. The oil trail is served on a silver plate here and the business relationships between the Bush and Bin Laden family are questioned. But Moore's efficient documentary strategy is also obvious, for example when, in following the oil trails, he can show that the White House has even censured his military papers, hiding the fact that he was a close friend in the military with the Bin Laden family tax advisor James Bath. Just as journalistically well documented is the discussion of the Saudi relation in a broader context and the very surprising move already on 12 September 2001 to target Iraq as semi-responsible for 9/11. This is done with experts and quotes from public mainstream press interviews with high-ranking persons. The use of the popular western classic *Bonanza* (1959–1973) at the end of this sequence, indicating the Bush administration's erratic cowboy policy, only adds to the point already made by journalistic means. To rub it in, experts also explain that the war in Afghanistan was really very inefficient, if the aim was to catch Bin Laden.

Deeply funny and satirical is also the part of the film (about 50 minutes from the start) in which Moore shows how the government, media and industries turned on the terror fear and then all kinds of people came forth with products to meet this fear: iron boxes to hide in, parachutes to jump from a tall building etc. Behind this also lies the serious journalistic debate on the consequences of the patriotic act on free debate and democracy, the process in which the War on Terror could become a war on democracy. An example is how anti-terror people infiltrated a perfectly normal group of citizens forming a discussion group. Moore's ability to combine classical, investigative journalism and satire and images taken out of popular American culture, his ability to document and make his point with rhetorical punch is what makes him unique. It takes strong measures to counterbalance mainstream media in the United States.

The final sequences of *Fahrenheit 9/11*, where Moore first shows the absurdities of the airport and coastguard security programme and then drives his little van up to Washington to confront senators on the street, asking them to get their sons to fight in Iraq, may seem over the top and populist. But seen against the well documented fact that it is the coloured and poorer people that pay the price in Iraq, it can be defended, and it certainly drives the main point of the film home: those in power serve their own interest, that is what this war is about. Perhaps even stronger is the way in which he lets us see the attack on Iraq from the viewpoint of ordinary Iraqi citizens and the cruel results of the bombings for them.

No end in sight: the military and political chaos

Moore's film is efficient satire, but it is also strong journalism documenting the political and military chaos before and after the attack on Iraq, and his film takes a lot of time to understand and document how soldiers and their families, the Americans who really know about the war, think and feel. In many ways, apart from putting himself at the centre, he is pretty good at combining elite discourse with popular discourse and the words and worlds of ordinary people. There is no doubt that Moore has become an institution in American public life and that he – despite the very strong opposition and even obstruction he has met – is one of the few documentary filmmakers that have challenged the dominance of the mainstream media in the United States. He has managed to create an alternative public sphere and debate around his films, and he has been successful in reaching both a mainstream audience and an alternative audience. He is by now also using the Internet very deliberately to create online communities for critical, democratic debate, and he has a very strong and active profile on, for instance, Facebook.

Charles Ferguson's *No End in Sight* (2008a) on the other hand is made in the investigative, journalistic form of a PBS Frontline documentary, and although the two films have much the same theme and perspective on things, they are very different in form and genre. Ferguson, before making this film, became an internet millionaire developing Frontpage and he was able to finance the film with his own money. But despite the solid budget behind the film and the obvious film quality, and the fact that the film won the Sundance prize as Best Documentary in 2007, the film belongs to the independent sector and has had limited success in reaching the mainstream media and audience.

The film – in Ferguson's own word – documents the incredible stupidity of America's war on Iraq, the almost incomprehensible lack of strategy and preparation, the tragic and criminal lack of knowledge of the country they invaded and its culture (interview with author, NY, October 2008). Although not satirical in tone, Ferguson starts the film with a diabolical sequence in which Rumsfeld praises President Bush for leading the incredibly complex and little understood first war of the twenty-first century. The following opening parts of the film very dramatically contrast the American strategy and declarations of victory with the violent images of an Iraq in open decline and chaos. We see pictures never shown in such detail on American mainstream television, and we hear statements from high-ranking Americans and Iraqis challenging the strategies behind the war. Many of the witnesses are former Bush administration officials, and they directly undermine many of the fundamental concepts behind the War on Terror and the reasons for the attack on Iraq. The pattern followed here is to give a voice to many of those people trying to go against the stream and offer alternative views, people who were not heard and eventually put aside. The film does the independent, journalistic work which the mainstream media should have done.

The point of the film is very much that an initial sympathy for the American invaders is lost when the everyday lives of ordinary Iraqis are declining by the hour and religious and ethnic violence is exploding. The American war strategy is based on wishful thinking and lack of knowledge, and the focus is much more on American interests than Iraqi. The film illustrates what is also documented in journalistic books like Rajiv Chandrasekaran's *Imperial Life in the Emerald City: Inside Iraq's Green Zone* (2006): that the American administrators lived in an artificial bubble with no insight in, or connection, to the country and the people they were supposed to help develop democracy and a new society. The number of mistakes is monstrous and incredible, the so-called ORHA – supposed to deal with human and civilian aspects – were completely incompetent and impotent, and the few people of knowledge like, for instance, the Ambassador Barbara Bodine, give evidence as to a complete lack of means, strategies and plans.

One of the most devastating parts of the film is where these administrators explain how the early lootings of Baghdad turned into a systematic destruction of major institutions and the infrastructure. The insights and stories from these people are contrasted with Rumsfeld trying to criticize American media for reporting on this and trying to reduce it to minor incidents. The film documents that among those institutions listed as important to protect by ORHA, the only public institution and ministry in Baghdad actually protected by the Americans was the Ministry of Oil. The insiders and experts conclude that this was where America lost the ordinary Iraqis because they found out that the war had nothing to do with their lives. As one civilian Iraqi says: 'Saddam was awful, but the Americans are worse.' The film also clearly documents that all experts point to the fact that a lot more soldiers would have been required to win the war and restore democracy, peace and a normal everyday life in Iraq. The film is therefore a heavy, well-documented journalistic story of why 'no end is in sight'.

Weapons of mass deception: media, spin and the War on Terror

Charles Ferguson tried to get Paul Bremer, Donald Rumsfeld, Paul Wolfowitz and others to give interviews for the film, but in vain. The Bush administration clearly tried to manage the media and public debate, but were not willing to answer questions from an independent journalist. This points to a side of the War on Terror that other documentary films have taken up: the direct deceptions and lies to the American public from high-ranking politicians. Robert Greenwald's *Uncovered: The Whole Truth about the Iraq War* (2006) deals with the whole political process that led to the decision to go to war. It is done in a very investigative, factual, journalistic form, with an impressive list of high-ranked persons that have inside information from the Pentagon, CIA and the Bush administration. Part of the film is also footage from mainstream media news dealing with this problem. The film can be seen as a journalistic counterweight to Michael Moore's much more satirical *Fahrenheit 9/11*. Greenwald clearly focuses on the whole of the media and uses media footage to illustrate many of his points.

But the most obvious meta-media critique on the War on Terror is Danny Schechter's *Weapons of Mass Deception* (2004). The film is very direct in the characterization of the media: we are not just talking about distortion of reality, we are talking about lies, which is also the point made in his book *When News Lies: Media Complicity and the Iraq War* (2006a). Greenwald's *Iraq for Sale: The War Profiteers* is a very revealing journalistic film documenting how strongly the privatization of the War on Terror has gone, with companies from all the allied countries, but primarily US companies, getting a very big slice of the cake and taking over functions that clearly used to be public, government affairs. The agenda here is, of course, to point to the role of profit and private economy behind what appears to be a purely democratic, patriotic act. In *Uncovered: The Whole Truth About the Iraq War* the focus is broader, because the film tries to unravel all the deeper reasons for going to war. The start of the film is characteristic: it is simply a line of presentations from all the witnesses, an impressive list of people from CIA, military persons and people in public office. Greenwald wants to signal that the film is not making claims about reality based on his own research among independent, alternative sources, who for political reasons are against the war. He relies on the testimony from people very close to the centre of power. The film confronts media statements from the Bush administration on the Iraq War with statements from these experts, which clearly undermines the official explanations and the 'fabricated' facts.

But the film also shows that parts of the intelligence community actually tried to go against the government. Compared to Moore's, Morris' and Jarecki's films, Greenwald's film is very much a classical, in-depth news background analysis dominated by thematically organized interviews with experts. Media quotes are systematically contrasted with interview statements, and the whole film is based on this structure and way of arguing: it is a film with a strong factual, rhetorical structure. Danny Schechter's *Weapons of Mass Deception* is a more personal and polemic film with a much stronger kind of montage of words and images. The focus here is on the media war and in the opening sequences of the film, Schechter – like another Moore – appears on screen using his own experience of the media war to start questioning the way American media reported on the Iraq War. He also uses his own historical experience as a reporter to consider how the stories on war have developed and changed.

He points to a movement towards embedded, live coverage, starting with CNN and the Gulf War coverage.

But although this film is more personal in its form and rhetoric, it is a film presenting a close factual analysis of the way the media dealt with the Iraq War. Schechter looks at aspects of the reporting in the American media, but he also reports on the academic analysis of media coverage and the critical self-reflection in the media as the early phases of the war are over and public opinion also starts to move in critical directions. An important aspect of the film is also to illustrate the role of new online communities and media in creating alternatives to the mainstream media. The film goes into the Pentagon management of the war and the way in which the Pentagon narrative was clearly adopted uncritically by the mainstream media, and it also demonstrates in detail how the programme for embedded journalism actually functioned. Many journalists express how they were treated in a way that influenced their views on the war and also how bonding between the journalists and the soldiers they were embedded with was very clear and psychologically understandable. Schechter's film does not endorse theories of conspiracy, but what he tries to demonstrate is more how a combination of Pentagon media management and commercial interests produces something that one might call 'militainment'. This, however, does not include Fox News because this channel is clearly on an ideological crusade for the patriotic and neo-conservative case and views of the world. Another important part of Schechter's film is the demonstration of how the perspective of the war changes within the cultural and political frameworks. The chapter on Al Jazeera shows this, but Schechter also points to the changes by FCC of the American media, the deregulation and concentration.

Other voices – new perspectives

As already mentioned, the agenda of the US media on the War on Terror began to change around 2006 and this meant that not just PBS and HBO and the independent documentary sector expanded the perspectives and depth of analysis, but also that mainstream media and books began to throw a broader light on the situation. Much more direct criticism comes forth in PBS programmes like *The Lost Year in Iraq* (2006), directly criticizing the politics behind the war, or *The Insurgency* (2006), on the erupting violence in Iraq. The development also opened up for reports from the other side, for actually getting voices from or behind the 'enemy lines'.

This is, for instance, the case with *Behind Taliban Lines* (2010) where an Afghan journalist reports on his ten-day-long stay with an Al Qaeda cell in Afghanistan, a very rare kind of documentary, at least in the American mainstream media. In 2011, PBS also made a documentary *Top Secret America*, based on and with the same title as Priest and Arkin's book from the same year. But looking at the development of documentaries on the War on Terror after 2008 and thus into the Obama period it is also clear that the immediate, political interest in this subject is declining and new agendas are taking over, although the tenth anniversary of 9/11 in 2011 of course spurred a lot of looking back and reflecting on the event itself and the subsequent wars and political developments.

A sort of dramatic political climax also came when Osama Bin Laden and some of his men were killed by an American Seal team on a secret mission in Pakistan. This incident is the final chapter in Priest and Arkin's *Top Secret America* and, even though Bin Laden's death may not be the end of terrorism and Al Qaeda, it is – together with the fact that American troops have withdrawn from Iraq in 2011 and the war in Afghanistan is coming to an end – an exclamation mark:

> Bin Laden's death was not the end of terrorism or even al-Qaeda. But it was a bold punctuation mark, the period at the end of a decade-long story (…) As his body was pushed into the sea (…) a chapter in the nation's history slid in after it. An era in which the fear of Bin Laden's theatrical brand of terrorism turned rational people irrational also sank to the ocean's bottom (…) (Priest and Arkin 2011: 261).

There is doubt whether the Obama administration has actually reduced the super-sized secret America that the Bush administration left behind, but recent developments nevertheless seem to indicate that public debate in the US is beyond the fear created by 9/11 and turning to other challenges created by the global financial crisis.

The political battle over a critical, Danish war documentary

The patriotic unity and the dominance of commercial mainstream media in the United States cannot be found to the same degree in Denmark or the United Kingdom, but nevertheless the story of how the well-known Danish documentary director Christoffer Guldbrandsen's film *Den hemmelige krig/ The Secret War* (2006) was received and met with deliberately planned spin from the government tells another story of Denmark than is usual for this fairytale democracy. And much the same story can be told about some of the British documentaries, for instance the both politically and aesthetically very controversial film by Mike Robinson, *Iraq, Tony and the Truth* (2006). In both cases the government attacked the form of the films, basically diverting public attention and debate away from the content and the well-documented criticism of government policy on the issues dealt with in the two films.

Guldbrandsen's *The Secret War* is a classical, investigative documentary dealing with the Danish military engagement in Afghanistan. The film focuses on and rather convincingly documents that Danish soldiers systematically captured and handed over prisoners of war to the Americans even though it was pretty obvious not just to the military, but also the Danish government, that the Americans did not follow the Geneva Conventions on how to treat prisoners of war. President Bush and other leading Americans had made public statements indicating that terrorists were not to be treated according to the Geneva Convention.

The main political argument of the film is that the Danish government consistently had denied that they handed over prisoners and claimed that they had clear guarantees from the Americans that the Geneva Conventions would be followed. So the Danish government had mislead parliament because of a very close alliance with the Americans, an alliance that, especially in the case of the Iraq War, clearly divided the Danish and the European governments and citizens.

Figures 4c and d: Christoffer Guldbrandsen's *The Secret War* (2006). Danish soldiers taking prisoners of war and George Bush and Anders Fogh Rasmussen confirming the alliance on the war on terror. Frame grab. Cinematography: Josh Nussbaum, Kasper Tuxen.

Christoffer Guldbrandsen has characterized the war in Afghanistan and Iraq, where for the first time since WW2 Danish soldiers were in direct combat in an international war, as 'a wake up call and shock for the Danish national mentality' (Guldbrandsen interview, Bondebjerg 2008c), 'a kind of move from images of Danes with blue helmets of peacekeeping forces to an image of combat, torture and death' (Bondebjerg 2008b). Guldbrandsen's film documents that Danes are no better than others when it comes to war crimes and political secrets and cover ups. The film shows how the Danish military, normally a quite open and communicative organization, suddenly would not give access to key persons, would not hand out important papers, or claimed that important papers did not exist. If they handed out papers they had deleted large parts of them so they became unreadable – with reference to national security. It also shows a government that will not give interviews and is not willing to give access to key information either.

So the filmmaker had to fight to finish this film confronted with a very clear cover-up involving both the military and the political complex. It is quite absurd that it is actually American experts, soldiers and journalists that give many of the final proofs and testimonies on the indirect Danish involvement in torture. The production circumstances of this film – as for many other films after 9/11 – indicates a problematic war on the critical media and free democratic debate. The story of how this film was received and debated is a clear example of this. Its structure and form is, as already indicated, that of the classical, investigative documentary. From the opening of the film we hear the director's own voiceover, commenting on a montage of TV clips with the attack on World Trade Center and the Danish Prime Minister, Anders Fogh Rasmussen. The voiceover and the clips indicate a close connection between not just the United States and Denmark but also Bush and Rasmussen. These clips are continued with the now famous Bush statement from his 2002 State of the Union Address: 'You are either with us, or you are with the terrorists.' Then sequences follow where Fogh Rasmussen announces the Danish involvement in the war in Afghanistan, explained as a humanitarian job and with guarantees that the Geneva Convention will be respected.

In the following sequences the film quotes a traditional State of the Union New Years Eve address by Fogh Rasmussen, where he stresses the wars in Afghanistan and Iraq as an important part of the War on Terror and the defence of democracy. But, by showing small authentic drawings of torture during the opening credits the film visually undermines this statement. The opening sequences thus combine a strong visual montage with a journalistic discourse, the visual and auditive framing of these opening scenes indicate that something is wrong, that the official explanations are not credible. In the following sequences of the film the journalistic discourse and argumentation becomes more and more factual and investigative. The film points to secret instructions on how to deal with prisoners and to reports documenting that the Danish military had knowledge about the American torture in Afghanistan, but nevertheless cooperated with them and handed over prisoners. However, in the film the director never manages to get anybody above a certain rank to speak directly about this, and all communication is monitored or declined. This is when the film takes an

'American' turn and, through that, is able to support the criticism and the points made in the Danish research.

After this very deep, investigative report on the facts of torture procedures and the Danish involvement in this, the film returns to the political agenda, the question of whether the government has deliberately lied to the public and to parliament. Going through the transcripts of the many times Fogh Rasmussen has answered questions on this and comparing these with the publicly stated American policy, the film clearly demonstrates the facts. An interview with the Danish Minister of Defence, Søren Gade, shows a remarkable lack of knowledge in the matter or sheer denial, just as the sudden amnesia of the military chief of staff is very strange. Visually the film combines this with sequences showing Søren Gade getting a medal from his American colleague Rumsfeld, and a Bush visit to Denmark where he publicly praises his very good friend and ally, Anders Fogh Rasmussen. This is not Michael Moore satire, but simply underlines the very close collaboration between the United States and Denmark on these matters, thus corroborating the journalistic story about a secret agreement on how to avoid the Geneva Convention in the fight against terror.

The Secret War is a solid piece of investigative journalism made despite very difficult working conditions where the system wanted to protect itself from investigation and open debate. The film has a strong case against a policy of War on Terror where the methods used are such that they threaten and violate the very democracy and the very human rights the war is supposed to protect. The film also clearly points to problems for the media in a time where politics is globalized, and where accountability and transparency is no longer enough on just a national level. The film addresses a Danish audience and a national public sphere, but it deals with matters that are really entangled in a global or transnational public sphere.

The debate on the film is just as interesting and significant as the film in itself. The government and the military had systematically undermined the making of the film by not collaborating and by censoring vital information in the case. But they staged a very deliberate campaign against the film involving several ministers and their offices and spin doctors. Their main strategy was basically to attack the form of the film, to denounce it as partisan and 'Michael Mooreish' in its use of stylistic visual and sound elements. Half the Danish media bought this story and in the weeks following first the theatrical premiere and then the TV premiere they attacked the form of the film and the filmmaker and did not deal with the factual content and journalistic critique. Also the Danish main public service channel broadcasting the film (although not on their mainstream channel) came under fire. But they not only defended the film and broadcast it again, but also produced a follow-up film broadcast in 2008 called *CIA's danske forbindelse/CIA's Danish Connection*. Here it is proven beyond doubt that Denmark was also in secret agreement with the Americans on the 'extraordinary rendition programme' that allowed the United States to arrest suspected terrorists on foreign ground and use foreign airports to secretly transport them.

In the end the debate on *The Secret War* led to an independent investigation of the film made by university specialists in journalism and professional journalists. The report (see http://politiken.dk/indland/article358495.ece) cleared the film of all accusations of being partisan and for not complying with journalistic norms and standards. It did, however, point to a problem having to do with the relation between film language and journalism. This problem, however, is not very convincingly described and in many ways the form of the film does follow standard formulas of investigative documentary film (see Bondebjerg 2008a). But by the time the report was published, the real debate about the film had died out in the public sphere. The spin strategy of the government had succeeded.

Guldbrandsen's film marks a change in Danish films on war and the military. Until around 2001 Denmark had not been in active combat outside Denmark since WW2 and the Danish self-understanding was mostly connected to a role as a peace-keeping nation and military force, not as an active military combat force. There has always been a rather dominant humanistic-pacifistic ideology and the military has often been met with scepticism in documentaries (Bondebjerg 2008a). The decision to join the allied coalition in the war against Iraq in 2003 was taken with the slimmest majority possible in the Danish parliament and clearly split the nation. But the more active role taken in foreign conflicts after 2000 also changed the way and the degree to which war and the military was dealt with in the media and in Danish documentaries. *The Secret War* represents the continued critical, investigative tradition, but Denmark's new active military profile since 2006 has led to an increased number of films on the countries global, military involvement (see p. 117f and 135f). As a small European nation in a very global world the period after 2000 in many ways meant a wake-up call and an increased openness towards the problems of globalization and understanding of global, military engagement.

Bush's poodle? Blair, politics and the War on Terror

In British politics and culture there is an uneasy relationship to the big American other, and as the second major centre of the dominant, English-speaking culture there is both a natural alliance and competition. Just as there seems to have been a very close relationship between the Danish prime minister and Bush, in the eyes of both the English and European public, Blair came out as an even closer friend and ally. From day one the European public and politicians were strongly divided on the question of Iraq: in the United States, and in the British press, the French and the Germans opposing the war came out clearly as cowards and Blair was a hero. But this soon turned around and the British media in general became very critical and there was a tendency to see Blair through the traditional, negative metaphor of a 'poodle' of the Americans.

But the difference between the European public sphere and the American is obvious when you look at the different role played by the public service media in the mainstream media culture. If we look at just two of the British main channels for documentary production, BBC and Channel 4, it becomes quite clear that the UK media, just like most other European media, keep a strong independent and critical distance to political power and that programmes in prime time are often used for investigative documentaries. In 2003, for instance, the BBC broadcast ten documentaries directly related to Iraq, and many of them were critical, investigative reports, not on just the development of war but also on the problems and background aspects of the war. Programmes like *Blair's War* (Robinson, Mike) and *The War Party* (Robinson, Mike, 2003) are very critical, with the latter one looking into the role of the American neo-conservatives in American politics. Channel 4 also has a long series of programmes, both of a critical, investigative nature and in their documentary series *Dispatches*, but they also specialize in going behind the scenes and looking at the human stories behind the war: the ethnic divisions in Iraq, the families torn apart, the life of British soldiers and their families and so on.

Programmes like this can, as already shown, only be found on cable channels and independent media in the United States, but in Europe they become a direct part of the everyday news coverage and the mainstream channels' background stories. This, however, does not mean that European politicians do not try to manufacture news and information and control or attack media, as the Danish case clearly shows. This was clearly seen in the case of the highly critical documentary *Iraq, Tony and the Truth* (Robinson, Mike 20 March 2005) in the BBC's famous *Panorama* series, almost precisely two years after the start of the Iraq War. The film was controversial because it directly accused Blair of misleading the British public and of manipulating and misrepresenting the information he was given by his own intelligence service. Whereas the intelligence reports he was given were either very sceptical of the existence of weapons of mass destruction or directly said they did not exist, Blair in apparently open collaboration with the Americans claimed that the evidence was clear and overwhelming. As with other investigative documentaries, the journalists could not get the political top figures to appear in the programme, so the programme used reconstructions – based on inside sources – to show what was said and done at crucial government meetings. What we see with this programme is thus a clear mixture of the classical investigative and authoritative documentary with a dramatization or reconstruction of certain aspects and characters.

The programme starts with the announcement to the British public of the war and then takes us deeper backstage in the political landscape, including devastating statements from former government officials and advisors. The crucial point is the fact that Blair needed a legal justification to go to war, a war he had already decided to engage the nation in. The evidence to do so had to be edited or fabricated. Strong evidence for this comes from Blair's own former Foreign Affairs Secretary, David Manning, and the former Foreign Secretary, Robin Cook, and from the papers and reports from the intelligence services. The programme gets the testimony of Rear Admiral Nick Wilkinson, secretary for the so-called D-committee in that period, and he is very clear: the intelligence Blair and the government was given did not support the American allegations of terrorist connections and weapons of mass destruction in Iraq.

Just as the Danish programme, *The Secret War*, already analyzed, this film indicates a very close relationship between Blair and Bush as one of the elements in the strategy and the decision for 'regime change' even without a strong legal justification. The programme does go into alternative routes that could have been taken, but also shows that already by early 2002 the UK military was deeply involved in military planning. The connection with Bush was apparently of such a nature that Blair was drawn into the very undemocratic and fabricated form of global power play, no matter what. The films points to the strange fact of a labour prime minister supporting a neo-conservative republican president, as Robin Cook puts it in the programme, and the strange procedure of a prime minister pressuring the intelligence services to come up with evidence that could legitimize a policy already decided.

The critical investigation of UK politics in Iraq was spread to other media and, quite unlike the US media, we actually do find a widespread critical agenda in the mainstream media, both before and after the Iraq War. But even though this BBC programme is a clear example of a TV channel proving its critical independence, the David Kelly case in 2004 points to a situation in which the British government clearly tried to castrate independent media voices in their reporting on Iraq. The Kelly case goes back to 2002 and deals with government activities getting intelligence on Iraq's weapons of mass destruction that would legitimize a war. When the first intelligence on this was published claiming that Iraq had weapons that made it possible to launch an attack on the United Kingdom within 45 minutes, the BBC ran a series of critical reports indicating that the government might have 'sexed up' the report. An anonymous highly placed source, later identified as the government weapons inspector David Kelly, leaked this information, but when revealed as the source he committed suicide.

There was an enormous debate on this, the BBC came under fire and a committee, lead by Lord Hutton, was asked to investigate the case. The Hutton report whitewashed the government and criticized the BBC, and as a consequence the BBC apologized to the government and the BBC director general, Greg Dyke, resigned. In an article in *The Guardian* from 2006 it is reported that:

> Greg Dyke called yesterday for the publication of documents that would reveal why the BBC governors 'abjectly' apologized to Downing Street after the Hutton report. Speaking at a freedom of information tribunal, he said the BBC governors made the 'embarrassing and unjustified' apology for the way in which it reported on the existence of weapons of mass destruction in Iraq. 'It was a betrayal of what the BBC stood for,' he said (Evans and Tryhorn 2006).

British documentaries and the politics of the War on Terror

There is no doubt that next to the American channel PBS, the British BBC is the world's leading producer of critical, investigative documentaries, mostly broadcast under the *Panorama* strand. With around 30 programmes produced a year, *Panorama* alone covers a lot of themes and problems. Since 2001, the BBC has covered the political dimensions of the War on Terror from a number of angles, and with critical focus on both British and American policy, as already indicated in the programmes analyzed above. But they also cover these issues in ways not found in the US media, where global voices and a global outlook is not very common. Also, the BBC was openly critical from the start, a few months after 9/11. In *Deep Down and Dirty* (2 December 2001), Peter Taylor deals with the offensive cowboy discourse in the rhetoric of the Bush administration and the intelligence community. The programme deals with this issue with quotes from high-ranking officials and people in the field, and in Taylor's own words the programme is about an old dilemma: 'September 11th has underlined the dilemma that always faces intelligence agencies in liberal democracies. How to resolve the conflicting imperatives of human rights and beating the terrorists' (Taylor 2001, programme transcript). In *License to Torture* (2009) the questions raised in this early programme are dealt with in retrospect and with a concrete, critical investigation into whether the US post-9/11 interrogation programme broke international law.

This political issue on the War on Terror, related to the question of democracy, human rights and international laws and conventions, has been constantly and much more directly on the agenda in the British media than the US media. But the critical focus is not just on the US but also on the British role in this policy and the anti-terror activities. In *Britain on the Brink: The Panorama Debate* (30 September 2001), only a little more than a week after 9/11, the question is raised how far the UK is willing to go. The programme is a debate lead by BBC's David Dimbleby and involves military persons, politicians, anti-war representatives and others. Compared to the patriotic unity in the US at this time, the debate is quite frank and open, although there is a clear feeling of the need to somehow engage. It also shows that the UK for years had their own terror problem in Northern Ireland. That this historical dimension is present in the British debate is obvious from several programmes after 2001, for instance *The Gunmen Who Never Went Away* (2009), where the internal terror problem is seen as still present. This issue of terror in the UK itself, of course, also arrived on the public and political agenda after the London terror incident in 2005, dealt with in the programme *London Under Attack* (July 2005).

Right from the start, the way the British media dealt with the issues concerning the war on terror was different from the American media in two ways: the critical tone and analysis, and a more global, multicultural perspective. It becomes obvious already from two programmes in 2001 on *Panorama*. In *Clash of Cultures* (October 2001) David Dimbleby is in charge of yet another debate, but this time on a much broader scale. The debate takes place between a live audience in New York and in Islamabad in Pakistan and it is the result of a cooperation between BBC and Al Jazeera. The question raised is whether we have a clash between cultures in the global fight against terror or whether the lines follow other principles. Here is Dimbleby's presentation of the programme, directly from BBC's transcript:

Good evening. Panorama tonight joins Radio 5 Live, the BBC World Service and on television BBC World. After two weeks of military action in Afghanistan to destroy the Taliban and find Bin Laden, the dilemma for the West is whether its actions are winning acceptance in the Muslim world or are increasingly seen as an attack on Islam. Is there a conflict of cultures and if so how can it be resolved? We're going to be hearing tonight from audiences in Islamabad with Venetia Pely, we're going to be hearing from New York with Nicky Campbell, and I'll be putting the arguments to a member of the British War Cabinet the former Foreign Secretary Robin Cook and to Richard Perle, Chairman of the Pentagon Advisory Board, and also to a prominent politician, former Pakistani Ambassador to the United States Abida Hussain.

It is quite amazing to listen to the debate in this programme, an actual dialogue between Americans, British representatives and Muslims, so shortly after 9/11. The debate clearly demonstrates stereotypes on both sides, but also manages to steer free of the divide so often present in the post-9/11 discourse. But this is not the only such debate on BBC in 2001, in another programme shortly before, *Koran and Country* (October 2001), it is the British Muslim community that is in focus. Vivian Scott's report shows both hostile and militant reactions from Muslims in the UK to the attack on Afghanistan, hate reactions against Muslims from non-Muslims in the UK and also Muslims supporting the fight against terror. But it is a unique look into a Muslim community in a Western country, a look which is clearly supplemented by those documentaries that go behind the war in Afghanistan, Iraq and other Muslim countries in order to give a perspective from the other side.

BBC and the internal and external critical dimension

From 2002 the BBC started focusing more on Iraq in their critical investigations of the political dimensions of the War on Terror. The question of weapons of mass destruction and the whole reason for going to war was being investigated from day one, for instance in *The Case Against Saddam* (September 2002), *Chasing Saddam's Weapons* (February 2003) or *Still Chasing Saddam's Weapons* (November 2003). Also the policy towards prisoners suspected of terrorism and the whole question of democracy and human rights is taken up, for instance in a programme like *Inside Guantanamo* (2003) and the follow-up *Shamed* (2004), about the Abu Ghraib incident. The gloves are also off in the programme *The War Party* (2003), a very critical, and deep analysis of the neo-conservative network of people in the Bush administration and in think tanks and other institutions outside, which voices in the programme claim have almost hijacked the White House. The programme takes us inside organizations like, for instance, the Enterprise Institute, a neo-conservative think tank with direct influence on the White House policies in the War on Terror, with statements on strategies directly taken from persons in that institute. The programme follows events inside the neo-conservative groups for a longer period, and documents not just the links to the White House but also the way this group operates in relation to the media. Unlike the US media, the BBC also asks early on what the outcome of an invasion might be and whether there is a strategy for a new Iraq, for instance as early as 2003 in *After Saddam*. In the US this kind of approach came much later, and first only in elite newspapers and books.

As already indicated, the documentaries dealing with the politics of the war against terror in the UK also have a strong focus on the Blair government and the somewhat strange alliance between a neo-conservative American president and a labour prime minister. *Blair's War* (2003) directly asks the question whether Blair could lose his job over the decision to go to war in Iraq. BBC's own presentation of *Blair's War* sounds like this:

> Could Tony Blair lose his job over the Iraq crisis? For two months Panorama has been following the opposition to him, in the anti-war movement, in the Labour Party, and in Parliament. This is the real-life political drama of a Prime Minister, accused in the past of being guided by focus groups, yet apparently now determined to override a million demonstrators and over a hundred of his own MPs – the story of the war on the home front (quoted from BBC News 2012a).

So, unlike the situation in most US media reporting, this programme goes deep into the oppositional groups outside and inside the government, and the programme also indicates a very special and personal relation between Blair and Bush, almost in the same way as the relationship between the Danish prime minister Fogh Rasmussen and Bush was dealt with in the Danish media. Sometimes global policies and connections can be tied to very personal relations. In the second programme, *Blair vs Blair*, BBC investigates the apparent disagreement between Tony and his wife Cherie Blair, so it is the global War on Terror taken into the private living room. The programme is based on public statements from Cherie Blair and other sources, statements like for instance the following:

> This is Tony Blair, on 5 August 2005: 'Let no-one be in any doubt, the rules of the game are changing.' And this is Cherie Blair, speaking as a Human Rights lawyer, on 26 July 2005: 'It is all too easy for us to respond to such terror in a way which undermines commitment to our most deeply held values and convictions and which cheapens our right to call ourselves a civilised nation' (quoted from BBC News 2012b).

The perspective on the war of course also directly deals with the British military strategy and presence in Afghanistan and Iraq, not just in the form of reporting from the frontline, but also the more political aspects. One example is *Troops Out* (2005), which – as the title indicates – deals with both public opinion and political attitudes to the military engagement. This theme is also dealt with in *Bringing Our Boys Home* (2006), reporting both from Iraq and from home. But this debate is also related to the question of how soldiers wounded and traumatized by war experiences actually get the kind of support and help they need, for instance in *Shock Troops* (2005), *Runaway Soldiers* (2007) or *For Queen and Country* (2007). But looking at themes and programmes after 2006 it is also pretty clear that the focus is shifting: more and more programmes that deal with the War on Terror are not related to Iraq but to more internal aspects, and the focus is now more on soldiers and the aftermath of the war. For instance, Iran and the Arab Spring now move to the centre in programmes like *Living With the Ayatollah* (2011) and *Fighting Gaddafi* (2011).

The American, the European and the global public sphere

The images of 9/11 are tragic visual icons of a globalized media reality, a sign of a new, fragile modernity that the sociologist Ulrich Beck has called the second or the reflexive modernity related to a global risk society (Beck 1992). In the twentieth century media and democracies were to a large degree defined by a national space or by controlled and institutionalized international collaboration, but in the still more globalized societies of the twenty-first century nation states and nationally defined media, cultures have come under heavy pressure. As Beck has pointed out (Beck 1992: 184ff), the traditional division and relation between a civic, public sphere and a private technological-economic sphere and the project of welfare and democracy through the public sphere in this period has become increasingly constrained by the globalization of corporate powers and economies. The explosive development of new world powers and the growing confrontation and dependency between developing and rich, highly developed countries have destabilized the global culture.

The growth of terrorism and the clash of Western and Islamic cultures, which 9/11 is a tragic symbol of, is not just a peak expression of an attack on the largest and most powerful Western cultural nation, but also a symbol of the new, global risk society. But reacting to this challenge with 'imperial' powers that undermine both democratic and moral values and international laws and principles is treating an illness with a medicine that may take away some of the symptoms, but will also kill the patient. The documentary films and programmes analyzed on the politics of the War on Terror all tell a story of a political system trying to manipulate facts and the media and of a very unholy alliance between government and private, commercial interest masked behind claims of legitimate war and defence of world peace. They tell a story of a politic undermining rather than enhancing global democracy and understanding. The story of how these films and programmes were produced and received is also a story of very problematic tendencies in our political culture and our media – both the commercial media and the public service media.

In her book *The Dark Side*, Jane Mayer comments on the 9/11 event as follows: 'Seven years after Al Qaeda's attacks on America, as the Bush Administration slips into history, it is clear that what began on September 11, 2001, as a battle of America's security became, and continues to be, a battle for the country's soul (Mayer 2008: 327)'. What she refers to is, of course, the undermining of democracy on a both national and global scale, which the political and military reactions to the attack made room for, and which involved a much too passive and uncritical public sphere and media in the wake of an understandable American patriotism and European sympathy. In the United States the problem is simply the lack of independent, critical media, and the fact that critical voices do not reach mainstream media, at least when we are talking about television. In Europe the problem is the self-commercialization of the public service media on the one hand, and the tendency towards political control and undermining of the critical, public service media on the other hand, as we see in the case of DR in Denmark and the BBC in the United Kingdom.

In 2008, after the election of Barack Obama as the next President of the United States, the truth about the war in Iraq has finally reached the mainstream media. Obama has consistently said that the war was a mistake and based on false premises. The voice of the few independent media and the public opposition behind the big public demonstrations in 2002 and within online media communities has finally become the official US voice, six years after 9/11. This leaves room for optimism: opposition, critique and dissident voices actually do make a difference. This is what James McEnteer concludes in his book on the political documentary, *Shooting the Truth: The Rise of American Political Documentaries* (2006), and also what Ben Dickenson tries to argue in his book *Hollywood's New Radicalism* (2006): the political avant-garde of Hollywood, with Michael Moore as a prominent example, have both played a vital role in the regime change that is now a reality. But he also points to the clear connection between the Bush administration's foreign policy and their systematic support for a further commercialization and concentration of power in the film and media business, not least the radical changes in the Federal Communication Commission's (FCC) policy (Dickinson 2006: 171).

Although the American political system and media system are rather different from those in Europe, we do, however, see the same tendencies threatening to undermine the role of independent and critical media and debate in the public sphere. In Europe there is another problem, namely the lack of a European public sphere. Europe was clearly divided on Iraq, with France and Germany strongly against, so clearly the European Union could not debate and react with one voice. National priorities and national political differences played a major role and thus prevented Europe from being a strong global voice for democracy and alternative ways of solving global conflicts. A European public sphere and a global public sphere are very difficult to establish in any systematic and institutional way. Even though global movements and demonstrations are important and the new media can help create global networks and social and political communities, the national media and critical programmes still have an important role to play. They are voices of dissent in a world largely dominated by big commercial networks and industries, and even though they can have a hard time, they make a difference. Many of the documentary film and television programmes analyzed in this chapter demonstrate the power of independent documentary voices outside the mainstream centre. Taken together they represent a more multi-vocal and plural agenda that transcends national spaces, and in many cases they also represent forms of mediation between opposing social forces and cultures across global divides.

Chapter 5

On the battleground: reporting and representing war

Reporting war is not just an important news genre and a strong part of documentary filmmaking after 2000. War is also drama, action and mainstream entertainment, and some American researchers have claimed that modern news reporting is deeply influenced by Hollywood aesthetics. In her analysis of how CNN and Fox News covered the invasion of Iraq, *Ugly War – Pretty Package* (2009), Deborah Jaramillo traces the 'high concept war narrative' in news. She points to a satirical film like Barry Levinson's *Wag the Dog* (1997) as a kind of direct reference to the alliance between Hollywood, the media and the military complex, a relation that is also documented by others (Kellner 2010; Prince 2009). There is no reason to talk about conspiracy and total control and fabrication of news, but besides the concrete connections between Hollywood and the military, there are more indirect inspirations and influences between news reporting and other ways of war narratives.

Narrative and dramatic structures are – as already indicated (see p. 40f) – not in themselves an indication of fictionalization. Narrative is a basic cognitive dimension in the way we perceive and interpret reality, and most documentaries use narrative structures in various ways. But especially in the US context, where the war and action film has a very strong presence and influence on the general ways of understanding and telling about war in the Hollywood mainstream film, a spillover effect to both news and other factual formats is more likely to occur. In comparison there is almost no tradition for national war and action films in Denmark, and the line dividing public service news broadcasting and feature film aesthetics is much stronger. A broad study of the coverage of the Iraq War in Danish news media (Hjarvard et al. 2003) – both television and newspapers – concludes that the coverage is very broad and factual, and that aspects of politics, combat and everyday life in Iraq are included. There is no indication of dramatization or high concept in Danish media. A recent case, where a Danish journalist on the main public service channel DR was fired for a rather minor 'staging' of his report from the combat zone – he added a little more sound to underline the dramatic effect – indicates that editing reality is considered a serious breach with the factual contract of news.

Contrary to this, Jaramillo's argument in the analysis of CNN's and Fox News' coverage of the Iraq invasion in 2003 is that high concept narrative techniques borrowed from Hollywood structure have deeply influenced news, but that the narrativization of the war reflects the story told by the military and the government:

> While CNN and Fox News Channel news personnel attempted to deliver war news as though it were objective reality, they simultaneously and explicitly referred to the war *as a*

narrative (…) an assumption that echoed the message of the Department of Defense (…) CNN and Fox News Channel depicted various occurrences as 'dramas', 'dramatic' and 'unfolding dramas' and Fox News Channel's Greg Palkot even referred to a specific form of drama with his description of a 'soap opera' in the Center of Baghdad (…) news anchors referred to events as 'plotlines' and 'storylines' (Jaramillo 2009: 52).

The point is that the narrative and drama created in the news stories corresponds exactly to the story the political-military system produced and sold to the media. This means that there was absolutely no critical investigation of the reality behind the war and that the story told was extremely decontextualized in terms of sources and areas outside the scope of the American military story. Jaramillo concludes that although the two 24-hour news stations had many similarities in the way they told the Iraq story, Fox News was clearly the most 'ideological' in the sense that they did not only buy the official story, they actually increased the drama, punchlines and statements (Jaramillo 2009: 86f).

The realities of war close up: transformations of a national stereotype

Contrary to the situation in both the US and the UK, Denmark is virtually without a tradition for war movies, both fiction and non-fiction. War is simply not an important reality of the Danish mentality and historical experience. Most war movies until 2005 were fictional historical movies based on the resistance during WW2. War was until recently only something that involved *others*, and if Denmark was involved in war activities at all, it was as UN peacekeeping forces, never as active combat units. This did, however, change for the first time with the Balkan war (1992–1995), but not on a broader scale before the wars in Afghanistan, Iraq and Libya, where the Danish mentality towards a more global, active and military engagement changed the whole agenda and the very mediatization of war. If Danes before had a rather idealistic and distant relation to war, maybe even a generally pacifistic attitude, this mental condition was certainly challenged and tested.

We have already dealt with Christoffer Guldbrandsen's *The Secret War*, which marks the shift in the public debate. Here the image of Danes probably involved in activities violating human rights, and a government covering up, divided the public, but also became a wake up call. The peacekeeping image of the nation and its military was clearly tainted, and suddenly war came close to what it often is – a dirty, complicated business. The involvement in the Afghan war backed by a UN mandate was broadly supported both politically and by the general public and so were the Libyan actions. However, the Iraq War clearly divided the nation and parliament. But if we look at documentary films dealing with combat and life on the battleground there are still very few, compared with the UK and US situation. In 2010 both of the main public service channels did launch series dealing with war, but it is very characteristic that the eight films broadcast were all focusing on the more human story and dimension, the relation between soldiers and the home front, and not the actual combat experiences and realities out there.

In fact only one of the films, broadcast on TV2, namely Janus Metz' *Armadillo*, was a classical war documentary, and it follows the story of one platoon of soldiers in the Helmand province in Afghanistan over a period of six months. The film has a classical, dramatic, narrative structure starting with the training and preparations before going to Afghanistan, the trip down there, the mix of dull camp time and dramatic actions with both wounded and dead, and the homecoming. The film crew was allowed free access to the soldiers, the camp and the military action and we get extremely close to the group as a whole, but especially to two very different soldiers. Some of the dramatic combat scenes are very authentic and filmed with helmet cameras that place us as viewers in the middle of the action. Janus Metz has clearly stated in public interviews that the debate following *The Secret War* made them prepare very carefully for the cooperation with the military, even though as a film *Armadillo* is quite different by not being an investigative, journalistic documentary, but an observational documentary 'drama'. Metz has also clearly stated that he is inspired by the American tradition of fictional war movies, and he wanted to make something other than a traditional, journalistic documentary:

> After all, a documentary film isn't supposed to be an extended news report, and *Armadillo* is a film that tries to grapple with some deep psychological issues and to deal with some aspects of reality that just can't be captured by traditional journalistic means. Even in those moments when the film seems to be most intensely engaged with the brutal reality that it depicts there are other and far more universal psychological dimensions at work. At the same time there are just so many mediatized images of war, and they're also at work in the film and undoubtedly influence our experience of the film's reality. As a filmmaker I've clearly, for example, been influenced by the classic fiction film tradition of American war films. You just can't get around those, even as a documentary filmmaker. Feature fiction films like *Apocalypse Now* or *Deer Hunter* are extremely realistic, truthful films, and their themes and perspectives on war are definitely discernible in *Armadillo*. (Janus Metz, interviewed by Ib Bondebjerg in Hjort et al. 2013).

Even though the producer of the film and Metz had managed to get an exceptionally good deal with the military and were able to film rather freely, conflicts did occur, and the film was at certain points nearly stopped because of this. But probably one of the reasons the military wanted to give access and the freedom to film can be directly linked to the bad publicity the military got after *The Secret War*, and some rather damaging public cases involving the military in the years just before Metz' film. According to Metz, the military viewed the making of *Armadillo* as a way of telling the public that they have nothing to hide and want to communicate the reality of war and of being a soldier. Metz also thinks that once this realistic representation was on its way to the big screen the military got cold feet, but eventually they gave in.

Stopping the film or censuring part of it could have increased the bad image of the military in the eyes of the general public. The fact that the film is not preaching a specific point of view but trying to reveal the reality of war to a nation that had never seen the like, at least not with Danes playing the leading roles, also made it difficult to criticize the film for being partisan. It is clearly a film telling how brutal war is, how damaging to those fighting, the enemy of course and the civilian population. The film also shows how little war has changed: it is images of an endless war going in circles. But the film was seen as a true, authentic film about the realities of war, a fair and balanced portrait – although the film is not loved as much by the military as by the rest of the Danish audience. But it was seen by 160,000 in the cinema in Denmark, more than a million on Danish TV, and the film is now sold to many international territories and has won eight international prizes.

Figures 5a and b: Janus Metz's *Armadillo* (2010). Danish soldiers in contact with the locals not always with great success. Frame grab. Cinematography: Lars Skree.

Armadillo is, as Metz himself indicates, both a very concrete story about a group of Danish soldiers in Afghanistan and a very universal story. The broad and collective drama is also constructed in such a way that prototypical individuals stand out and are used to create a symbolic story on a deeper, psychological level. The story is also a mental story of the transformation of our national self-image. It is about what Metz himself has called our new 'militant humanism' (Metz in Hjort et al. 2013), the fact that globalization has led to a new kind of global engagement which is built on an imaginary and problematic concept of exporting democracy which could be a dangerous illusion. *Armadillo* is clearly a classical, observational and very reality-driven film, but it uses both narrative and dramatic structures to focus the story, with it being also strongly character-driven. It tells the collective story of a group of Danish soldiers preparing for and eventually going to one of the toughest combat areas of Afghanistan, and most of the film deals with the social and psychological interaction between a group of men in a very tough, military macho culture.

But behind the picture of a group of men and the structures and hierarchies in a military culture like this, typical individuals with a broader symbolic and prototypical kind of representational value stand out. In the film two types of soldiers and men are the main characters: on the one hand the daring macho guy Daniel, constantly seeking out the more extreme, pushing himself to the limit, and on the other hand the softer and more reflective and sceptical Mads. The two characters can also be read as universal, psychological master types that are probably present at the same time in most human beings and soldiers in such a situation, but in different forms. By establishing such a character-driven symbolic structure the film allows the viewer to experience and interpret war on a much deeper level than most reports and journalistic representation of war experiences.

The film also very clearly opens up spaces of reality of a very different kind, again providing us with a close portrait of war. We have the *space of home and family*, represented in the beginning and at the end of the film, but also present through the contact between the soldiers in Afghanistan and home. This is a space of very familiar feelings and relations, we can all relate to the anxieties and hopes expressed here. We have the *base camp space*, the home of the soldiers abroad so to speak, a space that has both spots of privacy and intimacy when they relax, the space for military preparation and for debriefing after battle or other serious incidents. Social and psychological structures and feelings in this space are not as universal as the family space, but they elicit emotions and experiences that most of us know from work and from collective social structures and institutions. The most dramatic space is, of course, the outside *space of war and fighting*, this is the most extreme and darkest area, where sudden death or mutilation is just around the corner. But it is worth noting that the film clearly establishes a link between the fighting space and the *space of the local community and families*. The message and reality conveyed in the film is to a large degree that military actions do not really help the locals.

The use of story-driven, dramatic and narrative structures, inspired by fiction films of a strong realist nature, and the symbolic use of characters to represent different ways of experiencing and relating to war does not undermine the film as a documentary. There are a few reconstructions in the film, and the chronology has been changed a few times in the edited version, but basically there is a strong documentary quality and a feeling of authenticity. It is also very expressive in both the narrative and dramatic structuring, and in the visual style. Both the dramatic combat scenes and the more quiet scenes of the camp and the landscape around are filmed with a clear realism and a stunning beauty – especially some of the panoramic evening, night and morning shots – a style that tells a story of the qualities and possibilities in this tortured part of the world. Likewise, the dramatic scenes of combat or other military actions are often shot with very vivid camerawork, and heavy music underlines the kind of feeling, fear and pumping adrenalin created by combat. The film uses stylistic elements in a careful and balanced way in order to establish different forms of feelings and experiences for the audience, feelings and experiences with a solid basis in the reality portrayed.

American action and the realities of war

Whereas Danish film and media culture has virtually no tradition for war films and documentaries, the opposite is true for the American film and media culture. There is an incredibly diverse historical tradition of films dealing with almost all aspects of war. Even though American film culture may be mostly known for action-packed war films from the Hollywood mainstream tradition, the real picture is actually much broader. This is one of the conclusions in Stephen Prince's book *Firestorm* (2009), which deals with post-9/11 cinema. He points out that, at least for a long time, the traditional action movie will be more problematic to a mass audience for whom that kind of action and mass destruction has suddenly come very close to the reality at home. In some ways those films that took another road and focused on either the political climate after 9/11 or the way in which the war deeply influenced everyday life and families, were films that made a lasting impression and changed the agenda.

But in many ways documentary films from this period were the most direct and active in dealing with all aspects of the War on Terror, and they brought the war on the ground, the reality of war in action, much closer than most of the fictional war films in this period were able to. Between 2002–2011 more than twenty documentary films alone can be characterized as films following soldiers in combat in either Iraq or Afghanistan, and the films are made by both independent directors and film companies, by HBO or PBS, or by channels like National Geographic or the History Channel. The films furthermore represent different documentary genres and ways of representing war: from authoritative, informational films like History Channel's series *The Iraq War* (1–5, 2007), more critical behind the scene documentaries from the frontline like Stephen Marshall and Guerrilla News Network's *Battleground: 21 Days on the Empires Edge* (2004), more observational films on the drama of the casualties of war as in HBO and Jon Alpert and Mathew O'Neill's *Baghdad ER* (2006) from a military hospital, the more classical films following a group of soldiers like Tim Hetherington and Sebastian Junger's *Restrepo* (2010) or Old and Scott's *Occupation: Dreamland* (2005). Such films also include documentaries where the link between the battleground and those at home is at the forefront, like we see it in Jake Rademacher's *Brothers at War* (2009) or Bill Couturié and HBO's *Last Letters Home* (2004). Just as the post-9/11 fiction film doesn't just tell the traditional war story, the documentary films really take many roads in the covering of war after 2001.

Reports from the battleground

The most obvious American equivalent to Danish Janus Metz's *Armadillo* seems to be Tim Hetherington and Sebastian Junger's *Restrepo* (2010), winner of the Grand Jury Prize at Sundance Festival that year. In their introduction to the film, the directors have a very clear statement about what kind of film *Restrepo* is:

> The war in Afghanistan has become highly politicised, but soldiers rarely take part in that discussion. Our intention was to capture the experience of combat, boredom and fear through the eyes of the soldiers themselves (…) Soldiers are living and fighting and dying at remote outposts in Afghanistan in conditions that few back home can imagine. Their experiences are important to understand, regardless of one's political beliefs. Beliefs are a way to avoid looking at reality. This is reality (Hetherington and Junger, 2010; cover of American DVD, dogwoof.com).

The film follows a platoon sent to a remote outpost in Afghanistan's Korengal Valley, one of the most hostile places in the whole region. The structure of the film is classical, observational cinema, where we and the film team simply live together with and experience the daily life of soldiers over a 15 month period. But, unlike *Armadillo*, there is no strong, dramatic structure, but more a sequence of recurrent events, many of which are dramatic combat episodes with the almost invisible enemy, but there are also events in the macho camp culture or difficult and sometimes tragic encounters with the locals. The film is also characterized by a strong use of individual soldiers talking to the camera about their feelings and experiences. There are intense and emotional moments, for instance when soldiers are killed, or when they visit a local village where children and women have been killed by mistake by American bombings. The film has no partisan views or explicit ideological message, but maybe the underlying and indirect message is that this war is a surreal fight leading nowhere. We follow the soldiers going to the Restrepo post in the valley, we follow a fight that is not easy to understand and doesn't seem to move anywhere, and after 15 months they go back, with no visible change in the power structure, although an officer tries to say that they have changed the whole situation. But a text message at the end of the film just sardonically announces that 50 American soldiers died at the Restrepo post, and after the platoon we followed went back, the Americans withdrew from Korengal Valley.

This absurd feeling of an endless war that doesn't get anywhere is often found in the observational war films following the both dramatic and boring life of a soldier. These films document war seen from the perspective of American soldiers in the frontline, but not all of them follow a strict observational format and narrative strategy. PBS and Frontline programmes are not very oriented towards the observational format, they generally follow a more authoritative, journalistic form, in which observational sequences and material is inserted. In *A Company of Soldiers* (2005, PBS) we follow a special unit in Southern Baghdad called Dog Company whose mission it is to protect bodyguards that are themselves protecting high military rank personnel. This means we are witnessing the daily routines of a group of soldiers doing a very dangerous job everyday outside their camp. The style is embedded journalism with the company which means we see their reality and actions very close up, basically in an observational form, but with a guiding voiceover. But we hear and see the soldiers most of the time, both in real time and in a reflexive voiceover where they comment on what they think and feel. The programme documents a very dramatic period in Dog company's history, with killed and wounded, and also conflicts and contact with different local groups. A story illustrating how absurd the war can be deals with the Americans building a market for the locals, however they don't use it out of fear and the local sheikh is trying to make money on it.

The problematic relation between the American 'liberators' and the locals is also clearly illustrated in another PBS Frontline documentary, Arun Rath's *Rules of Engagement* (2008) on the Haditha incident, an incident also dealt with in Nick Broomfield's drama-doc *Battle for Haditha*. The Haditha case is a famous example of US-soldiers killing a large number of unarmed civilians under circumstances that some media reported to be in cold blood, others to be a result of the blurred line between civilians and insurgents in a war where the traditional military rules of engagement may be hard to follow. The PBS programme is a critical investigative programme of an incident that hit the media as a case of war crime. We are certainly not following a group of soldiers on the battleground, but all sorts of documentation, witnesses and experts are used to reconstruct the case and show how things really happened. The soldiers eventually on trial in the case belongs to the famous 31 Marine Corps, also known as Kilo company, and the programme also allows us to hear their side of the story in retrospect and through a dramatization of their witness to the military court. So we are both inside the soldiers reality on the battleground, but also outside through footage and witnesses from the locals in Haditha. It is a grim story of the dark side of war and how rules of engagement are clearly violated in a war with blurred boundaries and where soldiers under pressure lose human dignity and reason.

The Haditha case was slow to reach the mainstream media in the US, but after *Time* magazine put it on their front page the case exploded. It was also an incident that showed a military deliberately trying to hide the truth about what had happened. The outcome of the case did not satisfy the local, Iraqi human rights organization: two men were accused and condemned of voluntary and involuntary manslaughter, but not murder, and others

Figures 5c and d: Nick Broomfield's *Battle for Haditha* (2007). Dramatic reconstruction of a disastrous event during the Iraq war. Frame grab. Cinematography: Nick Laird-Clowes.

were given minor verdicts. But the Haditha case did result in a change of strategy, where the uprooting of the Iraqi insurgence should be conducted alongside efforts to win 'the hearts and minds of the Iraqi people'. The Haditha case was also the background for Nick Broomfield's drama-doc *Battle for Haditha* (2007), an attempt at reconstructing actual events with the use of real people and real locations, and as close to real time as possible. With the freedom that the more fictional approach gives, the film manages to get inside both the minds and worlds of the American soldiers and the Iraqi people. The film doesn't pretend to know the real truth of what happened, but the reconstructed incidents are pretty graphic. But, based on factual accounting it manages to draw two different worlds and cultures together to get a better understanding of the happenings along with the context and background.

Inside stories from the dark side

The documentaries already mentioned, and especially the two Haditha films, clearly show the dark and sometimes surreal sides of war. Many other documentaries also focus on this reality of war, and the way soldiers in combat deal with it. For instance, in Michael Epstein's independent documentary *Combat Diary* (2006) we follow the marines of the Lima Company during very tough times in the Anbar province in 2005, where 23 out of 184 marines were killed during the shooting of the film. As Stephen Prince has pointed out (Prince 2009: 194f) *Combat Diary* has elements of a first person observational film as it is based on video footage taken by the marines themselves. But this footage is combined with interviews with marines and their family after they have returned. The film therefore, to a large degree, loses the sense of being there and, following the marines over a longer time, becomes a reflexive personal film in rear view.

A much stronger example of a similar soldier's-point-of-view documentary is Michael Tupper and Petra Epperlein's *Gunner Palace* (2005), which follows an artillery group of soldiers in late 2003 and early 2004 with their home base in one of Saddam's earlier grand palaces. The film gives a vivid inside view of the war seen from the perspective of this group of soldiers, but the film also manages to show an almost surreal and absurd contradiction between the official rhetoric around the successful ending of the war and the reality the soldiers are living in (Prince 2009: 195f). The upbeat official rhetoric is clearly contrasted with the chaos and dark, absurd sides of everyday life in Iraq, although the Iraqi people are not very visible in the film, but are seen from a distance.

Perhaps two of the most direct examples of these observational documentaries seen from and following combat with a soldier's perspective are Ian Olds and Garrett Scott's *Occupation: Dreamland* (2005) and Deborah Scranton's *The War Tapes* (2006). *Occupation: Dreamland* has a classical observational pattern where we follow soldiers from the 82nd Airborne Division as they try to control the unfolding Sunni insurgence in one of the hardest combat places in Iraq, Fallujah, in the early months of 2004. Alongside the observational sequences on the ground we get stories from some of the soldiers, both as voice off commentaries and through on-screen interviews, about their background, why they ended up in the army, and how they experience being in Iraq. The eruption of serious violence in Fallujah in November 2004, where Operation Phantom Fury cost the lives of 100 Americans and over 1000 Iraqis, takes place after the shooting of the film. But the film does document how the soldiers feel increasingly isolated in their attempt to win the hearts and minds of the locals, and longer sequences clearly tell a story of the increased hatred against the Americans that in the eyes of the Iraqis are not liberators, but colonizers and an occupying power. The film, and the dialogue between both the soldiers internally and with the local population, shows a huge lack of cultural understanding and ability to communicate, and this points back to the general lack of a policy and strategy in the Bush administration for the post-invasion development.

An even more radical, observational format can be found in *The War Tapes*, where the director Deborah Scranton gave cameras to ten soldiers from Charlie Company placed at Camp Anaconda in the Sunni triangle in Iraq. The film is based on the video evidence these soldiers submitted, but out of the ten soldiers three soldiers come especially into focus in the film. As Stephen Prince has pointed out (Prince 2009: 200), the three soldiers are very different, one of them a Lebanese-American with Shiite Muslim parents, and the film therefore shows a perhaps more diverse and critical image of soldiers than normal. The film also gives a much more direct image of violence and the soldiers' way of reacting to it, because they capture reality on camera themselves.

But more critical reports from the darker sides of the War on Terror come out in films like Mike Shiley's *Inside Iraq: The Untold Stories* (2004), based on travels in Iraq in 2004 and showing both the combat and events seen from an American perspective through a visit to three different military bases and from the Iraqi perspectives through visits to schools and hospitals. The film is a fine example of American independent documentaries. It is a personal report told to the camera or in voiceover by Shiley, and in the beginning he states that his film should be seen as going behind the scenery that dominates the mainstream media and traditional news reporting. The film therefore, in many ways, moves away from the genre of battleground reporting and moves into the genre of everyday life reporting from the war zones that we find in a number of other documentaries. A different, but also very critical, approach to the Iraq War is David Russell and Tricia Regan's *Soldier's Pay* (2004) which is largely based on interviews with Iraq veterans that look back with a rather critical attitude, and also with journalists, politicians, activists and Iraqis, with inserted footage from Iraq between some of the interviews.

This broader documentation of the context around the battleground that we find in the documentaries mentioned is part of the search for getting the 'unseen' images and stories out that independent reporters and production companies are engaged in. *Battleground: 21 Days on the Empire's Edge* (2005), directed by Stephen Marshall for the Guerrilla News Network (GNN), is a solid piece of critical, investigative war reporting with a strong focus on what the war has done to the Iraqis and the whole environment and infrastructure of the country. GNN was created in 2000 with the mission to 'expose people to important global issues through cross-platform guerrilla programming' (Wikipedia), but the company closed down in 2009. *Battleground* is a film dedicated to giving space for other voices from inside Iraq and although we see battle scenes during the 30 chapters of the film, we mostly hear about the consequences of war on the country and its citizens. Dramatic images of suicide bombing are followed by images of the damage done by American bombs and tanks, polluting the area and creating long-term danger of sickness. We see how the whole infrastructure is not functioning, and hear the voices of the locals who are fed up with the Americans, but we also hear and follow American soldiers on duty, for instance on the huge Anaconda Base north of Baghdad with 15,000 'inhabitants'. It is an important film which gives a much broader and more detailed image of the battleground, its context and the many voices both on the American and the Iraqi side, and it doesn't come out as a partisan left-wing film, but rather as a well-documented report from a very complex situation.

The historiography of a war

The films dealt with so far are independent productions or TV programmes from stations other than the mainstream media, but more established channels like Discovery Channel, National Geographic and the History Channel have all been very active in covering the wars in Iraq and Afghanistan. Some of these programmes come in longer series and they often fall into the category of classical, authoritative history narratives based on an authoritative narrator, chronological narratives with perhaps a different thematic focus, and the use of experts, interviews with involved witnesses, data and graphics, sometimes with a broader historical perspective. One classical example of this is the History Channel series *America at War: The Iraq War* (2007, 1–5), following the preparations to go to war and until the fall of Saddam and the aftermath. Great emphasis is put on weapons, technology and military strategy. The series fits the general generic format of many historical series on the History Channel covering older, historical wars like the Civil War or WW2: they are fact-based, but also dramatic narratives and they are not critical investigations of the war strategies or the politics behind them, although series like this can certainly touch upon controversial issues and disputes of a political nature. The programme follows the invasion very closely, so we get close to the battleground, including both the American and the British armies, and aerial shots and maps give the viewer a feeling of overviewing the complete invasion. What we don't get from a programme like this is the view from within Iraq, the actual reactions to the war: this is a programme about military and political strategy and those that carried out the actions. Only in the last programme, 'The Aftermath', does it deal with the much more difficult task of installing a new democracy, and we do get some views from the Iraqis.

National Geographic has made several programmes on the War on Terror, including the more political and controversial aspects. The channel has a mission of global understanding, and programmes like *The Road to War: Iraq* (2008) have a much more critical edge than one would expect, just as is the case with *Inside Guantanamo* (2009). But, their film *21 Days to Baghdad* (2003) is a more classical battleground report, following the preparations for war and the 21 days of direct combat. It is yet another classical war narrative in the more authoritative, journalistic form and there is a rather strong focus on the advanced new weapon technologies. But the film also focuses on civilian casualties and the fact that those advanced weapons are not always as accurate and precise as expected, so we get close to the really ugly side of war.

However, one of the most innovative of these longer TV series is clearly Discovery Channel's *Off to War* (1–10, 2006), directed by Craig and Brent Renaud. The series is presented as 'a story about soldiers and the families they left behind' so the battleground in Iraq is combined with life on the home front and the link between those two spaces. We follow a group of the Arkansas National Guard as they prepare to go to war, during the war and during homecoming. The fact that the group of soldiers come from a very small Arkansas town, Clarksville, with only 7000 inhabitants makes this a unique series on the everyday aspects of going to war. Unlike all the others films or programmes we have seen so far, this film has a unique, intimate and very close-up focus on all aspects of war in a typical, rural and very traditional, religious and national culture and community. This is not the kind of place where you would expect criticism of the war, but as Stephen Prince has already pointed out (Prince 2009: 203), given that we are among real patriots, the films clearly show how 'corrupting the experience of war' is for the soldiers and their families.

A soldier's body and mind: the scars of battle

War is a very physical experience and your whole life is at stake, or permanent bodily harm can be inflicted on both you and your enemy, or even civilians caught in the middle. But we know for a fact that even for those that get out of the war without marks on the body, the mental marks are just as heavy and can be very damaging and long-lasting. On PBS's *The Soldier's Heart* (2005) one of the soldiers in the programme says at the very beginning of the film: 'You don't have to be an amputee to be wounded, there is a psychological side of this war that is no less debilitating'. *The Soldier's Heart* is a deeply moving human story about the psychological costs of going to war, based on the stories of four soldiers returned from combat and now fighting another, mental battle with their experiences. The format of the film is a mixture of the stories these four soldiers and their families tell to the camera, sequences from the battleground in Iraq and testimonies from military and psychological experts on Post Traumatic Stress Disorder (PTSD). The film has an authoritative voiceover narrator, and also presents a historical perspective on the development of the military and public attitude towards soldiers with PTSD, a mental disease formerly not recognized but often just seen as cowardliness or weakness. This is even illustrated as a contemporary problem in one of the case stories where the media accuse one of the soldiers of cowardice.

The case stories in the film show different degrees of PTSD and, in one case, the soldier committed suicide after almost a year of suffering. The rest manage more or less well, thanks to help from families, friends and professionals. What the film shows is that war is not only taking a heavy toll on people wounded in combat, but that the civilian casualties, in terms of human breakdowns, are in fact much greater than the physical wounds and casualties. The mental scars, the memories, the guilt over actions done, haunt soldiers and their families for decades after the actual fighting is over. This is also the message in an even more dramatic PBS programme, *The Wounded Platoon* (2010), dealing with the 'invisible wounds of the war', wounds that make soldiers continue their violent behaviour even after they have come home. The film deals with a platoon of soldiers from Fort Carson, Colorado Springs, and initially frames the story through an incident where one of a group of four soldiers back home from the war was killed by the others. But as the film points out, this is not an isolated incident at Fort Carson, where 14 soldiers have been condemned of manslaughter after coming back from war. The war continues both mentally and at the home front, and the number of soldiers with PTSD after Iraq has risen by 4000 per cent, and the misuse of drugs by 3000 per cent, even though the military macho culture tends to stigmatize psychological problems. The film is again based on different case stories of PTSD victims and how they made it through, or ended up with serious problems and criminal charges.

HBO often makes documentaries dealing with the human dimension of war, and they deal with suffering, injuries and the death of soldiers, and the way this influences their families. HBO is not on the battleground in the direct sense of the word, but they are on the emotional and psychological battleground and they show the ultimate sacrifice or injuries that the mainstream media do not want to touch. On Thanksgiving Day, 11 November 2004, HBO broadcast Bill Couturié's *Last Letters Home: Voices of American Soldiers from the Battleground of Iraq*, a simple, very moving documentary in which the core is reading of letters home by the families of dead soldiers. We get human stories covering different kinds of America through these stories, different families, different places and we see stills of the soldiers from their time in Iraq. The quiet, moving and almost lyrical melancholia of *Last Letters Home* is contrasted by the hectic, dramatic, messy atmosphere and graphic horror of HBO's *Baghdad ER* (2006) from the 86th Combat Support Hospital in Baghdad's green zone. Here limbs are cut off and dumped in the garbage can, anonymous soldiers in comas die in front of our eyes, or soldiers with names go through difficult surgery to survive and move on. The programme starts with a text saying that 'it is a tribute to heroism and sacrifice of the soldiers who are the patients and staff of the 86th Combat Support Hospital'. We are inside the nerve centres of this frontline of battle for recovery and saving lives and limbs, and even though the images are shocking we are told that 90 per cent of the injured do survive. We follow the operation teams, the helicopter teams, the staff meetings, we are on tour to IED-valley where dozens of soldiers are hit by terror bombs, we hear soldiers call their families and we learn how staff and soldiers feel. Amidst the horror we also meet black humour, and the wounded who can joke in the midst of pain. Another powerful documentary in this genre is Terry Sander's *Fighting for Life* (2007), focusing on military surgeons.

It gives credit to HBO as documentary producer that they have also made the Iraqi equivalent, *Baghdad Hospital: Inside the Red Zone* (2008), directed by the Iraqi journalist Omer Salih Madhi and shot under both dangerous and difficult circumstances. About his intentions with the film he says:

I hope this film will give Americans the real picture of what's going on there. There are no services, there's no electricity, there's no water, there's no fuel for cars, or generators. Life is really difficult, with no electricity, with no fans, with no air going, and in winter you freeze because there's no electricity for hot water. I'm hoping that by going public with this story I'll get more reaction from people, that they'll listen to me, they'll know

I'm from the inside, that I'm carrying the real picture, and I'm telling you the real story (quoted from HBO 2009).

Another graphic HBO programme on soldiers injured is *Alive Day Memories: Home from Iraq* (2007). The film has *Sopranos* actor James Gandolfini as host and director, and as a documentary it is special by mixing studio-based interviews with soldiers with serious disabilities, and their memories and stories about that day where they barely escaped death, the 'alive day' as it is called in contrast to the birthday. We hear and see their stories at home long after the incidents, but the film is also based on embedded camera footage and soldier camera footage from their stay in Iraq, or from their lives at home before and after their war disaster. We also get really close to the soldiers' injured bodies and their various prosthesis, to what they were before and became afterwards. The films want to normalize or at least demystify the horror of war injuries to give us a realistic image of what war can do to people. The same kind of dealing with the wounded and mentally injured soldiers can also be found in Richard Hankin's *Home Front* (2006), dealing with the story of the blinded Jeremy Feldbusch and his life after Iraq with his Pennsylvanian family, and in Patricia Foulkroud's *The Ground Truth* (2006). Both were focused very much on experiences of soldiers who had been involved in the killing of civilians – perhaps one of the most ugly war experiences for soldiers, since it involves children and women.

One quite original and unique perspective on war and battleground experience is Jake Rademacher's *Brothers at War* (2009). It is a film by the director about his two brothers, both serving in Iraq. The contrast between the director's initial scepticism and difficulty of understanding his brothers, and the very real insight into their life and situation in Iraq that he gets close to and documents with his film, is a quite different narrative from most other battleground documentaries. The film is a first person documentary where the director narrates the story and gradually involves himself more and more as an embedded journalist in the reality of his brothers Isaac and Joe. The film is very much about the psychology of war, of how you deal with the harsh combat reality, but also about parting with and missing those at home and thoughts about whether it is all worth the effort. The film is also a portrait of the average all-American family and different ways of relating to the army and war; we hear the story and voices of most of the family members. But through the eyes of Jake, the non-soldier in the family, we also get close to the harsh realities of war in Iraq, and meet those on the frontline, and through brother Isaac also an intelligence unit seldom described in battleground stories.

Another concept of war documentaries that brings us really close to both the combat reality and life after the war is Danfung Denning's Sundance winner *Hell and Back Again* (2011). In a interview after the film available on YouTube (www.youtube.com/watch?v= eewlUkDH9Nfl8U&list=PL228211FF04BBD9A0&index=22&feature=plpp_video) he talks about his intention of the film as an attempt to break the lack of knowledge and emotional understanding of the war in Afghanistan and the costs for those involved: 'We have been at war for ten years, but it doesn't feel like that (…) I try to bring this war closer to home.'

The way this is done in the film is to focus on just one character, 25-year-old sergeant Nathan Harris from the US marines Echo Company. In the first part of the film we follow him close-up during heavy combat in Afghanistan, a closer and more realistic picture than in many other combat documentaries because of the focus on one person. During combat he is seriously wounded and in the second part of the film we follow him back to his home town, family and wife Ashley in North Carolina, and his struggle with both the physical, psychological and emotional damages from war. It is a strong and very personal case story which makes the viewer identify with a soldier's story in a new and more direct way.

Public service media eyes on the war: BBC war documentaries

The major difference between the British war documentaries after 2001 and the American is not a difference in genre and perspective; they actually tell exactly the same kinds of stories. The difference is that the BBC is the mainstream media of British television. This means that while you do not see the close-up realism, the critical perspectives or the human horror stories on mainstream media in the US, but only on cable television and in independent film productions, you actually see them in the UK. Programmes from the BBC to a large degree influence and frame the public debate and speak to the general audience, an audience that was from the beginning much more divided than the American one, but soon became more and more critical. This is clearly reflected in the development of BBC programmes on both Afghanistan and Iraq. The first programmes were more classical, embedded journalist reports on the invasion, as we see in *The Fall of Kabul* (2001), *The Race to Baghdad* (2003) or *The Battle for Basra* (2003). But if we look at the last of these programmes, for example, sent on 27 April with BBC reporter Jane Corbin, we can see it has a structure which leaves much more space to the ordinary Basra men and women, who get to speak about how they look at the battle and the presence of the British troops. The BBC ethos is clearly not just to make embedded war journalism but to give a broader and more diverse picture of the events.

The same kind of rather critical reporting on how difficult it is for the soldiers to carry out the military and political mission they have been sent on, you also find in the Afghanistan programmes. This is very clear from a programme like *Panorama With the Paras* (2002), following the men of D company of the 2nd Battalion of the Parachute Regiment as they try to create order in Kabul. The troops are not just fighting the Taliban, they are also fighting the local scepticism and hostility of both ordinary people and authorities, and they cannot trust the helpers, for instance, in the local police. It is a war on all fronts and the programme lets us experience this with voices from both parts of the conflict, although it is of course a programme about, and mostly seen from, the British soldiers' perspective. We also see it in a programme like *The Price of Victory* (2003), on Iraq and the situation in and around Baghdad, after the official victory has been declared, but as the real and tough war seems to be starting. The BBC presents the programme, which is about the American army, like this:

This powerful documentary examines the nature of the resistance in Iraq, gaining access to American troops as they hunt down paramilitaries. This is a story of men who came to rebuild a country but who found themselves sucked into an urban guerrilla war instead. This is a story also about Baghdad's five million Iraqis whose gratitude over liberation is in danger of being squandered amidst a deepening unease over occupation. Throughout the programme *Panorama* scrutinises Iraq's new 'occupiers', questioning whether the world's most powerful nation is up to the task of rebuilding a country as effectively as it can defeat it in war (BBC News 2003a).

Soldier's stories – the war close up and personal

The perspective on a war that doesn't seem to reach the goals set, but ends up in endless guerrilla war against an invisible enemy and a hostile population soon translates to a number of political questions. This is obvious from a programme like *Troops Out* (2005) in which the BBC's David Dimbleby gathered people from both sides of the war at The Imperial War Museum to debate whether the war makes sense, or in Jane Corbin's report, *Bringing Our Boys Home* (2006), which reports from South Iraq where British troops are stationed and asks commanders and soldiers when British troops can pull out, but also what will happen after they do. But among the war documentaries on the BBC, the broader reports from the war, or the collective stories with a military or political perspective, are not nearly as numerous as those stories getting close to the soldiers' reality – not just stories of heroism, but also stories of all the dark sides.

One of those dark sides also clearly taken up in US documentaries is torture. In, for instance, *Shamed* (2004) and *On Whose Orders* (2008) the BBC reports from different places of torture incidents in Iraq and Afghanistan and asks questions on where the torture originated from. Torture techniques banned by the British authorities in 1972 were reintroduced in 2003. The programme cites lawyers and experts involved on behalf of Iraqi family members in a particular incident at the British Camp Abu Naji in 2004 where Iraqi prisoners died, claiming that they died because of torture. The programme also discusses whether the alleged torture techniques by British soldiers were permitted and supported directly by decisions taken in the British government.

But one thing is what actions on the border of, or beyond, legal war actions British troops have engaged in, another thing is the severe psychological damage war does to soldiers even long after the violent battle experience they are involved in ends. One of the first BBC programmes to deal with the traumatic effects of war is *Shock Troops* (2005), which takes a broader historical look at PTSD and goes deeper into a case story of a soldier still suffering from the memories of war in Bosnia. Also, a programme like *Runaway Soldiers* (2007) deals with soldiers turning their back on society after their war experience. In another very special and personal programme, *The Battle For Bomb Alley* (2011), a former British bomb squad member, Ben Anderson, follows the American Lima Company on duty in the Afghan

Sangin province, where many UK soldiers earlier lost their lives. The programme takes us on a very critical tour into this special military unit and the circumstances under which they work. The personal and emotional case story becomes a background for a more general critique of the conditions for soldiers in Afghanistan and Iraq.

A more classical battleground documentary following a unit of British soldiers in Afghanistan's violent Helmand province is *Taking on the Taliban – The Soldier's Story* (2007), with strong images of the harsh realities of war including close-ups of dead and wounded soldiers. But this classical battleground documentary spawned a follow-up where one of the most heroic soldiers in the first programme was given his own programme, *Jack – the Soldier's Story* (BBC3 2008), following him home after his latest stationing. His stay for a long time in this place called 'the heart of darkness' is shown to have taken a high toll on his ability to adjust to a civilian life. The programme follows him during his last couple of months in Afghanistan and on his way back to England. However, he is not able to make it after he is back home, the experiences of war haunt him, and this 'hero' of war is accused with assault and bad conduct, he is stripped of his military rank and condemned to four years in a civilian prison. The programme is a fine psychological portrait of the life and problems of an ordinary soldier.

A very special and almost surreal contrast between the life on the battleground in Afghanistan and 'normal' life at home is *For Queen and Country* (2010) following the 1st Battalion Grenadier Guards both on the ground in Afghanistan and at the same time preparing to be the leading, ceremonial battalion at Trooping the Colour, the Queen's annual birthday parade in front of Buckingham Palace. The contrast between the chaos and terror of war intercut throughout the film with ceremonial parade pictures is stunning and very British. But the majority of films on the home front theme stress another, more sombre and realistic tone, like we see in films like *Back on the Home Front* (2008) and *Forgotten Heroes* (2011).

Where the first programme just follows up on what happened to the soldiers portrayed in an earlier programme, *Forgotten Heroes* (2011) is a documentary kitchen sink drama on the serious social problems former soldiers can end up with. The programme is introduced like this on the *Panorama* website:

Colonel Tim Collins, whose eve of battle speech before the invasion of Iraq brought him international fame, meets the soldiers who return home only to find that their service for Queen and country counts for little on civvy street.

In a Panorama Special, Collins meets veterans who struggle to find work and housing.

He sleeps rough on the streets of Brighton with a former soldier who's spent much of the past six years either on the streets or in jail.

He meets veterans who fear for their sanity as they suffer flashbacks, night terrors and violent outbursts and talks to families who struggle to cope with the husbands and fathers who went to war, only to come home as strangers (BBC *Panorama* 2012).

That the programme deals with a problem people can relate to is clearly seen by the fact that the associated commentary site has about 100 entries from former soldiers, families etc. The war is not just about the battleground, it has serious long-term effects on a lot of people's everyday life, both in the war zone and on the home front.

The hard realities of war and combat

Unlike the day-to-day news reporting on war and its consequences, the documentaries dealing with the realities on the battleground in Iraq and Afghanistan go much deeper and wider. They raise tough, critical and political questions on whether the lives of so many soldiers are worth the effort, and they show us the cost paid by civilians in wars supposed to create a better life for them. These battleground documentaries combine critical investigative perspectives, very dominant in PBS and BBC programmes, with more observational human stories by HBO and independent directors on the hearts and minds of those in combat, those wounded and those at home that have to carry the burden of war many years after the end of the direct fighting. The story they tell is, perhaps, that we cannot avoid war in the kind of world we live in, but we may learn from our experiences and reduce the costs and mistakes of war. These documentaries also demonstrate the emotional dimensions of documentary reality construction, and the fact that films from three different Western countries have many things in common illustrates universal dimensions behind global realities.

Chapter 6

Behind the headlines: documentaries, war, terror and everyday life

In a modern world of increased globalization and mediatization of both politics and everyday life, war and acts of terror in all parts of the world hit the front pages and headlines daily. But news often only deals with the dramatic and the catastrophic in a way that represents a distance perspective or a perspective guided by very stereotypical notions of actions and the various actors involved in the reported incidents (see Tumber and Palmer 2004; Katovsky and Carlsson 2003). In the United States, the United Kingdom and Denmark documentary programmes and films showing quite another perspective on the wars in Iraq and Afghanistan were also made. These films give voices to other actors behind the headlines and dramatic incidents of war and terror, both on the home front of the soldiers going to war in distant places, and among the ordinary people of the countries invaded.

They represent not just another way of reporting on war, they give space to the voices of everyday life and deal with the question of how to continue a life under extreme pressure. These films can also be seen as part of a discursive, documentary project on democracy. They represent a *documentary glocalization* of an otherwise more homogenized global media sphere, and although often made by Western journalists and media (but mostly in collaboration with locals) they challenge the dominant news order – for instance, by letting even Islamic fundamentalists and terrorists have a voice among others in the war zones of everyday life. They also represent a difference simply by doing independent reporting under difficult circumstances on how 'victims' and 'enemies' are also ordinary citizens and human beings trying to live a normal everyday life. If war journalism has a tendency to distance and stereotype 'the other', these documentaries try to draw on universal, human dimensions that we all share, they try to normalize 'the other'.

Media, globalization and everyday life

Many studies of recent developments in documentary genres have pointed to the rise of different forms of observational formats with focus on the subjective and everyday life. In his book *The Subject of Documentary* Michael Renov points to a 'new foregrounding of the politics of everyday life' (2004: 171). Jon Dovey much along the same line in his book *Freakshow: First Person Media and Factual Television* (2000) looks into the huge growth of television formats dealing with the reality of ordinary people and different lifestyles, both in more reality TV show formats and in more observational docu-series. Together on TV and in films, documentary formats seem to have shifted from investigative journalistic or authoritative formats to more ethnographic, subjective and observational forms (Bondebjerg 2008a: 353ff).

A move from traditional politics to a politics of everyday life viewed in a broader context can be seen as a problematic undermining of critical, investigative journalism and documentary film production. In both an American and a European context this is indeed to a certain degree the case, and in the mainstream media critical formats have been under heavy attack. Critical documentaries on the War on Terror in the American context have had a hard time finding both financing and distribution, and in Europe this topic has not been held in high esteem by those deciding production and programme scheduling (Bondebjerg 2009). But documentaries dealing with everyday life in those countries influenced by the War on Terror must also be seen as an extremely important and valuable contribution to the global and intercultural dialogue. In relation to the mainstream tendencies in both the average war news reporting and to the way nations in the Arab and Islam world are represented in Western media, these films and programmes glocalize the other and bring both specific cultural knowledge of difference and the universal dimension of human commonalities into the global media culture. They operate in the dialectic zone of social cognition between individuality, group cultures and universal culture.

Backstage war reporting and the documentaries on the everyday life in war zones or on the home front help shift the frame and context of global reporting on war. By shifting from the dramatic and unusual, from generalized observations of battles between forces and nations to the usual and universal questions of individual and family lives, these stories situate war in a new social and cognitive perspective where the relation between individuals, groups and humans in general come to focus, as already discussed in relation to Zerubavel's cognitive sociology (Zerubavel, 1997). In the last chapter of Farnaz Fassihi's book *Waiting for an Ordinary Day: The Unraveling of Life in Iraq* (2008) she puts it like this: 'War happens to people, one by one. War doesn't just happen to the military whose soldiers are fighting, or to the government, who wages it. It happens to people, one by one, house by house, and family by family' (Fassihi, 2008: 273). In standard war reporting, individuals only occasionally get a voice other than the voice of pain and suffering. As we have seen in some of the documentaries dealing with soldiers on the battleground, we do occasionally see things from an individual's perspective and family life at home is linked with the unusual life as a soldier. But in the observational reporting behind the lines, and in documentaries bringing ordinary people's life to the front, the narrative and reality of war gets a whole new dimension.

Since the birth of observational documentary cinema in the 1960s, everyday life has been a particularly important focus and trend in modern documentary film and television. In fact, one of the real strengths of documentary cinema is the ability to document different life modes and forms of everyday life, both in a national context and in a transnational perspective. Documentary formats as an entry to the understanding of everyday life are important for the development of a deeper global understanding of social and cultural phenomena. According to several sociologists and philosophers, everyday life mental structures, and social and cultural imaginaries, play a fundamental role in the way we understand both 'us' and 'them'.

As already mentioned, Charles Taylor (2004) points to the role of social imaginaries in the way we construct social and cultural identities as groups, nations and individuals. He points to both the ways in which ordinary people express and imagine their social life, the role of images, stories, legends and other symbolic mediated forms along with the common practices that form a 'widely shared sense of legitimacy'. Taylor points to the fact that social imaginaries are both 'factual and normative' (24), and they are often deeply embedded in the way we live our lives and not always very explicit and outspoken.

In some ways Taylor's concept of the forms of social imaginaries, embedded in everyday life, reflects Berger and Luckman's much older and more general concept of everyday reality as an almost taken for granted reality in *The Social Construction of Reality* (1966). Berger and Luckman present a form of phenomenological sociology in which the reality of everyday life is given a special priority as the 'reality par excellence' (Berger and Luckmann, 1966: 21). In Berger and Luckman's words:

> I apprehend reality of everyday life as an ordered reality. Its phenomena are prearranged in patterns that seem to be independent of my apprehension of them and that impose themselves upon the latter. The reality of everyday life appears already objectified (…) The reality of everyday life further presents itself to me as an intersubjective world, a world I share with others (…) The reality of everyday life is taken for granted reality (Berger and Luckmann, 1966: 21 and 23).

Berger and Luckmann's way of talking about everyday reality refers to a notion often called upon in sociological and anthropological studies of social and cultural phenomena, the notion of the everyday as 'banal' (Billig 1995) or the invisible, 'unnoticed, the inconspicuous, the unobtrusive' (Highmore, 2002: 1). By focusing on this fundamental but often invisible dimension of society and culture, documentaries become a kind of reflexive contribution to a deeper understanding of society and culture. Precisely by focusing on both the specific and universal aspects of everyday life in different national contexts these documentaries *glocalize* global structures of understanding. The documentaries analyzed here thematize the sociological dimensions of our lives and create a kind of global, inter-cultural dialogue of everyday life dimensions under the most extreme of tensions – the dramatic tensions of war and terror, a dialogue bringing our common life as human beings behind the headlines and frontline to the centre.

Bringing it all back home

As we have already seen in the analysis of battleground documentaries, many of these films include a home front perspective on the war. We learn how soldiers think of home and communicate back, we sometimes move between war sequences and home front sequences or get opinions and emotions from those at home. A number of the films also deal with the difficulty for soldiers of returning and adapting to their former everyday life. They carry the experience of war inside or they carry the open scars and mutilations of war. But bringing it all back home, experiencing the gap between life back home and life out there, can also lead to a political radicalization among otherwise very patriotic citizens. A strong example of this can be found in Ellen Spiro and Phil Donahue's NBR winner as best documentary, *Body of War*. The film follows the paralyzed Iraq War veteran Tomas Young after his return from war, his increasingly passionate and critical attempt to find out why the politicians sent the soldiers to war, and his struggle to get used to the very new body and life his war experience has left him. The personal, everyday life dimension in the film is brutally honest, in the sense that Tomas lets us see how it really is to be paralyzed and in a wheelchair. But this is also part of a direct, political dimension in the film, in which (step)father and son fight over patriotism and support for the war, with the father as an extreme conservative patriot and the son a more and more liberal opponent joining Iraq veterans against the war. The mixture of the home front situation and family 'politics' is powerfully linked to the political debates in the senate and speeches from pros and cons. It is a film about the bitter aftermath of going to war on a false basis and not finding out until it's too late.

But perhaps one of the films that gets closest to the life in families with a strong tradition of patriotism, and the costs of the war on the American home front, is the Danish director Jørgen Flindt Pedersen's *A Family at War* (2004). The film is about a traditional patriotic, American family whose son is killed in Iraq and who gradually start feeling betrayed and asking questions about the reasons for going to war. It shows the consequences and the mental blows and changes seen from an American perspective. The film has been shown on more than 100 stations in the USA, and it has a strong emotional and intellectual appeal through focusing on the costs behind the patriotic headlines of stories of war heroes.

The film has an efficient, informational and emotionally strong structure. The first part, in very short montage sequences, sets the political framework for the war, then the camera slowly zooms in on the house of the family we are about to follow for a year, a year after they lost their son in Iraq. The camera slowly pans the memorabilia; the pictures and we see a live family-video of the son's childhood. The ordinary, patriotic American family, in this case a traditional, conservative family with long military traditions, and their reactions and emotions, are set against the political agenda of the War on Terror. It's everyday life against big politics; it's a film about a patriotic loyalty that is at last tested when doubts about the foundation of the whole policy behind the war hit the family, especially the mother. All through the film we get glimpses of the media coverage of the war or suspected threats of new terror attacks on the US, illustrating the kind of anxiety and tension created by the Bush administration of terror lurking everywhere.

A powerful element in the film is the split and tension inside the family between the father and the mother, and it gradually becomes a film about the mother's search for the 'truth' behind all the arguments for the war in Iraq. She is a normal teacher, a fact person, she says, as she starts her search and gets more and more confused because the facts are not there. The feeling of having sacrificed a son to an unjust and unnecessary war becomes stronger and stronger. The father, on the other hand, is more automatically a supporter of the military and the government: in this way the film juxtaposes views and feelings that clearly also represent the divided American public. Just as the film takes us into the mind's of the family members, it also does take us into different sectors of everyday life around the neighbourhood and the different kind of people living there. But we also witness truly patriotic Americana events for veterans and fallen soldiers, and the son Jeff's marriage. The film goes deep into the mentality of average American patriotism with a clear observational, analytical purpose not hampered by a specific framing.

Just like the stories we find in American and UK films and programmes, Danish documentaries around 2009 start exploring the home front perspectives of war and how it influences everyday life. War becomes a human story, as it is clearly indicated in the Danish TV2's announcement of the series *Our War* (1–6, 2010):

> Denmark is at war. Hundreds of Danish soldiers, professionally trained and armed for battle, kill and get killed. But this is not just about guns and ammunition. This is also about human beings and emotions, it is about a war reaching far into the lives of Danish families. This is what TV2 wants to show in six documentaries starting 3 January 2010. Six directors, among them Ole Bornedal, have been given the assignment: make an engaging and moving film about Denmark's participation in the war in Afghanistan. The film must be a human, character-driven story and give a new perspective on this world, only normally communicated by journalists (TV2 2009, my translation).

The titles of the films are also revealing: Mads Ellesøe's *Far, far krigsmand/Going to war* about Søren, dedicated to the life of a soldier, but also caught between that and his family life; Lauritz Munch-Petersen's *Skynd dig hjem/Hurry home* focusing on the wives left behind; Anders Gustafson's *Drengen der ville i krig/The boy who wanted to go to war* about the fraught relationship between a father and son, and Ole Bornedal's *Kære Elena og Niels/Dear Elena and Niels* about a soldier killed in Afghanistan seen through his letters and the eyes and memories of his father and mother.

Also the two programmes broadcast during a theme week, *Denmark at war,* on the DR1 channel in September 2010 illustrate how much war has become a part of a national, mental framework and is entering everyday life in a new and much more concrete and symbolic way. The two documentary programmes made as part of this theme week, *De sårede/The wounded* by Louise Kjeldsen and Leif Jappe) and *De faldne/The fallen* by Poul Erik Heilbuth deal with loss, death and injuries as part of a public mourning ceremony that is completely new in Danish film and media history. A new patriotism as part of a collective community discourse is clearly visible, in a culture normally characterized by lack of grand

feelings of nationalism and patriotism, in the way DR presents the week and the two programmes:

> In Iraq and Afghanistan young Danish soldiers have lost their lives. Here we portray some of them – told by the people nearest to those who died in combat. With the theme week DR take part in the national event (...) express our compassion and sympathy for soldiers and their relatives (...) express our recognition of the effort made by our soldiers in one of the world's conflict areas (...) we have chosen to use the week leading up to our national saluting the flag day to tell stories about people that are influenced by the war. These are important stories about Denmark and Danes, no matter what your attitude towards the war is (DR-Web 2010, my translation).

If this kind of patriotism is rather rare in Danish film and media until recently, the long US history of war of course makes this discourse much more widespread. A very emotional, ceremonial representation of that can be found in Jon Alpert and Matthew O'Neill's HBO documentary *Section 60 Arlington National Cemetery* (2008), which is the place where the fallen soldiers in Afghanistan and Iraq are buried. The two directors also made *Baghdad ER*, but here they bring the war home to the grieving families we meet at the cemetery, and the film is full of strong emotions, although we do not see the political reactions manifest in other films. O'Neill's and Alpert's own comment on the film highlights the intention:

> It's important to remember that there are many, many families out there that continue to confront the wars in Iraq and Afghanistan as a concrete reality that they are dealing with on a daily basis. And you see it in Arlington Cemetery, and you see it at military bases across the country. These families are largely invisible to most Americans. (...) we've had an agenda with all of our films, which is to bring awareness and to raise people's consciousness about what's happening in Iraq and Afghanistan and what's happening here at home as it relates to the wars. Because it's really, really important that the American people think about who pays the price when we wage war. We shouldn't go to war if we are uneducated about that cost. We shouldn't let people make decisions for us. And we should think about the people who sacrificed, and the fact that it could be your next door neighbour or your son or your daughter someday. But you shouldn't have your eyes and ears covered (interview quoted from HBO 2012a).

The imperial life and the messy life: two perspectives on everyday life in Iraq

It is important that the media report on the consequences of war for the soldiers in the frontline and at the home front. It is vital for our images of war that all the political, social and human dimensions, which may disappear when actions speak louder than words, are reported and experienced. But it is equally important to see war from the perspective of those you fight and the people living in the countries hit by war and terror. It seems, based on books and reports from the wars in both Afghanistan and Iraq, that the allied did not really understand the societies and cultures they were fighting against and for. But a number of documentaries in both America, the United Kingdom and Denmark have also gradually taken up the everyday life perspective from these countries and given voice to very different groups and perspectives.

In 2006 the *Washington Post* correspondent in Baghdad, Rajiv Chandrasekaran, published a book about life in the American 'green zone' that turned out to be a national bestseller and, perhaps more than other media stories beginning to appear later in the war, put the absurdity of the Iraq project on the map for ordinary Americans. The book *Imperial life in the Emerald City: Inside Iraq's Green Zone* documented how those people with inside knowledge of Iraq were pushed aside in the job to rebuild the country and win the other war, the war for a democratic, functioning, civil society. The book demonstrates how those in charge and command lived in complete isolation from the reality of the Iraq now bombed to pieces and torn apart from civil war.

The book is a critical analysis of the strategy, or lack of it, behind the American efforts, a series of portraits of people trying to do a job, giving up on doing it or simply not caring for anything else but their own self-interests. At the same time it is a very narrative and graphic tale of everyday life in an American 'bubble', a virtual 'Zanadu' outside time and place. 'Versailles on the Tigris', as Chandrasekaran's first chapter is called. The book has a series of almost cinematic scenes, scenes from a more and more absurd and surreal reality in and around the artificial 'emerald city': the hunt for sex and alcohol, the internal fight between democrats and republicans for everything from economic benefits and influence to bumper stickers and T-shirts, the absurdity of local pizza dealers like Walid that want to deal with the Americans, but are not allowed, because everything inside has to be by American delivery, the absurdity of some press conferences, etc.

The absurdity of the artificial 'American' everyday life established in the green zone and in the former palaces of Saddam Hussein is not just journalistic reporting in the form of satirical comedy. The analysis of the reality of the everyday politics of the Bush administration brings to the fore what many news reporters could not: the book unveils a complete lack of social and cultural knowledge about the country they had invaded, a very arrogant form of ethnocentric behaviour and lack of recognition of a different culture and ancient civilization. To show the everyday side of politics outside the battle zone proves to be very revealing. One of the strongest elements in the book is how it demonstrates that the few people with knowledge and good intentions are simply set aside, and that the only real political agenda of the green zone administration seems to be to protect American business interests (Chandrasekaran 2006: 45).

But life outside the green zone has also been documented by an American journalist, Farnaz Fassihi, who ran the *Wall Street Journal's* Baghdad bureau from 2003–2006. Her story, *Waiting for an Ordinary Day: The Unraveling of Life in Iraq* (2008) takes us into the hearts and lives of ordinary Iraqi citizens, many of them positive at the outset about the overthrowing of

Saddam. In the book, Fassihi, to a large degree, tries to give the voice to the Iraqi's themselves, and she observes everyday life in public and private. The more observational parts of the book are also framed by information on modern Iraqi culture and society. Fassihi also goes into contested areas of Iraqi life, like the relation between Shiites and Sunnis, so she is not just a passive observer and reporter. Many of the people she interviews belong to the Iraqi middle class, but even among the well educated she finds little support for the Americans after the invasion and the complete breakdown of normal everyday life:

> The more I speak to Iraqis and Americans, the more I am aware of a widening gap and a strong disconnection between Iraqi reality and American ideology. It is astounding that the Americans seem so oblivious to their surroundings, with an inherently selective eye for what's occurring in Iraq. The occupation seems doomed from the start (Fassihi, 2008: 66).

Some of the most fascinating parts of the book are when she, even though she is a woman, is able to move in the religious circles and get inside stories of religious everyday life among several of the Iraqi groups. Her point here again is in line with her other observations: you need to know the culture and society you operate in, you need to be able to understand everyday life discourses and forms of life. Pushing away Islam just because it is another religion will not help: dialogue and negotiation and common understanding is the only way forward. But the book also has vivid descriptions of the rising chaos in the Iraqi cities, the increased difficulties of making even the most simple things work in everyday life. And despite the inside perspective, Fassihi clearly takes advantage of her position as a well educated women with Iranian background to raise questions and even provoke the Iraqi surroundings on the question of women's position in society. Very strong evidence of life behind the war headlines is also the visit to hospitals, prisons and torture facilities, places where the consequences of war are fleshed out in terrible details and human suffering. But the book is also full of stories of romance, hope, and living despite terror and war – the kind of evidence always characteristic for the dimension of everyday life: the drive towards normalization, the instinct of living despite everything.

Loosing the war for democracy: narratives of daily life under strain

Both the wars in Afghanistan and Iraq were officially launched to free those countries of terrorism and install freedom and democracy. But numerous documentaries have shown how the population, which may from the beginning have saluted the invasion, have turned against the allied troops as chaos set in and daily life gradually deteriorated and internal fighting erupted. In Zeena Ahmed's *Iraq – the Women's Story* (2006, UK, Channel 4, *Dispatches*), the focus from the beginning of the film stresses the search for the ordinary, everyday life under extreme circumstances. The director's voiceover indicates that she has lived in Iraq for over 40 years, that she is not a trained journalist and that she travels and films dressed as any normal Iraqi woman and travels without security escort in an ordinary taxi. The introductory sequences show the well-known images of an Iraq in chaos and ruins, but also of women trying to hold things together, to continue a normal life.

The basic structure of the film is embedded journalism in the reverse: what Ahmed does is to follow a number of women, representing different types of life and social groups, through a typical day. The first woman is a highly educated pharmacist working in the difficult areas of Baghdad in a pharmacy, but she also travels into different neighbourhoods and even dangerous villages outside Baghdad where she goes to help and judge the situation. This approach of course gives us a unique insight into different forms of dangerous everyday life.

The specific focus on the female dimension of Iraqi everyday life is also underlined in the second portrait in the film, showing a female doctor in the typical rural village Qaem who has established a clinic to treat women. Again, this is a choice of a well-educated, elite woman standing out in comparison with the strong suppression of women in general in Iraq. The sequences focus on the destruction of hospitals, schools and ordinary homes: the American bombing is clearly portrayed as a destruction of ordinary life, a destruction turning the population against 'the liberation'. But even under these circumstances the portrait and the images focus on the continuation of life despite all this.

The journey in the film continues to Basra, 500 miles south of Baghdad, a former very wealthy city now bombed to poverty. Among the ruins we meet groups of families who are now long-term unemployed. The theme followed here is also the radicalization of Islamic groups in Iraq as a direct consequence of the war, and the destruction of normal life and the crushing of future hopes. What the film more than indicates is that, especially for the women, this Islamic radicalization is a clear threat to their life unless they comply with the traditional role for women. The point the film makes is that in fact the freedom and liberation of women under Saddam Hussein was stronger than after the war. We talk to mothers and female teachers, and we visit a school where girls are witnessing bigger problems, not just with how to dress, but with what they are able to study and what kind of activities they can participate in.

Ahmed's film is based on three months of filming all around Iraq, and it tries to give an impression of how ordinary women in Iraq experience the war and the developments in their daily life. The overall impression is quite clear, that three years after the invasion, life is not better and, especially for the women, has in fact become much worse with the possibility of living a freer life deteriorating day by day. There are no American voices in this film, nor any official Iraqi voices – this is the voice of apparently quite ordinary Iraqi women from different parts of the country and with different social positions, education and family roles.

'Saddam and the American – they are all the same' these are the words of the 19-year-old Iraqi Haida, who was one on the young people saluting the fall of Saddam and the coming of the Americans. As a Shiite he belonged to the suppressed groups under Saddam. But now he has turned against the Americans, who have mutilated him, just as Saddam mutilated and killed his father. In Haida's perspective the American and allied troops did not really invest in the rebuilding of a new Iraq, and when he was shot by Americans – taking him for a terrorist he turned against them, just as thousands of young Iraqi's do everyday. The battle against the former regime was quickly won, but the battle for a new democracy, for a new everyday life for the ordinary Iraqi, was lost day by day on a still larger scale starting half a year after the invasion.

Haidi's words and story are part of the opening sequences of the Iraqi journalist Sharmeen Obaid-Chinoy's Channel 4 documentary (*Dispatches* series) *Iraq – the Lost Generation* (2008). In the words of Sharmeen's voiceover double, this story is unfortunately prototypical for the majority of the young generation, at least in and around the major cities of Iraq. His film is shot under very dangerous circumstances in Iraq in 2007–2008 and takes us into the lives and minds of typical representatives of this generation, both those that stay legal but gradually give up and want to leave the country, and those that take an active road of terror counterattacks. We are in both Shiite and Sunni areas and we get very close to some of those figures that are normally just viewed as scum of the earth. Where other war reportings are embedded with the Americans and allies this is embedded with the interior enemy. The film certainly does not endorse their actions, but it tries to report on how they think and live.

The film shows how the everyday life of the young generation, the children and their families is falling apart and how this destruction of the basis of their life is experienced, and seen as a consequence of the occupation by the foreign coalition. The perspective in this film is very much on the young male generation, but also young women join – as indeed we know already from the news reporting on suicide bombers. But the film doesn't just portray the young terrorists, but also those that try to keep up a fight for a better daily life. The young doctor Mohammed is one of these, and his story takes us into the hospital sector on the verge of complete breakdown. We meet people like Ahmed, who was taken prisoner in 2003 and put in the infamous Abu Ghraib prison, but despite this has not turned to terrorism. He is seriously psychologically damaged and has had big parts of his young life taken away – but no violent reaction, just resignation. We finally also meet and get close to entrepreneurial young people, like the mobile phone seller Kamal in a more affluent part of Iraq. But also here abduction and terror is part of normal everyday life.

Iraq – the Lost Generation is a story of everyday life as civil war on all levels. It is also a story of losing a generation – as the title goes. Either because they do not get a life and an education at all, because they sacrifice themselves in vain, or because, like for instance the doctor in the film, they leave Iraq as 1.6 million people have done since 2003. It's the intellectual, creative and business elite that leave, only to deepen the crisis of a country with a dysfunctional everyday life, and on a difficult road towards an uncertain future. The closing pictures showing schoolchildren, just like they are everywhere, are accompanied by the journalistic voiceover talking about the result of the occupation: 'anarchy, religious division and ethnic cleansing has become the legacy of occupation, anti-Western feeling, even in the next generation is the inevitable result'.

Fragmented and divided nations

BBC journalist John Simpson has a long history of reporting from Afghanistan and in 2001 before the allied and UN-backed invasion he visited the country again and made *Afghanistan – The Dark Ages*. The film is about the long history of occupation of this country by shifting countries, and about a divided nation which he calls a 'wild place' and a 'black hole in the world's consciousness' (BBC programme transcript). His final words in the programme represent a both realistic and quite disillusioned analysis of an ongoing war that will never end and only have one victim, the ordinary people of Afghanistan:

Afghanistan is scarcely a country any more, it's just a blank space on the map where outside nations, Russia, the United States, Pakistan, India, have been able to interfere and fight each other by proxy with the enthusiastic co-operation of the warring Afghan factions. I'm here now to report on the next turning point, the destruction of the Taliban regime, it's just now starting. It's the most obvious cliché in the book to say that the innocent are always the victims of war, of course they are, but it's stark fact in Afghanistan and the most basic reason this terrible downward spiral of war and terrorism is that Afghanistan has become a killing field in the interests of other countries. If all the Americans and their allies do now is to smash the Taliban, destroy Bin Laden's terrorist network and then promptly forget about this country all over again then they won't have achieved very much that's serious or worthwhile and the terrible suffering Afghanistan has gone through will just begin all over again (quoted from BBC programme transcript: http://news.bbc.co.uk/hi/english/static/audio_video/programmes/panorama/transcripts/transcript_07_10_01.txt).

Simpson's words are unfortunately very prophetic and documented in many other documentaries from both Afghanistan and Iraq. For instance, in American director James Longley's strong, beautiful and at the same time terrifying observational documentary *Iraq in Fragments* (2006) we see daily life from three perspectives and three stories. In the first story, *Mohammed of Baghdad*, we follow a fatherless young boy of 11 in school and working for a very authoritarian garage owner, it is a story of the fear imposed by the war and invasion and of an everyday life that has not improved one bit, but rather got worse. In the second story, *Sadr's South*, the perspectives are even worse as we enter the religious centre for the rebellion against the American led invasion, headed by the Shiite leader Mohammed al Sadr. The preaching against the invaders is very violent and so is the fighting we witness. In the third story, *Kurdish Spring*, we find the only semi-positive report from the country, since the Kurds are very positive and are developing their democracy already. In this part of the film the images suddenly change to peaceful, beautiful pictures of landscapes and people at peace with themselves. Taken together the three stories in the film give a seldom seen and nuanced image of a fragmented and divided Iraq seen from the inside. As Stephen Prince has already pointed out (Prince 2009: 225), the film stands out because of its very poetic and observational

Figures 6a and b: James Longley's *Iraq in Fragments* (2006). Four stories from everyday life in Iraq during the war. Here the hard and fearsome life of a boy in Baghdad. Frame grab. Cinematography: James Longley.

style, not just in the Kurdish story, but also in the use of graphic matches, dissolves and fast digital grading of some sequences.

The documenting of fragmentation, division and decay in the war zones is also clearly demonstrated in American independent director Laura Poitras' *My Country, My Country* (2006), based on filming eight months in a primarily Sunni district in Baghdad. Focusing especially on Dr Riyadh al-Adhadh, an Iraqi medical doctor, father of six and a political candidate for the Sunni faction. The film tells a story of how the Iraqi middle class is gradually loosing faith in their own country and democracy after the invasion. A film like *Voices of Iraq* (2004, US) is on the other hand one of the few films in which the many voices heard are almost all positive. Giving Iraqis cameras so that they could film themselves and give the camera on to friends and family made the film. Partly the same collective approach to filmmaking can be seen in *About Baghdad* (2004) following the return of an exiled poet, or *The Dreams of Sparrows* (2005) where people are given cameras to document the consequences of the bombing of Baghdad.

But a much stronger and intimate family portrait of life in Baghdad after the invasion is to be found in Kasim Abid's *Life After the Fall* (2008), made for British Channel 4. Abid is born in Iraq, but has lived in exile for more than thirty years, but in this film he goes back to his Shiite family in Baghdad, and through four years he films his family's everyday life as the situation gradually deteriorates. This subjective dimension of the film and the fact that he, as an exiled person, is both inside and outside the culture he is describing add to the special quality, authenticity and broad scope of the film. It is a film with a positive dynamic in a family all set to participate in the forming of a new Iraq and engaged in politics, but it is also about disillusion, about losing faith in a new future.

A very rare inside, dramatic story of an Iraqi family is Andrew Berend's *The Blood of My Brother* (2005), dealing with the drive for vengeance in a family where the eldest son was killed by the Americans for no reason. The director got extremely free access to film not just the everyday life of the family, but also the Shiite insurgency groups around Moqtada al-Sadre and his Mahdi army and political, religious movement based in southern Iraq. The film has violent scenes of insurgency actions and rallies and also scenes with hostile activity towards American forces. The youngest son Ibrahim dreams of getting revenge by joining the insurgence, but his responsibilities towards the family are more important. The film is therefore in many ways a film that contrasts everyday family life with the development of a still more divided and fragmented Iraq, an Iraq where violence erupts between groups and between these groups and the American led invasion force. The film underlines the same point as the other films: the failure of the Americans and other forces to address the basic problems and needs of Iraqis and to understand the culture and the everyday life perspective. The cultural and communicative barrier between the Americans and other foreign forces leads towards the rise of resistance against an invasion which some of the Iraqis, at least originally, saw as a liberation.

Politics and everyday life in a war zone

Surprisingly enough, since the main purpose of invading both Afghanistan and Iraq officially was to topple a terrorist regime and install a new democracy, there are rather few documentary films dealing with the political dimension of life inside these countries. The theme does of course pop up in documentaries about the war and everyday life in general in these countries, and the political also from time to time dominates Western news reporting. But a deeper and more close-up analysis and documentation of politicians, political parties or the view on politics among ordinary citizens is quite rare. One such example is however Channel 4's *Vote Afghanistan* (2009), directed by Havana Marking and Martin Herring, which follows three presidential candidates, opponents of Hamid Karzai, but also draws a broader picture of Afghan politics through the sometimes apathetic view from the street. The film is a classical, observational documentary, following the candidates around and taking in the cheering and

Figures 6c and d: Eva Mulvad's *Enemies of Happiness* (2006). Developing female equality and building a new democracy in Afghanistan. Frame grab. Cinematography: Zillah Bowes.

enthusiastic crowds, which indicates that, despite all, there are some positive political powers in this war torn and divided country. But images from both Kabul and around the country also show that people are sceptical and have a very pragmatic outlook on things. They are not used to anything good coming from those in power, and they are more concerned about improvement of their daily life than grand visions of a new Afghanistan.

The other important film about politics is Danish director Eva Mulvad's film *Enemies of Happiness* (2006), which certainly deals with the many problems of establishing a democracy in Afghanistan, but which is also a positive and optimistic story of women in Afghanistan taking matters into their own hands. It is also a story of politics and the relation between politics and everyday life, because we follow the main character in her life in a remote province of Afghanistan. The film is a portrait of the courageous, world-famous first Afghan woman elected for parliament, Malalai Joya. But following her around in Afghanistan the film also becomes a portrait of everyday life and particularly the life of women in different parts of the country. The film is shot during the election campaign in 2005 where she is elected, and clearly demonstrates how dangerous her political project is: she is heavily protected by bodyguards because of several threats to her life, she has to be extremely careful when moving around, and she is constantly attacked in public by the male clan groups dominating Afghan society.

In her presentation of the idea behind the film, the Danish director Eva Mulvad stresses the need for other narratives, narratives that go behind the well-known headlines and challenge the monolithic views of the Islamic world:

How does the story we choose to tell affect our society, our world? The great 'mono-narrative' has to be broadened. The world hungers for more dimensions, more voices so that we can create our own opinions, our own sense of awareness about what is really happening in the world – especially when it comes to Islam. This film was made to tell another story from one of the world's most talked-about regions: Afghanistan. The stories we hear are always full of bombs, torture and terrorists, stories full of apprehension that create distance: between 'us' and 'them'. The world is not about villains who lurk outside awaiting us. The world is more than that – full of everyday people who fight everyday battles for their and others' right to life, dreams and happiness. Muslims are not a monolithic villainous entity, just like we in the West are not. We can understand each other. There are many who profit from making us think that we cannot. But in them we cannot believe. They create our apprehension for the world and each other, an apprehension that leads to distance (from original press release 2006, quote dated September 2005).

The film received international awards, reviews and reports from screenings around the world that clearly indicate that it has precisely functioned as a path to a different public image of life in the Islamic world. Both for an American and a European public, the film, simply by getting inside the everyday life and mind of a particular person and her context, helps viewers to construct images of 'the other' that bring the culturally specific and the universally common much closer together.

The film's opening scene is from 2003 and a tumultuous parliamentary gathering where Joya strongly attacks the war lords and the suppression of women and is expelled from parliament. The film follows her fight to return and her campaigning and other activities in the Farah province, where her base is. A radio voice at the start of the film, where Joya once again changes house because she is threatened, tells us that the election is the first in 35 years and the first ever where women can vote, and this voice also informs us that Joya has survived four murder attempts. The film genre is clearly the classical, observational form, there are no authoritative comments or explanations at all, just the voice of Joya commenting on her own life and story, and sequences where we see her talking to different people in the province. The film is a strong and informative inside story with both political and ethnographic qualities.

The style and aesthetic form of the film clearly contributes to this ethnographic inside image of life in a remote Afghan province. Unlike many of the already mentioned films from life in war zones, this is not a film about conventional war, it is a political war, a war of mentalities. The film's cinematographer, Zillah Bowes, captures the beauty and colourful life of the Afghan nature, provincial city life, people, buildings etc. in breathtaking shots. With original Afghan music underscoring the pictures, the visual side of the film creates a sort of utopian dimension of hope beneath the fight to death for democracy and equality.

But more important than this visual presentation of a country usually reported through images of violence, destruction and human suffering, is the portrayal of strong and charismatic people with often incredible stories. One old woman walks a very long way just to pay tribute to Joya and her fight for women's rights, and the very graphic and emotional tale of her own fights in life is very moving, and puts the whole thing into a historical perspective. Strong scenes also take place when a very young girl already married to an older man comes to complain because she is threatened and very ill-treated. The film gives a deep insight into women's difficult and often humiliating life in Afghanistan. The film shows how difficult it is for even a women like Joya to get legitimacy and to negotiate and try to solve deep-rooted social and cultural conflicts with the men and clans involved.

The film gets very close indeed to the main character: we follow her almost everywhere in different situations and emotions, but the camera also respects a certain distance and the one time in the film where she is overcome with fear and fatigue, the camera only captures her from far and from behind. Given the character of Afghan society and the lack of pervasive media coverage of everyday life, the film is a quite unique documentation of daily affairs, politics and the ways in which the ordinary Afghan woman in particular thinks, acts and feels about the basics of life.

As observational documentary, *Enemies of Happiness* takes place in chronological time as the election campaign unfolds. Even though the film focuses mostly on the quite non-spectacular dimensions of everyday life in the remote province of Farah, it also has elements of a political thriller, an intense and dangerous human drama. But just as the film starts in Kabul in 2003, as Joya is expelled from the national assembly, it closes with scenes from Kabul and the newly elected parliament gathering and, among them, Joya as the first-ever elected woman in Afghan history. Despite the human drama and danger, despite the politically influenced terror threat against her, personal courage pays off.

Gender and everyday life in an Islamic culture

The image of women's and ordinary Iraqi life after the invasion in *Iraq – the Women's Story* (see p. 138) is a sinister and dark tale of decay and destruction, of an endless fight against all odds, as is clearly illustrated in the classical shot of the dark burkha women lamenting their dead husbands and relatives at the end of the film. In *The Beauty Academy of Kabul* (2004) the spirit is quite opposite: a comedy-like clash of cultures between a Hollywood 'makeover culture' and entrepreneurial spirit and the rather non-glamorous culture of Kabul women, recently suppressed by the Taliban and now living in a transitional war zone. We are again in an almost completely female world, and in the opening sequences women in the American-driven beauty school, opened in Kabul in 2003, state their work and personal presence there as part of a rebellious act against their men and the oppressive attitude towards women in Afghanistan. This is also indicated by shots from streets and neighbourhoods in the city with heavily veiled women.

The beauty academy is set up by a group of Afghan-American women that fled from Afghanistan in the 1980s. The start of the film shows both the contradictory cultural signals of the post-Taliban Kabul and the historical changes and different political regimes since the 1970s. There is a certain element of a reflexive cultural consciousness in the film, adding to the overcoming of the generic elements of the comedy of 'the good American women coming to save their suppressed and underdeveloped sisters'. Mixing the actual and contemporary story with footage of Afghanistan's very complex history and different cultures gives the film a broader context. The fact that the women starting the beauty academy have a background in Afghanistan adds to this reflexive, historical dimension, because we also get their history and perspective: when they left Kabul in the 1980s it was a modern city, where the rights and norms of women were quite different.

Where *Iraq – the Women's Story* combined an observational, road movie style with more traditional journalistic elements of a more authoritative and investigative nature, *The Beauty Academy of Kabul* is much more classical observational, a chronological narrative unfolding as a story of the establishing of the academy following events and giving voice to the active participants, with the initiators in a more privileged position as commenting witnesses. A special case is of course made of the difficulties facing the women on the logistics side, since Kabul is a complicated place to start a new business, especially for foreign women. Focus is also on very concrete gender conflicts and the rather sceptical attitudes of male relatives and partners. The film systematically illustrates streets and other places of everyday life in Kabul and catches the opposing images of women on posters and in reality – pointing to inherent contradictions in the Afghan mentality.

An interesting side-narrative is the story of Nafisa's hair salon, established seven years ago and thus stretching back into the Taliban period. Nafisa is a traditional Afghan woman who was born and raised in Kabul, married to her cousin with five children. But still she was able to establish her own business with her husband's consent. Her story adds to the reflexive and complex picture of women's life in Afghanistan and she can tell of even Taliban wives getting their hair done at her salon, although secretly without their husband's knowledge. Nafisa's story is followed by other stories of women that have gone their own ways and tested the borders of a woman's life. In this way the establishing of the beauty academy is put in a local context: it is not just imposing American ways and ideas on the Afghans but merging two cultural approaches that may benefit from each other.

The humorous qualities of *The Beauty Academy of Kabul*, the entrepreneurial spirit of the women involved and the sometimes soap opera-like portrayal of female life in a contradictory, male-dominated culture, show the optimistic, oppositional forces of everyday life, and the importance of daring to act and challenge the borders. Many incidents from Islamic countries show how dangerous this may be. But this film is both a feel-good documentary based on the Academy story, and on the other stories of Afghan women following their independent paths despite the difficult social framework.

An unusual and impressive film from inside the world of women in Afghanistan is *Afghanistan Unveiled* (2005), filmed by 14 Afghan women, trained by AINA Afghan Media and Culture Centre, travelling around the country outside Kabul and talking to and showing how the women live and think. This kind of going deep into a women's world is also found in two just as extraordinary documentaries made by the British Channel 4. In Saira Shah's *Beneath the Veil* (2002) we get terrifying inside pictures from the Taliban terror regime before the UN-backed invasion, and in 2007 Sharmeen Obaid-Chinoy's *Afghanistan Unveiled* follows up on the first story, trying to document whether the situation has improved after the overturning of the Taliban regime.

Beneath the Veil is a film made by a very brave, British journalist with Afghan background. She travels to places in Afghanistan which are directly dangerous for foreigners and women, she is several times threatened by Taliban representatives and taken in for questioning, and she has to go undercover and film with a hidden camera throughout the film. If anyone should doubt that the UN-backed invasion had legitimate cause to intervene to protect simple human rights, this film will document why beyond doubt. This is a regime where mass executions take place on a daily basis and is used for mass entertainment at stadiums, where women are not allowed any public rights, cannot work and are punished and executed for 'indecent' behaviour, where girls older than 12 are banned from school and where the most basic needs in ordinary life are almost impossible to fulfill. The film shows begging women on the street, and children and women eating garbage, and they show the Taliban hitting down hard on all non-religious cultural expressions and media. It is a country in ruins, a scary terror regime where the representatives even boast of their terror.

In Sharmeen Obaid-Chinoy's *Afghanistan Unveiled,* made five years later, we are no longer in an Afghanistan under the Taliban terror regime, and on the surface the situation for women and daily life has changed for the better. But the film shows that although Kabul has become a kind of 'showcase' for women's rights in Afghanistan, with a burgeoning world of shops and culture, the rest of Afghanistan tells another story. The liberation and new freedom is only for the elite and chosen few, while women in the rest of Afghanistan are very much dependent on men in all spheres of life, for instance they need written permission from their male guardian or husband to go to hospital. Even in the outskirts of Kabul reality is different. Obaid-Chinoy goes undercover with a local woman and a hidden camera to show how women are treated as second class citizens.

In the film, Sharmeen Obaid-Chinoy also travels to the Western province of Heart, to the far north to Taloghan and to one of the most remote and isolated provinces of Takhar. Life here for women and ordinary families is quite different from Kabul and she finds stories of a growing number of female suicides and self-mutilation, a final way of escaping violence, rape and suppression in the families. She finds some hope in the growing education of girls, but there are only very weak signs that the Western invasion has improved life for women and ordinary families. In the last part of the programme she concludes:

> The liberation of Afghan women is mostly theoretical: it was naïve to think that the country could be transformed quickly, when the oppression of women was the consequence of centuries of tribal and cultural practice – not the sole invention of the Taliban. The West should be asking hard questions about where all the millions of aid money has gone, with so little to show (transcript from Channel 4 2012).

That ancient ways of looking at women are difficult to change is also demonstrated clearly in Tanaz Eshagin's HBO documentary *Love Crimes in Kabul* (2011), a portrait of three Afghan women jailed for immoral behaviour. Eshagin surprisingly got access to the notorious Badam Bagh Women's prison and Kabul Men's prison, and she was also able to film in several courtrooms following cases like those of the three women. The openness towards an American documentary film team indicates that something has happened in Afghanistan since the invasion, but at the same time the stories told in the film show how far from gender equality, and freedom of expression and behaviour, we still are. The 'crimes' these women are accused of, and which could give them up to 20 years, are trivial cases of love relations that go against the norm of family-arranged weddings, and the view on marriage and love these women have is simply just the modern, individual view which is not accepted in Afghanistan. In an interview before the premiere of the film the director said about the situation in Afghanistan:

> It's a country in transition. The girls would get different sentences depending which judge they went in front of. Each judge has his own authority, but they all have the basic understanding of Islamic family law and Sharia law, where you can't be with a woman

you're not married to who isn't your sister or mother. A woman can't be with a man who's not her brother, her father or husband. All that is understood – there's no fluidity when it comes to that (HBO 2012b).

Growing up in a war zone: chaos, culture and daily life

The most moving and terrible images from a war zone are no doubt those of the dead, molested, desolated and deserted children, documentary war films are unfortunately all full of such images. But few documentaries document in a deeper and broader way how it is to grow up under such circumstances, how daily life is and how – after all – children and young people somehow manage to live a life and have dreams and hopes. But one very unusual film doing exactly that is *The Boy Mir: Ten Years in Afghanistan* (2011), made as an independent film by British director Phil Grabsky and the Afghan journalist Shoaib Sharifi. The film follows an Afghan boy, and his family, from the age of eight to 18, and it has amazing footage from the life of this very poor family in a very remote province of Afghanistan. We experience their lives almost without filter (they were, however, not allowed to film the daughter), the discussions and quarrels of the family members and their daily routines. The director himself did not speak their language, but through both local translators and his Afghan co-director Sharifi, it was possible for the film crew to live among them and connect and communicate rather freely. The development of the boy Mir is not necessarily a happy one and a sign of progress for the Afghans. He goes through different phases, also phases that a boy in other parts of the world would go through. But daily life is hard, he has to work for and with the family, but he is also educated. His ambition of being a teacher one day is, however, contrasted with the fact that life seems to become more and more dangerous as the years go by.

Grabsky and Sharifi's film about the boy Mir is not the unfiltered truth about everyday life among ordinary, poor Afghans in the more remote provinces. But the film goes a long way by bringing the camera close to these people and by reporting their life based on many hours of filming and a rather long stay. In an interview Grabsky has pointed out that they actually decided to pay the people they filmed and also set up a fund for the education of Mir, something he says could be called unethical for a documentary film, but which he defends as the right thing. Grabsky is well aware of the effect a Western camera crew, although in this case small, can have on reality, and as a Western filmmaker, travelling round in a dangerous place, he could not, like so many other directors under similar circumstances, travel without protection. But still, he defends the film's picture of Afghan everyday life, as impressed in this interview and presentation of his project:

You must not think that because you have a camera and you're from the West, somehow these are little people that should be grateful because you show up. Grabsky's subjects had been through war – they had lost relatives, and seen others tortured. They lived traumatized lives. He found that most adults by that time were exhausted and depressed – but their children – like most children – still had hope. Still, the challenge of creating an honest film required establishing a level of trust with his subjects – and a recognition of Grabsky's own impact on his surroundings. 'I think that the minute you pull out a camera you are intervening, and actually it's much more realistic to think to yourself, "How do I manage the intervention?"' (quoted from Blogcritics 2012).

Daily life is difficult in a war zone like Afghanistan and Iraq, so is a good and free education for all. But also cultural expression and the possibility of expressing yourself through music, or other forms of culture, can be difficult:

> Most people in Baghdad don't leave their houses at night. They don't rent movies. They don't go to bars. Mostly they sit huddled in dingy shacks and wait and watch and hope that the occupying army will lift its curfew and everything will become safe enough for them to go outside one day. Fat chance (Gideon Yago, *Vice Magazine*, January 2004).

These words by an American journalist come from an article dealing with the Iraqi heavy metal band *Acrassicauda,* and they once again, from a more cultural point of view illustrate the destruction of a normal everyday life that the war caused. Eddy Moretti and Suroosh Alvi's documentary *Heavy Metal in Baghdad* (2007) tells the quite incredible story of this band and their endeavours to use the liberation from Saddam to launch their career. But even though the band would have had a chance in a truly liberated and democratic Iraq, and the more global, Western cultural trends they represent do strike a note with the young Iraqi generation in the big cities, they eventually had to flee the country.

As the occupation created the conditions for a new religious and ethnic war, the war against an 'americanized' culture like heavy metal became a clear target for sectarian violence. The film is a tale of the American film crew trying to search for the band in 2006, three years after they first met them in Baghdad. This means the film becomes an odyssey into a country in dissolution. There are endless pictures of destroyed neighbourhoods, road blocks, former beautiful hotels and mosques now heavily damaged, security forces and military all over the place – but no sign of everyday life it seems. Everyday life is there, as the film shows, but a life like that in a nightmare. What the film crew finds out concerning the band is that most of the members have fled the country and many of their supporters are dead, disappeared or fled. But the story is also a story of a band that finally get a breakthrough outside Baghdad and a new audience both in the US, in Jordan and Syria.

Heavy Metal in Baghdad deals with an Iraqi youth culture phenomenon highly influenced by the global and American media culture. As such the film indicates how very regional subcultures merge with global media cultures and how youth everywhere in the world dream the same universal dreams. In this way, more universal entertainment formats can be part of a new cultural liberation. This is clearly shown in the American documentary *Afghan Star* (2008), directed by Havana Marking, a UK-Channel 4/Afghan-produced film that follows the Afghan version of American Idol through the eyes of the audience and the contesters, and which demonstrates the effects of such a popular culture phenomenon on both everyday life and the media and culture of this country. The release of *Afghan Star* was a major cultural event in 2008, because the former Taliban regime and even the present more secular regime is not in favour of this kind of popular, Western-influenced culture, and especially not the participation of women. As the press material for the film says directly: 'this is much more than just a TV show … you risk your life to sing'. The film documents that the show is a major, cultural event followed by almost all groups of society and in all parts of the country (11 million viewers, or one third of the population saw the finale), and in some ways it is a programme that works as a cultural unifier in an otherwise very divided country. But the show is also very much about youth culture in Afghanistan, and the main characters we follow for three months before the show and through to the finale are all between 19 and 25. Especially 21-year-old Setara, a young woman from the Heart province using Bollywood style, who becomes a controversial star of the show. The programme clearly challenges the traditional norms for women. The strength of the programme is that we get really close to people and audiences around the country who are all obsessed with the show. It is a documentary that truly combines a view into a media phenomenon with a look into the daily life of its audiences.

This is also the case with the HBO film *Baghdad High* (2008), which underlines a social and cultural dialogue in an intense portrait of the everyday life of four Baghdad High schoolboys during a year. The film tells the story of a very specific ethnic and religious culture and at the same time a very universal story of the things young people dream about and the way in which they take cultural elements from a global media context. The film is based on video diaries from four Iraqi teenagers in a Baghdad high school during a whole year and the style is very much the video nation video diary style and aesthetic, with us following them around and them speaking in close ups to the camera. Ivan O'Mahoney, who directed and produced the film with Laura Winter, has said about the film:

> The daily news about Iraq was so relentlessly depressing for so many years. It was therefore fantastic to realize while making this film that there is normality amidst all the violence, and that people do lead normal lives, despite the mayhem around them. It gave me a lot of hope to see kids be kids (quoted from HBO 2009).

The film is based on 300 hours of footage shot by the four teens, and the four boys (Hayder, Anmar, Ali and Mohammed) represent a life like most normal young people all over the world: they dream of careers as singers or football players, they think of girls, but at the same time they are stuck in a nightmare of violence and suicide bombings in a seemingly neverending war. We see them in family situations, in school situations, we follow their interest in rock and pop, dance, television and film, but we also see them performing specific religious rituals and relating to, or reacting to, the local political situation, the media and the state of affairs in the country. Bringing everyday Iraqi life – the daily situation for ordinary people like you and me – home to the American audience was clearly a deliberate strategy taken on by alternative directors and cable channels like PBS and HBO. Given that the average American probably has an image of Iraqis as hateful terrorists and fundamentalists, this kind of documentary representation of the 'normality' of Iraqi youth and the life and dreams they have is part of changing the global image and discourse on us and them.

Figures 6e and f: Ivan O'Mahoney and Laura Winter's *Baghdad High* (2008). School life seen through video diaries of life in Baghdad during the war. Frame grab. Cinematography: Ivan O'Mahoney and Laura Winter.

Universal and local dimensions of everyday life

The documentaries dealt with in this chapter illustrate how important it is to get the media behind the battle line and into everyday reality, which is the more hidden and unnoticed part of a conflict. War is, of course, in many ways fought on the battleground and it has to do with power and politics. But behind the dramatic tales of fights, power and politics, there is a life and an everyday reality that has to go on, despite the war. Part of the war is about the images and the agenda the media create of the war – on the home front and on the battleground, in the minds of those that support, those that are being fought against and those caught in between. A war can be won on the battleground, but be lost in the years after combat has ended, because the means to change a culture, a society and a way of life was not created.

The reality of Iraq and Afghanistan and indeed much of the Arab and Muslim world has been influenced greatly in Western media by the terrorists and the radical elements of these countries and cultures. This reality clearly has a foundation in what is happening, but behind the image of the radical Islamist there is also another image in which the people living there are just human beings like the rest of us, with much the same dreams and hopes. Documentaries going behind the headlines of war and conflict have a mission to tell this story, of using images of everyday life to confront the stereotypes indicating that the Muslim world is fundamentally different from ours. At the same time these films about everyday life, even more than other documentaries, demonstrate the power of narratives of reality to give global conflicts and challenges an emotive and human dimension.

PART III

A new global order: political, social and cultural challenges

Chapter 7

Politics and spin in a mediated world

Politics have changed dramatically because of the development of a very pervasive and dominant media culture. Researchers talk about a 'restyling of politics' (Corner and Pels 2003) in which the mediatization of politics and the convergence of the private and the public, and the popular and the serious, is increasing. On the one hand the number of media makes it much more difficult for the politician to 'hide', and critical scrutiny of politics, and not least politicians, has increased. On the other hand the mediatization of politics, (Bennet and Entman 2000) creates a counter-initiative in the form of political spin and increased strategic media communication. The relation between power and visibility in the modern media culture (Thompson 2000) makes political scandals more frequent, but scandals are not always linked to important, political issues. In fact some researchers point to the increased entertainment factor in modern politics (van Zoonen 2005). The development of a new, mediated and increasingly global culture thus has both problematic and positive aspects. The fact that the balance between national and global politics has begun to shift adds to the increased importance of media coverage of politics, a politics bringing politicians and the global dimensions closer.

Changing forms of mediated politics

'Every generation gets the Thomas Jefferson it deserves (…) The Jefferson today is one of sex, scandal and hypocrisy,' Ellen Goodman in 1998. She was referring to a shift from political substance towards a kind of politics more occupied with the backstage area – both the private gossip and the 'game' of politics. The strong commercial nature of American media and, not least, the fact that political advertising on television has been allowed to develop in the way it has in the last decades probably means that American politics has gone in that direction much earlier than European politics. But this change in how politics is mediated is in reality a global phenomenon. Paul Krugman, referring to American politics almost ten years ago (Krugman 2003), satirically suggested some ground rules for future covering of politics in the media: (1) don't talk about clothes, (2) actually look at the candidate's proposal, (3) beware of personal anecdotes, (4) look at the candidate's records and (5) don't fall for political histrionics. But we can all conclude that, after almost ten years, nobody listened to the advice.

The documentaries dealt with in this chapter are characterized by both following the trend backstage whilst at the same time putting it under reflexive scrutiny, and they are part of a long, historical tradition of political documentaries that have dominated both US media and European media. It was the breakthrough of television around 1960 that initiated this development globally, and as Michael Schudson, among others, has pointed out in *The Good Citizen* (1998: 182 ff), this new medium and the new ways of mediating politics was not a sign of decline, as such. It was on the contrary, a sign of a widening of democracy, an opening of the link between politics, politicians and the voters and citizens. But just as newspapers do things differently, TV stations equally represent different forms of mediation: there is quite a difference between the world according to PBS and according to Fox News. But on both kinds of channels the exposure of politics and politicians has become much stronger than it was before television existed, and the coming of 24-hour news channels and constant updating on the Internet has put the pressure up even more.

Politicians are under constant observation, constant crossfire, and the need for political drama, visual reporting and storytelling has created a new mediated political persona. In this persona the private sphere and the public sphere have become deeply intertwined and this increased merging of previously more distinct spheres has strongly influenced modern communication and public opinion formation (Corner 2003). Some researchers see this development as the potential decline and complete change of 'rational' politics, a politics of reason where the arguments are at the centre (Bennet and Entman 2001). Others, such as Lisbeth van Zoonen in *Entertaining the Citizen: When Politics and Popular Culture Converge* (2005), have pointed to a longer historical coexistence of a popular culture strand and a more rational, discursive strand in politics.

What van Zoonen points out is that politics has always, in some form or other, drawn on rhetorical performance, drama, narrative, and that the personal factor has also been very central. This is in fact supported by modern, cognitive sociology and studies of political communication. In Drew Westen's large-scale empirical study of how American voters react to political communication, *The Political Brain* (2007), the main message is: 'The political brain is an emotional brain. It is not a dispassionate calculating machine, objectively searching for the right facts, figures and policies to make a reasoned decision. The partisans in our study were, on average, bright, educated and politically aware (...) And yet they thought with their guts (...) There is however a good side to this story. Most of the time emotions provide a reasonable compass for guiding behavior' (Westen 2007: xv).

The often stereotypical notion of emotion being the enemy of reason is clearly dismissed by Westen. They work together, so what is happening in modern mediated forms of politics is not a decline caused by emotional rhetoric in politics. What is happening in the modern media culture is that the control of this performance and the public exposure has changed rather dramatically. The old form of political meetings, often locally, the report from politics through a press linked to political organizations or a more distanced general nature is now taking place much more intensely in the media and across platforms from the printed press, television and to new digital and very decentralized social media. The rise of a new and much more diverse media power has of course led to a more complicated struggle over the media agenda, media images and the presentation of politics, and political performance and persona. The political system developed its own staff of spin doctors in order to match the increase in media exposure and demand. As Corner (2003: 73) points out, the strategic projection of political and private identity into the public became more important, and the branding of politicians became more and more professionalized.

One aspect of this mediatization of politics and political figures was that politicians allowed camera crews and journalists backstage. Exposing the political process became more common, as 'openness' could be perceived as a sign of democracy and honesty. At the same time, the branding of the political 'persona' as a private person became more clearly integrated into the projected image of the politician in public, and it was no longer just the tabloid media that dealt with the political persona in that way. What could earlier have been seen as tabloidization or infotainment (Corner and Pels 2003: 4f) is now often merely seen as a restyling of politics. The shift is underlined by the fact that when Eisenhower in the 1950s hired a Hollywood actor to advise him before his first television appearance, it created a huge public debate. Today American politicians and presidents routinely receive intensive media coaching and are constantly judged for their media performance (Meyrowitz 1985: 303).

But what is the case in most nation states with a developed, modern communication system is also a transnational phenomenon. Leaders of other nations and leaders in transnational organizations become global figures, much closer to us than ever before. Documentaries dealing with modern politics contribute to this development, by circulating narratives of politics across borders, and by taking up the challenges of a global nature that politics are facing today. The films on war and terror demonstrate the shortcomings and problems of war as a solution to global conflicts, and since 2010 people living in Europe, the USA and other parts of the world have witnessed how global financial corporations and powers have challenged nation state solutions. Migration and climate change are other large-scale, global problems that call upon a new form of global politics.

Close-up politics: national and global dimensions

In *No Sense of Place* (1985) Meyrowitz points to the rise of visual media as the cause of this development. Prior to the breakthrough of television as the main medium for news for the broader public, the distinction between political content and public message, and personal and private style and persona was much clearer. Obviously, the way politicians spoke, wrote and conveyed their message could reveal elements of a more personal style and rhetoric, and journalists would certainly from time to time include more personal elements in portraits of politicians. However, the intense media exposure of political figures in public and the visual presence of the politician as a person closer to us, and with all the elements of body language and marks of personal style belongs to the modern media culture. It became more and more important to be able to combine elements of the politician as an ordinary human being, with the politician as media person and communicator. In the words of John B. Thompson

(2000: 33ff) this modern mediation of politics has to do with a 'transformation of visibility', a transformation taking place at a more national and a more global level.

On a national level the politician and the political system get much more deeply intertwined with a new multimedia society in which mass media take politicians much closer to the individual, private citizen through, for instance, television news – now more and more often broadcast 24 hours around the clock. This means that we start to engage with and relate to political figures with the same emotional and communicative patterns we find in face-to-face communication. But just as the media start presenting and dealing with politicians in a much more personal way, combining their political and private figure in news reporting, so do politicians and their spin doctors. Politicians try to meet their voters on a new and more personal and direct level, where they also use controlled narratives of their personal stories. With the rise of web pages and also social media like Facebook and Twitter we see both political parties, political movements and individual politicians addressing their voters in a more direct way, outside the gatekeeping control of mass media. At the same time the media start using the information on social media and we have already seen a number of cases where 'private' postings on social media enter the public domain and create problems and scandals. But at the same time social media have developed as a potentially new gateway for a new public sphere for democratic activism and debate – as we have clearly seen during the so-called Arab Spring.

In the modern media society, the clear distinction between frontstage and backstage and between the public and private sphere in the Habermas sense (Habermas 1989) becomes increasingly blurred. This blurring of boundaries opens a broad space for what Meyrowitz calls the middle region, a region taking elements from both frontstage and backstage behaviour and communication. The middle region is a strategic region where political communication takes place as a kind of strategic game about winning time and space in the media, and getting political messages through by combining personal and more general political dimensions. But if the divide between frontstage and backstage becomes blurred, this increases the need for a deep backstage, in a both private and political sense. The game is on about how you create a shield, and a space not exposed to the gaze of the tabloid media. It also necessitates a certain amount of strategic thinking and preparation before you enter the frontstage with the new stress on performance of this more mixed stage. Social media are part of this, but we also see politicians increasingly entering entertainment programmes in order to use a personal fame factor.

The changing forms of mediated politics we see on a national level are to a large degree repeated on a global scale. Just as national politicians connect and communicate in public in new ways, world leaders and politicians are also entering our daily life and living rooms in the same manner – if not necessarily with the same intensity and closeness. Global politics is therefore also to a large degree formed by 'personalities' that can make a difference. President Bush was not a very popular character in Europe and his media performance did not go down well there. On the other hand Obama created a clear 'Obama-effect' in Europe, not only through politics, but also through a new style and personality and a very clever use of, among other things, social media. Global politics is of course about global, political challenges and about collective dialogue and action. But in modern, mediated politics symbolic politics play an important role. The fact that former Vice President Al Gore personally entered the global debate on the climate crisis, and that rock and film stars become symbols for global causes, has an impact on global politics.

Modern documentaries, politics and politicians back stage

The way politicians were portrayed in documentaries in the early 1960s has changed dramatically, and the hunting for private and sensational stories and the private persona behind the politician has increased. In the 1990s Bill Clinton was chased relentlessly by the press, and no president before or since has been exposed to such humiliating interrogation on a rather private sex issue. But even though Clinton became involved in several scandals during his election campaign and under his presidency, he was also considered a president with a strong media appearance, as is clearly captured in PBS's documentary *The Clinton Years* (2001). This is a documentary following Clinton all the way from the first election campaign in 1991 and through his two periods as president, and it is a documentary clearly showing the conditions for politics and politicians in a heavily mediated world.

These conditions and the transformation of the relation between public and private have been the object of many portraits of politicians in recent years. In the Danish documentary portrait of the former Minister for Social Affairs, Eva Kjer Hansen, *Eva's store udfordring/ Eva's Big Challenge* (Lars Høj, TV2, 2005) the TV stations express the dilemma for modern politicians in the following way:

> Ministers today must appeal to the hearts of the Danes with their entire lives and stories? Politics is not just sold with arguments; it is also necessary to appeal to the voters' feelings. It is therefore of utmost importance how politicians look, how they live their lives, what their family life is like, how they are with their children, and it is of paramount importance that they are capable of communicating the right image of themselves to the media (official press release, TV2, 2005, my translation).

There is no doubt that female politicians especially get to feel this in public media exposure, but the conflict between public and private is also visible in different forms in documentaries dealing with male politicians, and this change is not just visible in documentaries. In his analysis of the historical changes in Danish television news since the 1960s, Stig Hjarvard (Hjarvard 1999) has shown that news reporting on politics and politicians has fundamentally changed. Where the media earlier had a more message-oriented approach to reporting on politics, and were also less independent and critical towards the political system, the media today have clearly taken the role as the voice of the ordinary viewer with a more critical and direct approach to politicians. At the same time, the political agenda has shifted towards softer and more human interest oriented perspectives, and the critical edge in mainstream media is often of a more populist nature. Politicians need to be able to communicate directly and more strategically towards both the media and the ordinary viewers, and to be able to combine a public and private discourse in the way political issues are discussed.

Two recent Danish documentaries about one of the leading social democrats during the last four decades, Mogens Lykketoft, clearly deals with both the nature of the modern, political persona, and the dilemmas of power, media and the public and private life of a politician. In Poul Martinsen's *Mogens og magten* (DR1 2003, 'Mogens and the power) the focus is on the brutality and costs of political power and the way the media expose and narrate those stories. In the second documentary, Christoffer Guldbrandsen's *Lykketoft finale* (DR2 2005), the focus is on losing power and on a politician's very hostile relationship to modern media and his attempt to protect his privacy. This is underlined quite strongly in DR's official press release for *Lykketoft finale*:

Lykketoft finale is a film about a political system under change. The presentation, the political slogan has defeated the political argument. Mogens Lykketoft is caught between his idealistic self-image and the media image of him as an elitist politician, greedy for power. The film thus portrays the modern Danish election campaign as a media circus in which form and presentation is everything. The political consensus is created through the ability to speak in headlines in front of the camera. The exit of Lykketoft is the exit of the idealist (DR, official press release 2005, my translation).

The two documentaries deal with the same person and theme, but they belong to two different documentary sub-genres. Poul Martinsen's documentary is more critical, investigative and has a mixture of a psychological and a political approach. In parts of the film we have observational sequences following Lykketoft and his wife (also a well known Danish Social Democrat) on tour to a very important meeting where Lykketoft will win a long power struggle and become the leader of the party. But the framing of this tour and the meeting in itself is distant, critical distance: the party anthem is played in a weak and fragmented style, and while we watch him prepare his speech and talk about his political career on the train, a montage of negative splash headlines from the press suddenly appear. In an interview with Poul Martinsen in the Danish Tabloid *BT* on the day of the broadcasting (April 23 2003) he comments on the making of the programme and the fact that Lykketoft set strict rules for the film crew in order to protect his privacy. Martinsen was neither allowed to film in his private home nor his office in parliament, and Martinsen also reveals that he found Lykketoft more reserved than he had expected: 'It is difficult for him to step out of the politician role and into the private person Mogens Lykketoft. He will have huge difficulties in being popular, and that may ultimately cost him the seat as Prime Minister.'

The interesting thing here is that the integration of the personal into politics, the fact that it is not enough to be a very competent politician, has clearly been established as a norm for documentaries and journalists dealing with politics. The conservative newspaper *Berlingske*

Tidende (24 April 2003) repeats this message in the review and commentary the day after the programme was broadcast. They see it as a programme about a politician without genuine passions and feelings, 'so self-controlled that this quest for power almost seems like sleep walking'. This analysis of Lykketoft as a political and private persona is not just underlined through the framing of the observational parts of the programme, but also in those parts of the programme where two journalists and experts on the Social Democrat's history and long power struggles, Hans Mortensen and Arne Hardis, comment on the present situation. While on the one hand we have Lykketoft's own story and Martinsen's discrete, critical framing of it, on the other hand, through the two commentators, we go much further backstage in to Lykketoft's political career, and the very long and brutal struggle between the left and right wing. In the unravelling of this story through both visual and written documentation we actually get very close to both the private and the public story, and we go behind the scenes in both sides of the story. So the programme manages to go into the deeper psychological dimensions of both politics as a power game, and the life and career of a politician going for the ultimate, political power.

As already indicated in the quote from the press release of Christoffer Guldbrandsen's *Lykketoft finale*, this film frames the story differently and also tells it in an almost clean, observational form, although with many forms of metaphorical visual elements and a quite striking use of montage. In interviews before the film was released on television Guldbrandsen clearly stated that he sees Lykketoft as an 'old school' politician, who believes in the argument rather than rhetorical form and personal charisma (*Jyllands-Posten*, 11 March 2005). The starting point for the film, to a large degree, was to portray a person and his staff of advisors facing hostile media during an election campaign, where the media often focused on style and lack of ability to communicate, and Lykketoft tried in vain to talk about political substance. The film is a portrait of a powerful politician who loses the battle to become Prime Minister, but is very much a portrait seen from inside Lykketoft's world without critical comments and analysis.

This point of view of the film is clear from the outset when we see Lykketoft in front of the computer in his private home, preparing the speech where he will announce his resignation as leader of the party after having lost the election. He is seen from a distance while a very sad, frail music plays, and as the camera goes into close up on his face and the computer screen, we see a tired and defeated person about to make his exit as number one. From this the film goes back to the image of a very young Lykketoft in a taxi with one of the former leaders of the party, then to him and his wife in a taxi on their way to the farewell meeting and speech, and his meeting outside that place with the aggressive hordes of journalists, and finally images of his speech to the party. Those images are crosscut with brief images from former times and conflicts, and after this very symbolic intro the film moves back in time to the tour round the country during the election campaign. A clear focus is on the relation between politics and the media, it is about the confrontation between the old school politics of Lykketoft and the modern media circus of style, rhetoric and personal charisma.

In 2009 one of the other central figures in the Social Democratic Party of Denmark, Svend Auken, died of cancer. When he died, he had been married to one of the leading Danish documentary directors, Anne Wivel, for a number of years, and in 2011 her portrait of him, *Svend*, came out. The film is subtitled 'filmed and remembered by Anne Wivel' and this indicates that we are dealing with a very personal and political portrait. It is a film with a very reflexive and autobiographical dimension, where the personal life story and feelings of an approaching death influence the experience of the film. The film was started before his cancer broke and the intention was to make a portrait of a politician with an idealistic, global agenda, fighting for global understanding and the environment. The mood of the film is therefore not just melancholy, but rather optimistic and forward-looking, and we follow a very active politician around the world. It is in fact much more of a manifesto for modern, global politics, a politics above the level of national controversies, which Svend Auken has been a very active part of. But although the focus of the film is the global politician the national and local is not forgotten, and during the shooting of the film a national election in Denmark takes place, and we follow that closely. The portrait is also very intense on another level, because we see Auken around the world facing the globe's magnificent nature (Africa, Greenland) and thus the environment he is fighting for.

Fighting power – using power

The very first modern documentary about politics and politicians followed an election narrative, and this narrative and drama is, of course, as we see in the Danish portraits, still a central part of documentaries on politics and politicians. This tendency is repeated in different forms in US and UK documentaries on politics as well. But politics is also about creating political results and transforming visions to reality, and many political documentaries deal with this dimension in an investigative, critical way. The BBC Panorama programme *The Labour Years* (2001), for instance, is a portrait of Labour and Blair after four years of government, and aired just four days before the national election that would give Blair four more years. It is a rather critical programme looking back on the powerful rhetoric and promises of Blair and his new 'third way' policy and comparing it with the actual results and reforms of British society. It is a classical BBC documentary with a very diverse representation of voices from Labour, from political opponents, from experts and from ordinary people. But the globalization of politics and the fact that UK and US politics are often directly connected also makes it natural for the BBC to make a classical portrait of the newly elected President Bush in *The Accidental President* (2001). This portrait is much more a biography of a person and politician, an attempt to define his background and ideological position, and not a programme directly on a concrete, political agenda. But the intense battle between Bush and John Kerry in 2004 also resulted in a political election drama like *The Chosen One* (2004).

Critical documentaries on politics are, for natural reasons, much more direct and specific when it comes to national politics, although the War on Terror and other rising, global political agendas are beginning to change that. But the UK documentaries on politics and politicians are clearly more abundant with national figures. The BBC's *Tony in Adland* (2002) focused on alleged misuse of public money for party political advertising, whereas a programme like *Eurovisions* (2003) dealt with the European scepticism of the UK and the question of whether to join the euro or not. But even though the UK is a member of the European Union, programmes on issues related to this kind of transnational politics are much more rare than national political documentaries. A further example of that, and of the critical agenda towards large national policy issues, is *What Has Labour Done for the NHS* (2005), looking at the problems in national health care, a problem also taken up in *The NHS Blame Game* (2006). More person- and political portrait-oriented is *Does it Have to be Gordon?* (2006), pointing towards the change from Blair to Gordon Brown as Prime Minister and focusing on how different they are as politicians and leaders. A direct link to this portrait can be found in *Tony Blair's Long Goodbye* (2006), which is a backstage political documentary following the process in 10 Downing Street for developing the ideas and initiatives to reform the welfare society, a theme also dealt with in *Tony Blair's Quest for a 'Big Idea'* (2006).

But perhaps one of the best documentary political portraits in UK was made by Andrew Rawnsley for Channel 4. His two part series *The Rise and Fall of Tony Blair* (2007) is a powerful story of the person who more than anyone else transformed Labour and the British political agenda after years of conservative dominance. It is the story of a man with new visions for a modern welfare state, but also the person who brought the UK into a highly controversial global alliance on the War on Terror. But it is also a story about the merging of style, form, and the personal and the public, taking place globally in politics in a media-saturated culture. Blair as a mediated political figure was, however, also interesting in the sense that he was both a British and global icon. As a political figure he was almost as familiar to people in Europe and the US as the national, political figures.

Obamania and other American political portraits

Blair was no doubt a brilliant rhetorical performer who knew how to use the media, and in that sense he points towards Obama and his rise to power in 2008. Blair showed ability in addressing the public mostly through the traditional mass media, but Barack Obama became the symbol of the president in a new media culture where social media had become central as part of the appeal, especially to young voters. He became the symbol of a modern-times politician with both a substantial new political agenda and a new form of communication that also had to do with being a charismatic public figure and speaker. At the same time, perhaps even more than Tony Blair, he has also become a global political icon, not just because the US is still the number one superpower in many ways, but also because he has managed to develop a discourse and image as a politician on the global stage.

US documentaries on the battle for election and the political process of being in power have great similarities with the Danish and UK documentaries, but there are generally fewer of them in all forms. However, the political portrait and the election documentaries are clearly represented after 2000. In 2002, for instance, HBO's Alexandra Pelosi made *Journeys with George*, based on her footage from following George Bush on his election campaign in 2000. It is an observational documentary following George Bush on his first election tour, filmed with one of the new small, digital cameras (Sony TRV-900). This almost non-professional, cheap camera influences the nature of this political portrait and introduces a kind of 'casual, irreverent attitude' to a public political figure and a close-up kind of intimacy often connected with the family album (Kahana 2008: 278f). Compared with the already mentioned observational political portraits from the early 1960s, where the breaking down of the barrier between front stage and backstage starts, this film gets much closer, and the juxtaposition of shots from the frontstage parts of the political campaign with the backstage parts, seem to indicate a rather cynical or reflexive attitude to what modern politics is all about. A more classical and broad election documentary and political portrait can be found in John Butler's independent film *Going Up River: The Long War of John Kerry* (2004). The film is a direct response to false accusations during the 2004 presidential campaign, that Kerry had lied about his military career in Vietnam. The film documents this and shows how the conservative apparatus, all the way back to Nixon, has tried to discredit Kerry. The film also gives a broader portrait of Kerry's later political career and political standpoints.

But the films on Obama are many, both made in the US and the UK, and some of them rather interesting. The BBC made *Obama and the Pitbull: An American Tale* (2010), dealing with the election campaign and the role of Sarah Palin. The BBC also looked at race and politics in the US in *Is America Ready for a Black President?* (2007), which takes a look at a president that doesn't want race to be of importance and who has a modern, cosmopolitan profile. The programme is made in a classic, authoritative form and talks to ordinary people, experts and political commentators, and we get an inside view of his campaign and his strategy and rhetorical discourse. But we also get historical and contemporary examples of how deeply race is still embedded in American culture. The UK programmes on Obama deal with global challenges that are also challenges for Europe. In 2009 the BBC made *Obama and the Ayatollah* (2009), dealing with the question of Iran.

In 2010 BBC 2 made the two-part programme *Obama's America*. The programme has Simon Schama as the classic journalistic narrator, often talking from places of symbolic importance, and with an often broad historical and social perspective on Obama's politics. In Part One, *The Price of Freedom*, the question concerning the War on Terror is central. The start of the programme clearly states that Obama was not just popular in America, but that he also clearly addressed a global audience, but reality has set in, it's difficult to cash in on all the visions and promises. The programme takes us back to WW2, using the celebration of the D-Day invasion to reflect on the nature of modern wars and why we fight them. The programme constantly makes this historical reflection and compares Obama with other presidents like Kennedy and Truman, but zooms in on the War on Terror as a modern example of the US in the role as a global player. In the second part of the programme, *The End of the Dream*, Simon Schama turns to the economic and social agenda of Obama and the problems arising from the financial crisis. In Schama's way of making political documentaries a wider context and deeper reflection is dominant; this is not just a political portrait, it's an essay on national and global politics.

PBS started its programmes on Obama, and his political career and context, with *The Choice 2008* (2008) about the election campaign. It is a two-hour programme that goes deep backstage through footage and interviews with key people on both sides of the campaign. But the programme clearly gets it's dramatic drive from the Obama figure and what PBS calls 'a race that pits the iconoclast against the newcomer, the heroic prisoner of war against the first African-American nominated by a major party. Frontline's critically acclaimed series *The Choice* returns this election season to examine the rich personal and political biographies of these two men' (quoted from PBS 2012a).

In 2009 PBS made a more personal-political portrait of the new president called *Dreams of Obama*, but they also started focusing more critically on his political agenda and challenges in, for instance, *Obama's War* (2009) on the War on Terror, or *Obama's Deal* (2010) on the tough political fight behind the health care reform. *Dreams of Obama* is a classical political portrait of Obama's rise to power, structured like a chronological narrative diving into his family background and his education and political career before and after his decisive speech at the 2004 Democratic convention. This speech is used as a kind of red thread throughout the programme, where an authoritative narrator guides us through images from his life, interviews with friends, colleagues and experts, quotes from his books or television media excerpts. Where this portrait gives us an image of a visionary, charismatic and different American president, the two other programmes deal much more with the critical reality of a president faced with serious problems abroad and at home, and a declining majority in House and Senate. *Obama's War* is more a film on policy and strategy than a political portrait. It deals with the launch of the counterinsurgency strategy in 2009 and takes us out on the ground in Afghanistan, but also into the political scene where support for the war is decided, and it deals with the complicated political alliance with Pakistan. *Obama's Deal* is about another big challenge, the vision of creating a universal health care system in the US, but it is also a programme concerning the hard pragmatics and strategies of getting political results. It is about how a president's idealism has to face the realities of a pretty hostile political system. It is also a programme taking us from the established political system and out into the debate among ordinary people at town hall meetings, or the powerful lobby groups and their attacks.

HBO, otherwise not very productive in directly political documentaries or portraits of politicians, also made an Obama film, *By the People: The Election of Barack Obama* (2009), directed by Amy Rice and Alicia Sams. The film has 28 scenes and basically follows the dramatic events of his election in 2008 with long jumps back to his earlier life and career, but at the same time, it tries to capture the image of a president of a new generation, focusing on the way he communicates and reaches out to a broader audience. The film is in line with the observational, political tradition: we are inside the campaign headquarters and we follow Obama and members of his staff very closely. We are behind the stage, we are in the machine room, we are also in the Obama family sphere, we go back in his personal family history. However, through media clips, vox pops, and staff and expert statements we also see Obama from the viewpoint of his collaborators and from the outside. The film also shows the skepticism from many in the beginning, the disbelief in his potential to win, the dirty tricks from opponents and the sweeping change of the race that brought the victory.

Critical tales of twentieth century global political icons

One of the most remarkable political portraits in recent documentary film history is Errol Morris' Academy Award winning *The Fog of War* (2003). The subtitle of the film, 'Eleven lessons from the life of Robert S. McNamara' illustrates that this is a portrait of a key figure in American foreign policy in post-WW2 history. But as often in Morris' works, the eerie music of Philip Glass indicates the moral, existential and critical undertone in this dialogue and portrait of a global power player. As the film moves forward, the main character seems to be hit by increasing uncertainty about his own life and career as a politician and key strategic figure for presidents since the 1960s. The portrait of one man becomes the portrait of the politics of a superpower. This structure is underlined by the fact that the voice of McNamara is heard throughout most of the film, either in direct address to Morris and his camera, as a voiceover to archive footage, or in historical media footage with him in his different positions since the 1960s.

But Morris also uses a more reflexive and complicated form of montage as part of this portrait. In a form of media montage of text and images he creates a historical context around his main figure, and by zooming in on text fragments he makes an interactive connection between then and now, between statements and interpretations made by others and the statements and interpretations put forward by the film. Instead of the classical, authoritative voiceover this is a visual montage commenting on the character and his time. But it is also a film bringing new material on politics to the public, not just through the long, intensive interview with McNamara, which is the core of the film, but also through the intensive documentation of phone conversations, radio and television interviews and written material. The film works on many layers of presentation and historical data to portray what Morris in his synopsis calls an 'idealist who gradually rose from humble origins to the height of political power' (see www.sonyclassics.com/fogofwar/indexFlash.html, accessed 10 May 2012).

The film is very much a portrait of global politics seen through a key figure, and most of the film is about McNamara as a public figure. But there is also a broader and more personal story that adds new and social dimensions to the political story – a man and politician created by his background and experiences. In this sense the portrait is in line with trends in the political portrait documentary. The film very much focuses on the costs of global conflicts and wars, and in both visual and verbal discourse confronts the rational calculations and decisions made by world powers and world leaders and the realities and consequences for ordinary people. At times the moral and existential dilemmas raised here are illustrated by both symbolic montage and extreme close-up shots of McNamara's troubled face.

The portrait of McNamara is one of a central political figure, both in the frontline and as the architect behind much of the modern US foreign or economic policy. Although the film deals with a political past, it delivers a contemporary message as well. 'Our understanding of the world is not adequate,' is McNamara's closing lesson. A similar, but very different, portrait of a contemporary strategic mind for the republican right is PBS's *Karl Rove – The Architect* (2005), a much more straightforward, traditional and authoritative journalistic portrait. The programme describes the background, career and mentality of Rove as a highly revisionist, conservative thinker and political strategist, going back to the Nixon era, and describes his work for the Bush family and administration from around 2000, but with strong focus on the 2004 campaign and election.

More spectacular documentaries of a rather different nature deal with Henry Kissinger, again one of the most influential global politicians of the twentieth century. The most critical of the films is Eugene Jarecki's *The Trials of Henry Kissinger* (2002), based on Christopher Hitchen's controversial book with the same title from 2001, in which the author claims that Kissinger is guilty of war crimes and crimes against humanity for his Cold War-dominated foreign policy doctrines. Jarecki's film is more cautious and neutral in its critical approach, and becomes a broader political portrait of a man and his times. But it is clear that this political portrait enters the same kind of critical discourse on global politics as the McNamara portrait. These documentaries deal with transformations in doctrines of global politics from the Cold War era to the new global era after the fall of communism. Niall Ferguson's *Kissinger* (Channel 4 2011) is quite different and based more on the concept of going inside the mind of Kissinger. Ferguson followed Kissinger on trips abroad and interviewed him over a two year period. So if Jarecki's film is a critical montage on Kissinger, mostly seen from the outside and through different observers, Ferguson like Morris lets the man act and speak for himself.

Global politics and the challenges of cosmopolitanism

Politics was never really just a national case, and not even the traditional division between domestic and foreign policy can be seen as an adequate way of defining politics in a global world. This is certainly very clear when we look at Europe, where the increasing transnationalization of political areas and European integration is challenging the notion of what national politics is. But even though we do not really have a global political sphere, the transnationalization of politics is also visible outside Europe, partly because instability and crisis in one part of the world very often directly influences the whole world, and partly because global media does create a greater awareness of common global problems. Documentary film projects in the new digital media culture illustrate the potential for cosmopolitan film productions where professionals and ordinary users interact. In 2010 YouTube hosted a project called *Life in a Day* where established directors and producers like Kevin MacDonald and Ridley and Tony Scott asked YouTube users around the world to send in films made on one day and based on this they created a cosmopolitan, collective documentary film. In 2012 this cosmopolitan experiment was repeated by Kevin Ruddeck in *One Day on Earth*, screened in 165 countries on the same day, Earth Day, 22 April 2012.

Some sociologists and anthropologists such as Ulf Hannerz (1996), Ulrick Beck (2006) and Gerard Delanty (2009) have argued that we are entering a social, cultural and political phase, where a cosmopolitan mentality will expand, although national backlashes will certainly also take place. Following this observation media scholars such as Alexa Robertson have pointed to the importance of *Mediated Cosmopolitanism* (2010). Alexa Robertson mainly deals with the globalization of television news and her main point is that we both have a development of news channels with an increasingly global outreach and audience, and a globalization of national news. By constantly reporting in smaller or larger news broadcasts on global matters, news frames a cosmopolitan imagination and narrative, and gradually connects local, national and global levels of experience. This narrative may not be positive and utopian, for it often deals with transnational institutions (like the UN) that cannot act or navigate together, or catastrophes and crises that seem very difficult to tackle and overcome. But principles and attempts at cosmopolitan governance and movements and organizations dedicated to the strengthening of cosmopolitanism are also important parts of the story. The fact that global dialogue is now taking place not just through transnational institutions, organizations and movements, but also via digital platforms and social media has clearly enhanced the role of media in a broader sense in the construction of a mediated, global sphere.

As Alexa Robertson has documented in a comparative analysis of European news, there is in fact a rise in global reporting, but different channels have different national profiles (Robertson 2010: 30ff) and narratives vary; the same also goes for news on Europeanization. But even though the framing of a cosmopolitan imagination and narrative happens in different contexts and national interpretations, we are still witnessing a kind of universal trend towards a greater cosmopolitan outlook. This is also visible in forms of production and distribution in documentary filmmaking that goes beyond the traditional model as demonstrated in the already-mentioned global, collaborative documentary projects *Why Democracy?* and *Why Poverty?*

The Danish contribution to *Why Democracy?*, Karsten Kjær's *Bloody Cartoons*, is a film about the Danish Mohammed crisis following the Danish newspaper Jyllands-Posten's front page drawings of Mohammed. This crisis can indeed be seen as a symbol of the challenges for cosmopolitanism, and the crisis among other things illustrates the conflict between universal principles of freedom of speech and certain cultural and religious norms. The film has an almost Michael Moore-like structure in the sense that Karsten Kjær directly seeks out and confronts those persons in the Muslim world that were active in the condemnation of Denmark and Jyllands-Posten in this case. He shows them the cartoons in question and it turns out that many of these persons haven't actually seen the drawings and are surprised when they see them. The film shows that in Arab countries there is actually a long tradition of pictures of Mohammed, just as satirical drawings of Jews and Christians are common. The film traces the various media narratives in the Arab world on the Danish Mohammed drawings, and is able to find different attitudes and often overlooked nuances here. This is also the case in some of the meetings with ordinary Muslims, with whom the journalist almost becomes a good friend. The film in itself is thus a sort of cosmopolitan dialogue, an attempt to bridge cultural differences and to show deeper universal bonds between people – if they can actually meet and communicate.

But the reality of politics in a more and more global world is that global decision-making and global action can be frustratingly difficult. In the Danish documentary by Rasmus Dinesen and Boris Bertram *Diplomacy: The Responsibility to Protect* (2008) this is clearly documented by following a Danish attempt to get a Dafur resolution through the UN security council in order prevent civil war and genocide. It is a dramatic and intense story demonstrating how slow and impossible the functioning of global politics is. A similar film is Anders Østergaard and Anders Riis-Hansen's *The Vanguard of Diplomacy* (2004), following the Danish star diplomat Torben Getterman and the almost impossible attempt to rebuild Iraq and establish a Danish embassy in Baghdad. Global politics is a constant battle with internal and external conflicts. A dramatic expression of that is the bombing of the UN headquarters in Baghdad, and the killing of the head of the UN there which took place during the shooting of the film.

Invisible Europe

The focus on the complex and almost impossible task of creating a global dialogue on a large scale is only one of the new areas of documentaries on modern politics. Another form of global political documentaries is on more regional and transnational forms of collaboration, not least the EU. Strangely enough, the European project has not created a lot of documentary creativity or scrutiny; it seems to be anchored more in the day-to-day news and dealt with from a clearly rather sceptical point of view. This in itself points to the problems with a more global politics and cosmopolitan outlook. Despite more than 50 years of European collaboration, the national dimension in many policy areas is still rather strong, and the actual Europeanization of many areas of life, for more than 500 million Europeans, is often rather invisible.

There are only three Channel 4 or BBC documentaries after 2001 on EU politics and they have a clearly EU-sceptical attitude, focusing on the threat to UK national interests, or fraud and misuse of EU money. *Riding Europe's Gravy Train* (Channel 4 2010) is about EU members of parliament misusing per diem and travel costs in the EU system, and adds to the image of the EU as a bureaucratic monster. *Eurovisions* (BBC 2003) deals with the development of the euro and why the single currency is not a healthy project, and finally *Battle for Europe* (BBC 2005) revives the ancient battle between France, England and Germany for dominance in Europe. On the whole the fact that so few documentaries deal with this issue is in itself a very clear sign of the difficulties of transnational politics, and the themes and tone in the programmes further contribute to a feeling that globalization in the form of the EU is not really getting into the national agenda and the everyday concerns of Europeans – on the contrary, the national framing is very dominant.

In Denmark, Christoffer Guldbrandsen has dealt with the EU in three rather different documentaries. In *Fogh bag Facaden/The Road To Europe* (2003) – which won the European documentary award Golden Link – we get a rare glimpse behind the scenes at the EU during the very difficult negotiations under the Danish chairmanship in 2002 (under Danish prime minister Anders Fogh Rasmussen) as to whether the integration of the former communist countries, and the enlargement of EU to EU27, should take place. In the film we follow the Danish presidency in all phases of the preparation, we see informal and formal meetings in the EU system, and we follow the dramatic meetings and negotiations during the Copenhagen summit, where an agreement as to the inclusion of Eastern Europe is decided, but where we see national interest and clashes of political egos and leaders. Seen in a broader European perspective, the insight this film gave as to what politicians on the broader European scene say frontstage, and do and say backstage, was almost unprecedented.

In another film based on the same material, *Europa på spil/Europe at Stake* (2002), we follow three very different characters during the Copenhagen summit: an anti-EU demonstrator, the Danish prime minister and the chief of police in charge of security. Here the different perspectives on Europe and European integration are made into a democratic dialogue or debate. But Guldbrandsen made an even more spectacular and unusual EU documentary, *The President* (2011), which follows the backstage procedures behind the election of the first European 'president'. Some of the central players in this process, for instance the former chairman of the European Commission, Romano Prodi and also the elected 'president' Herman van Rompuy, are surprisingly open and candid in their statements and viewpoints. The film has a kind of ironic, humorous tone and the whole project of Europeanization is clearly undermined by national and personal rivalries, things that also exist in national politics, but which here develop to absurdity because of clear national conflicts and power struggles that undermine, or at least challenge, the transnational European project.

John Pilger: a critical global watchdog

A key figure, and personification of journalism and documentary film as a critical global voice and watchdog, is the Australian-born John Pilger, who since the 1970s has worked mostly from the UK. He has focused on global politics and the media reporting of conflicts and suppression in most parts of the world. One of his first influential films that helped form global opinion was *Vietnam – The Quiet Mutiny* (World in Action, ITV, UK 1970) that showed the American meltdown in Vietnam. But he has made inside stories and critical reports from other global conflict zones like Cambodia, Nicaragua, Timor, Burma, Palestine and Iraq. He has continued his reporting to date and in films after 2001 he has dealt with such topics as the US-Latin American relations in *The War on Democracy* (2007) and with how the media has covered global conflicts in *The War You Don't See* (2010).

The films Pilger has made since 2000 are still very characteristic of his ability to find hidden, global scandals. In *Paying the Price: Killing the Children of Iraq* (2000) he deals with the consequences of the global sanctions towards Iraq, and in *Stealing a Nation* (2004) the story is about the population of the Chagos Islands, where the UK brutally expelled the original population to make way for an American military base. Both films focus on the often invisible or unknown effects of global powers and global politics, and they raise both political critique and moral questions based on fundamental human rights. This is also the case with the film *Palestine is Still the Issue* (2002) – a film that he first made in 1977 and updated in 2002 – which has a strong story about, and defence of, a people without a country, caught as a pawn in global politics. The film has shocking images of a Palestine being systematically destroyed and the consequences of a conflict with global dimensions that endlessly damages ordinary people, families and children. The film mixes everyday life stories and images with pictures and information of a more general and political nature.

Taking the ground-level perspective of global politics and global conflicts is characteristic of all the films of John Pilger, including his film *Breaking the Silence: Truth and Lies in the War on Terror* (2003). The film joins many other critical films on the War on Terror but the special aim of this film is, as in all Pilger's films, to search for the consequences for ordinary people. So if the War on Terror is said to be fought for people in the US or Europe, let's look at what it does here, in this case Washington. If we fight the wars in Iraq and Afghanistan for democracy and for the people of these countries, then let's look at what the war does for them. This critical, humanitarian, but also strongly political approach makes Pilger the moral voice of globalization. This is also the case in his early film on financial crisis, *The New Rulers of the World* (2001), which is characterized like this on his personal website:

> The film turns the spotlight on the new rulers of the world – the great multinationals and the governments and institutions that back them such as the IMF, the World Bank and the World Trade Organization under whose rules millions of people throughout the world lose their jobs and livelihood.

The West, explains Pilger, has increased its stranglehold on poor countries by using the might of these powerful financial institutions to control their economies. 'A small group of powerful individuals are now richer than most of the population of Africa,' he says,

> 'just 200 giant corporations dominate a quarter of the world's economic activity. General Motors is now bigger than Denmark. Ford is bigger than South Africa. Enormously rich men like Bill Gates, have a wealth greater than all of Africa. Golfer Tiger Woods was

paid more to promote Nike than the entire workforce making the company's products in Indonesia received' (Pilger 2012a).

But Pilger's special take on the problem is not just to analyze this development from a macro perspective and by the use of politicians and experts. Instead he goes deep into everyday life in Indonesia, and other parts of Asia, to look at the concrete and experienced dimensions of economic globalization and dominance.

John Pilger's long-running critical examination of US global policies manifests itself once again in his first cinematic documentary *The War on Democracy* (2007), based on research into the US policy in Latin America and the US attempt and success in overthrowing democratically elected presidents and governments. The documentation in the films is based on interviews with several former CIA agents and other centrally involved people. Pilger himself has said that the film 'is about the struggle of people to free themselves from a modern form of slavery'. These people he says,

> describe a world not as American presidents like to see it as useful or expendable, they describe the power of courage and humanity among people with next to nothing. They reclaim noble words like democracy, freedom, liberation, justice, and in doing so they are defending the most basic human rights of all of us in a war being waged against all of us (Pilger 2012b).

The film confronts the words of American presidents and politicians about the alleged ideal reasons for interventions with the realities and the secret operations. It shows the role of interest politics and the ongoing tendency in global politics to stereotype Latin American politics as left-wing, authoritarian ideology. Besides interviews with CIA people, the film also tells Latin American history and gives a voice to leaders and other Latin American representatives. In line with Pilger's other films we also follow everyday life in different parts of Latin America, and we hear the stories of ordinary people, such as Mariela Macada in La Vega in Venezuela. In this Venezuelan town we also witness collective citizen movements. The new Venezuela of Chavez is thus seen from above and from below, and Pilger is also critical towards the corruption and bureaucracy still dominating despite Chavez's new policy. Pilger also visits the new rich in Latin America and the media images of a strong commercial culture in opposition to the government. By taking all sides and points of view into consideration the film clearly paints a much more nuanced picture of Latin America than we usually get, and by going behind the facade and dynamics of regional and global politics Pilger once more acts as the critical global voice.

Lectures on the dynamics of globalization

John Pilger's films clearly demonstrate a global regime where big corporate and political interest play a crucial role, and where the front stage global activities are not always what they seem. In *War on Democracy* Pilger, like many others, points to the role of conservative ideologies and especially the economic theory of Milton Friedman as figures behind US-led politics before and after 2001. In 2009 UK director Michael Winterbottom and Mat Whitecross made a film on this school and its role in globalization, *The Shock Doctrine*, based on the book of the same title by Naomi Klein. The film is a powerful historical analysis of the Chicago school and its influence on politics and economy from the 1970s onwards, with the post-Allende Chile and Thatcher's England as some of the historic examples, but also present-day politics in the War on Terror and the global financial crisis.

The film starts with Naomi Klein talking about the importance of using the present crisis to trace our roots, and the film immediately moves back to 1951, where politicians secretly met with academics. The agenda of the meeting was how to cause deprivation of the senses in human beings by different forms of shock therapy. This is the birth of modern intelligence interrogation, which we see developed fully in the war against terror. The film compares this with the economic theory of Friedman based on economic shock treatment, a sort of radical form of liberalism later tried out in Chile after the overthrowing of Allende and in Thatcher's England in the 1980s. The Chile case is dealt with in detail, in itself a shocking example of how high-level interests work behind the stage in the battle of globalization, and where the Chicago school had written the blueprint for the economic shock treatment. In Milton's own words it was a move from a communist economy to a free market economy, but the results were disastrous, especially for the poor and the lower middle class, and the free economy went hand in hand with a military dictatorship.

The Shock Doctrine is an authoritative, critical history lecture – marked by the occasional pictures of a lecturing Naomi Klein. It connects dots in a global network and a school of thought going back to the 1950s and into our present decade, claiming this to be of vital importance for the understanding of globalization as a radical liberalism with rather devastating effects. The historical network of ideas and political strategies continues in republican, American neo-conservatism around Nixon, Kissinger, Reagan and Bush, and the film points to links to the War on Terror and the ways of promoting corporate interest around the world and also the lack of understanding of climate problems. It is thus a highly critical film about global politics, and the hidden agendas and interests behind a specific ideology of globalization. In the film this is seen in contrast to another main trend, the Keynesian tradition from Roosevelt in the 1930s, a political trend more in tune with the strong European tradition of a balance between market and public intervention, a tradition of a more global dialogue.

At times, *The Shock Doctrine* seems to rest on a kind of conspiracy theory, and in this respect the film has a certain similarity with Adam Curtis' three-part television documentary *The Power of Nightmares: The Rise of the Politics of Fear* (BBC 2004). The dominant perspective in the series is basically the same. Those with political power, or other forms of power, have used the effect of creating fear in the population to carry out their plans, a politics of fear as the first part is called. Here the story starts in 1949 with the Egyptian Sayyid Qutb, usually seen as one of the ideological founding fathers of modern Islamic thought, based on his criticism of individualism and Western decadence, and moves on to

Figures 7a and b: Michael Winterbottom and Mat Whitecross' *The Shock Doctrine* (2009). Graphic illustration of the corporate dimensions of war. Frame grab. Cinematography: Michael Winterbottom, Mat Whitecross, Ronald Plante and Filippo Viola.

the neo-conservative ideologist Leo Strauss from the Chicago school, who at the same time gave birth to thoughts dominant in post-9/11 politics. Moreover, Strauss was opposed to liberal thoughts of individual freedom and in favour of nationalism and religion as the basis for a modern patriotism, and in favour of the moral supremacy of America. The series thus confronts two apparently very different ideologies that have both informed contemporary global politics, and which according to the programme, have many common traits even though they have been engaged in a fierce global fight.

The series is clearly an authoritative, critical investigation of power structures and ideologies, and has a classical voiceover and use of interviews to document the main points. It also uses a rich diversity of archive footage and montage from both actuality genres and fiction, for instance when 1950s western series and films are used to illustrate basic concepts in neo-conservative thoughts, or equivalent tendencies in Islamic countries. The TV series is a very solid and well documented history of the foundation of modern, global politics, moving between American politics, and the political developments in the Arab world or the communist block. The first part ('Baby It's Cold Out There') follows developments till the Reagan area and the fall of communism, in the second part ('The Phantom Victory') we move up to the time of Clinton and Bush, and in the final part ('The Shadows in the Cave') we enter the post-9/11 era. The series shows striking parallels between the way in which the neo-conservatives argue against the Soviet Union, and create public fear of their weapons of mass destruction and their actual military power, and the later arguments used before the attack on Iraq. The politics of fear was created early and has been used for a long time.

New forms of global awareness

Some of the documentary films and programmes mentioned already have focused on the negative aspects of globalization, the divisions and power struggles in a global world with big differences. This points in the direction of a broader breakthrough for a global awareness through documentary, a move away from the former, more nationally oriented, critical agenda. There is no doubt that the rise, since the 1980s, of new 24-hour news channels with a pronounced global agenda, and branches not only in the West but also in many other parts of the world, has contributed to this globalization of our knowledge. International news has of course been around in journalism and news for a much longer period in both print media and radio, but the rise of more permanent live coverage and instant access to the global world has created a new framework. Just as important for this development are the digital and mobile media that allow ordinary people to communicate directly in global networks, a fact that the professional media have been quick to respond to and use. The events during the Arab Spring, the oppositional movements in Iran or in China, show that it is increasingly difficult to control the flow of news and images. Even very closed regimes like North Korea have been opened up by clever documentarists.

In his multiple prize-winning documentary, *Burma VJ* (2008), Danish director Anders Østergaard, demonstrates how one can combine images generated by protesters in Burma during the bloody and violent uprising in 2007, with classical documentary modes. The film has a subjective point of view and a voiceover by one of the media activists and demonstrators, and is in its basic form a film with an inside and from below perspective. The images of the film are to a large degree based on actual footage shot by the demonstrators, but a number of scenes and sequences are based on reconstructed material that follows the original. The style is authentic, with often shaky and blurred images taken in secrecy and under great danger during the events. The images document the organizational centres of the uprising, the often very violent images of demonstrations and the military in action, but we also see images of a more quiet and beautiful Burma and ordinary everyday life. As a whole the film combines the expressions and images of amateurs, and the people involved with the professional editing and montage of the director and his team. The film is thus a clear example of a new kind of mediated globalization where professional filmmakers can collaborate with people in faraway and very closed societies. It is a piece of global dialogue and activism which shows that it is increasingly difficult for authoritarian and closed regimes to suppress freedom of information and the spreading of truth in the global media sphere. The film has won more than 35 international prizes and has been shown in more than 100 countries, at festivals, on television and via other platforms.

A similar example of the meeting between images from within a popular uprising and a professional producer and director can be found in HBO's and Anthony Thomas' *For Neda* (2010), about the iconic images of the Iranian demonstrator shot during a demonstration. The image of her dying on the street is one of the most powerful examples of viral video in recent year. Via mobile phones, the pictures of her went almost instantly around the world. The film points to other images like that: the little Vietnamese girl hit by napalm, the Chinese man in front of the tanks, the Abu Ghraib images etc., but the instant global spread by ordinary bystanders or protestors makes a difference. The film shows how Neda's death spurs a surge of global protests, where masks of the live Neda become a symbol. The film also shows images from inside the Iranian revolution, but first of all the film goes behind the scene to paint a portrait of Neda. The scoop of the film is that it manages, through an Iranian living in the US, to get inside Iran, make direct contact and conduct interviews with Neda's family. No journalist inside Iran has been able to do that, so it is again an example of the new global media power of the joint forces of amateurs and professionals.

The film develops not just as a portrait of Neda and her family, but also very much as a film about women's suppressed and humiliating situation in Iran, and other similar Islamic countries. Unlike *Burma VJ*, this is a film that combines the more observational inside images with a more authoritative, journalistic form based on the use of experts and witnesses. But perhaps one of the strongest elements in the film is that it shows how the private life of Neda and her friends is completely different from the official side of women's life in Iran. She becomes a human being with all those universal desires and wishes that women throughout the world have. We get quite another image of everyday women's life than the one we would usually be allowed to see. This also eventually shows in the demonstrations, where women are at the forefront and dare to challenge the regime and its norms, a fact that may be a reason for her death: the regime cannot stand open, female beauty.

The Egyptian revolution was of course an important event – and an example of this new, global media phenomenon. In Danish-Palestinian director Omar Shargawi's ½ *Revolution* (2011), a film that won the main prize at the Aljazeera International Documentary Festival in Doha, Qatar in 2012, we see the director going to Egypt, initially to make a film about street children in Cairo. But he soon became part of the revolution together with the friends he stayed with, and with his camera he was both filming, reflecting on what he saw, and taking an active part in it all. The film is a dramatic, observational documentary with a very authentic representation of both the happiness of people coming together and fighting for freedom and democracy, and also the brutality and killing of people. The director was also arrested for some time himself. The images from inside the demonstrations and along the streets, often dangerously close to people getting shot, wounded and killed, are both scary and uplifting, and the film also includes short statements from demonstrators on what they are fighting for. But it also has sequences from the flat Omar is living in with discussions and reflections, and images of joy and everyday life. The film even has elements of a poetic style and mood, where the use of slow-motion images and music signal the emotional side of revolutionary hope for a better future. The filming ends sevens days before the fall of Mubarak, when the director is forced to return to his Danish family. The film is a dramatic snapshot of history in the making.

PBS also dealt with this in *Revolution in Cairo* (2011), just as they have taken up the case of the famous Chinese artist and activist in *Who's Afraid of Ai Weiwei* (2011) and the Syrian situation in *Syria Undercover* (2011). *Revolution in Cairo* looks at the revolution mainly through the eyes of the April 6th youth movement, a movement of bloggers and internet activists started in 2008, and one of the backbones of the later revolutionary movement. What they did was simply to start to systematically document oppression and torture by the regime – using YouTube, Twitter and Facebook – and post it to a vast network of users inside and outside Egypt, so it is yet another film about the strength and potential of new social media. *Syria Undercover* has a similar focus, with PBS reporter Ramita Navai undercover in the middle of the uprising and being able to get both the opposition to the front and also draw up a critical portrait of the Syrian President Bashar al-Assad. These PBS programmes are all excellent examples of how professional media can connect to oppositional voices otherwise only able to communicate through internet and mobile media, and still keep a balanced, critical perspective.

New global order – very old problems

The documentaries on new democratic movements and uprisings is one side of the documentaries dealing with global politics outside the Western world. But globalization has also affected nations in the former communist block and in old colonial Africa, both global regions with very fragile democracies and societies in general. *Should We Be Scared of Russia?* asked BBC in a programme from 2008, a programme even airing the fear of a 'new cold war'. The programme looks at the support for a strong man on the streets of Moscow and around the country, investigates Russia's aggressive policy in Georgia and Ukraine, and the fear and envy of the West that still haunts the minds of Russian politicians and ordinary citizens. It is a classical *Panorama* programme with solid journalistic research and a combination of interviews with Russian politicians, experts and ordinary Russians.

A very different documentary dealing with the new Russia is Danish Lise Birk Pedersen's *Putin's Kiss* (2011), a much more observational, inside portrait of the young, well-educated Russian generation behind, and in opposition to, Putin. In the film, two characters are portrayed: on the one side the critical journalist Oleg Khaskin, and on the other, the initially very strong Putin supporter Masha Drokova, as the main character. The strength of the film is that we get so close to the young Putin supporters and the youth organization for Putin's political party, NASHI, and that the film follows the life of a young person who gradually loses her faith in her hero and gets closer to the critical views of the journalist. We get a close-up feeling of the mentality and beliefs of Putin supporters, but also the clashes with the opposition in the streets of Russia or in the media. What the film reveals is a very immature democracy with beatings and imprisonment of the opposition, unfair media control and widespread corruption, and also how political opponents try to prevent others from demonstrating and expressing their opinions. The deeds of NASHI are therefore often of a violent, criminal nature, shown in a series of dark/white night pictures. In the last part of the film Masha is gradually transformed by her meeting with the critical journalist and people around her: her democratic, humanitarian side wins.

But corruption and authoritarian tendencies in Russia are nothing compared to the pictures painted by documentary filmmakers of new countries in Africa, or life inside one of the world's last communist dictatorships, North Korea. BBC's *Mugabe's Blood Diamonds* (2011) brings us inside a torturing system of suppression and exploitation, based on the global sale of diamonds. But in Danish director Mads Brügger's drama-documentary *The Ambassador* (2011), the critical unravelling of widespread corruption in Africa is not just tied to one country and one dictator, but to a network also involving Western countries and interests. The film is unusual in that the director appears under a false identity as Liberian ambassador to the Central African Republic (CAR), an identity bought through European middle men, and on top of that large parts of the film are shot with hidden cameras. His fake project is to establish a match factory in CAR, and in doing so he bribes his way through the system. But through this fake documentary arrangement we get into the circle of corruption on a global scale, both inside and outside Africa; the director manages to go where no open journalist could ever go. The film demonstrates, according to statements made in it, that there is a global war in Africa between the new and upcoming power China, and the old powers of Europe and the US. It is a film about continuation and change in global exploitation of underdeveloped countries, about the reconfiguration and transformation of imperialism.

In his other drama-documentary *The Red Chapel,* the undercover dimension and hidden camera is abandoned, but the director and his crew travel under false pretences. He is given access as a journalist from the Danish public service broadcaster DR – which is quite true – but he claims to be interested in cultural exchange and in setting up a comedy show in North Korea. Mads Brügger negotiated the project and the conditions for the filming inside North Korea for several months but finally got the permission. During the whole stay the crew was, however, under constant surveillance, all their film material was checked every day, and on top of that, they were constantly filmed. Nevertheless Brügger succeeded in demasking an inhuman, authoritarian society in ways not seen before, and the film made an impression as shown by the fact that it won the Nordic Panorama and the Sundance Film Festival main prizes for best documentary. Through the use of humour and an innocent face of friendship, and by using Danish-Koreans as part of the crew, *The Red Chapel* managed to get as close to ordinary North Koreans as is presumably possible under the present circumstances. The film also managed to document how the system and its representatives stage reality and control the life of every single individual.

Corporate globalization and global crisis

If it hadn't been before, the global economic crisis that hit in 2008 has made it crystal-clear that we live in globally integrated and intertwined societies and economies. The fall of a major bank in one country, the burst of even a small national economy can send shockwaves through our lives and start a political process on a regional and global basis that is more intense than anything seen before. The earlier crisis of the 1930s and the global war that followed was already a sign of this, but since those days the corporate globalization, and the political and media dimension of globalization, has grown dramatically. Charles Ferguson's academy award-winning *Inside Job* (2010) is a very critical portrait of corporate globalization and the political crisis management that goes with it. But films on this topic have been made by both PBS, the BBC, Channel 4 and more independent filmmakers.

Inside Job takes the Iceland case as a pedagogical starting point. Iceland is one of the smallest, most developed and well functioning societies in the world, with a high living standard and a very clean environment. But when the government started a broad deregulation of the economy, allowing big multinational corporations to move in, and followed up by privatizing major banks, the result was a shock to society that made the country bankrupt in the space of a few years. The argument in the film is that the privatization and deregulation created an economic bubble where banks and investors borrowed more than ten times the total state budget abroad, and invested it in dubious and partly global projects. The film points to the greed of institutions, investors and individual financial speculators, and to a lack of global control and overview. Unemployment tripled and many people lost jobs, houses and savings – widespread protests and a political earthquake followed.

Figures 7c and d: Charles Ferguson's *Inside Job* (2010). Global financial crisis and the failures of global politics and control. Frame grab. Cinematography: Alex Heffes.

This initial case points to the film's basic arguments and documentation of the US and global crisis in general – the same mechanism at work. But the film demonstrates the global spread and details of the crisis through a careful media montage of clips demonstrating the basic facts and it also takes us back to the history of crisis and financial politics since the 1930s, and especially points to the republicans' deregulation philosophy from Reagan onward, a deregulation politics continued by democrats. Part of this policy was to allow huge mergers between companies and sectors, thus creating very big, global corporations that eventually played a central role in the 2008 crisis. A large part of the film deals with an analysis of the patterns of a very unhealthy loan and investment policy which gradually created the bubble economy that burst. Part of the critique raised by the film is also that these big corporations have laundered money for, or sustained, very dubious political regimes around the world, quite apart from being condemned for different forms of fraud and corruption. It's a film about global corporate capitalism running out of control, about a financial capital based on false, fake or weak values, and also about a corporate financial lifestyle that has gone over the top. But it is also a film about a political system that seems unfit or unable to perform the kind of national and global control and regulation that is needed.

Inside Job is, despite a very outspoken, critical tone, a very well documented film with lots of statistical data, interviews with those involved and experts, and with clips from a huge number of congressional hearings and from media coverage of the global crisis. The film has a broad, structural analysis of corporate globalization, as does a film like Mark Achbar and Jennifer Abbott's *The Corporation* (2003), while other films have a more focused approach to one type of corporation and their problematic role in globalization, for instance, Danish Frank Piasecki Poulsen's *Blood in the Mobile* (2010). The Canadian film *The Corporation* has a rather unusual social-psychological approach to the understanding and criticism of the modern corporation, and seems to deal with corporate culture as a kind of deviant psychopathic behaviour. Through a rapid, and sometimes almost satirical montage of images – including some from fictional films and commercials – and by drawing on a huge number of historical parallels and developments, the film puts forward a diagnosis of a corporate culture growing like cancer on the body of global society, a global network of personalities and institutions with incredible power. Despite the satirical tone of the whole film and the collage of sounds and images, *The Corporation* gives us serious historical and contemporary information on corporations in society through interviews with a wide spectrum of experts.

Michael Moore, who is actually interviewed in the film, is of course a central director in the criticism of modern corporate capitalism and the corporate dominance of politics, finance and the everyday life of ordinary Americans. Already in *Roger and Me* (1989) he went for General Motors and their role in ruining Moore's own hometown Flint, Michigan, one of the central places for automobile production. But this more local and national story of a big American corporation is expanded to a larger, global picture in *Capitalism: A Love Story* (2009) – following the 2008 crisis. In Moore's usual bulldozer style and with heavy use of satirical montage and footage from a wide variety of sources, the film tries to pin down those responsible for the meltdown in 2008, both in the political sphere and in corporate America. Like *The Corporation,* there is also a broader historical tale of the development of modern, corporate capitalism, but the film has a more political, activist tendency that seems to play into the later Occupy Wall Street movement. The satirical tone is clearly indicated during the opening texts where we see bank robbers, followed by images of ancient Rome, mixed with modern corporate images. We get the message: bank robbers are running the American empire.

The satire is thick when Moore enters big banks and corporations in Wall Street to claim back the money he and the American people have lost, or when he puts police tape around some banks to indicate that they should be arrested. But the real social message of the film is also clearly indicated as we witness ordinary people being evicted from their houses, kicked out of their jobs and living on next to nothing. The film is an intelligent, satirical and historical critique of the development of capitalism, made with clips from a broad variety of popular culture images, but also interviews. It's corporate America against ordinary people's America, as always in Moore's deeply critical documentaries.

Poulsen's *Blood in the Mobile* is extremely critical toward the activities of global corporate players, and goes deeper into the actions of one particular company. The film looks at the consequences of their business behaviour on the environment and working conditions of people in developing countries. Poulsen's film combines a classical journalistic strategy with a Michael Moore-like presence of the director. The film deals with the excavation of minerals in the Bisie mine in Congo, minerals necessary for mobile phones. But as the film points out, the minerals are excavated without respect for even the most basic security and safety of workers, among them kids working in these mines. The mines are run by unscrupulous warlords who kill, torture and keep workers and their families almost as prisoners, and the money from the mines is used to finance regimes without respect for democracy and human rights. It is a story about big, global corporations in the Western highly developed world who indirectly support authoritarian regimes and undermine the lives of ordinary people. Poulsen puts himself into the film by trying to confront his own mobile phone company, Finnish-based Nokia, with this reality and make them change strategy – without achieving anything and without even getting any real contact with those responsible in the corporation. After the premiere of the film, Nokia did, however, react and declared they would start looking at the problem. Sometimes film can make a difference.

Examples like this show different strategies in more independent documentary films dealing with the global crisis and global corporate culture. However, PBS, the BBC and Channel 4 have also made a great number of documentaries on corporate culture and the crisis. PBS seem to have made this one of their major themes after 2008, with programmes like *The Madoff Affair* (2009), *Inside the Meltdown* (2009), *Breaking the Bank* (2009), *Bigger than Enron* (2010), and most recently, *Money, Power and Wall Street* (1–2, 2012). The BBC made, for example, *The Year Britain's Bubble Burst* (2008) and Channel 4, *The Ascent of Money* (2009). *The Ascent of Money* is a whole series of six programmes with Niall Ferguson, professor of economic history, as the anchor person. The story told, and the realities documented, in these television documentaries are basically the same as in the more outspoken, independent and critical documentaries: it is about a global capitalism going into overdrive, about a deregulation by politicians that has stripped the old financial system of all its safeguard mechanisms, and it is about greedy CEOs and companies pushing everything to the limit, and eventually, over the top. This characteristic can be found in the voiceover to PBS's *Bigger Than Enron*, dealing with one of the biggest scandals and showing that big companies often seem to be more in the fiction business than in an economic reality, but which also demonstrates that the political system was as much to blame for not acting. The Enron affair was a spectacular and symbolic example of what was going on already before the general crisis in 2008. The affair is also told in a very dramatic documentary by Alex Gibney, *Enron – the Smartest Guys in the Room* (2005) for HDNet. The fact that this company could go from being the seventh biggest company in the US to bankruptcy in just one year and the very clear ties between Enron, the Bush administration and key politicians, makes this story one of the most clear and spectacular examples of corporate capitalism gone wrong. Gibson tells the story with a focus on the business strategies that led to the downfall, the psychology and lifestyle of the people involved in leading the company, and the congressional hearings after the fall. The film leaves the impression of the key persons in this financial sector living recklessly in the fast lane without thinking of the costs and the social consequences, and it shows a political system whose mechanisms of control are malfunctioning or simply not in place.

Colonial past and global presents

Part of the global heritage is the colonial past, the exploitation and suppression of countries in Asia and Africa by Western countries. The colonial past still frames and influences much of the structures and power relations in the present global era. In the former colonies authoritarian and brutal local regimes have often taken over, sometimes in combination with global corporate or political interest, but workers in these parts of the world are also trying to cope with globalization and to develop new democratic societies. This is the theme of American-Danish director Joshua Oppenheimer, whose global documentaries also represent new experimental forms, and ways of giving a voice to people in the global periphery. His most spectacular experiment so far is *The Act of Killing* (2012), which is about the decline of the Indonesian democracy after the de-colonization and independence in 1945 and the cruel suppression of the political opposition in the 1960s. The unusual thing about this film is that Oppenheimer lets the executioners, those that did the killing with the blessing of the military, the police and the authoritarian regime, tell their story. And it is even more amazing that they still seem proud of what they have done. In front of the camera these men stage a reenactment of what they did, inspired by American musicals and gangster films. The film lets us inside the mind and mentality of killers, but also shows us what seems to be the beginning of remorse and psychological breakdown.

The Act of Killing is about the globalization of politics in the sense that it brings a problem that is connected to a colonial past, and part of a global problem, into the Western documentary tradition. But in Joshua Oppenheimer and Christine Cynn's remarkable documentary *The Globalization Tapes* (2003), we have an example of a film made in close collaboration with plantation workers and their union in Sumatra, and developed as part of what the film calls 'an inspiration to workers around the world to take control of the globalization process'. The film takes the national fight for a welfare state and democracy to a global level, and confronts a liberal, free trade business- and economy-based concept of globalization with another more collective understanding of global solidarity and control of markets and finances. By taking up this perspective, the film contributes to an alternative global development where the imbalance in working conditions and worker's rights between the developed and developing countries is seen as part of the problem, a difference used by the global firms, for instance to outsource.

The Globalization Tapes is a significant and different film about globalization, because it shows workers in the developing world as producers of the story of their own lives, and because the film clearly illustrates that they have clear ideas and strategies for their future. The two directors in a way act as co-directors with the workers, but at the same time they have added a broader context to the film, in terms of a more professional visual language, for instance when the film illustrates how important the plantation products are for consumers all over the world. The workers also show a pretty good knowledge of ownership structures and economic structures in the business they are working in. The film demonstrates, with both realistic images and stories from the workers' everyday life, and with satire and irony, how old forms of global exploitation of developing countries are now replaced by more hidden economic mechanisms and forms of exploitation. Authoritarian regimes in developing countries are establishing relations with global corporations in order to exploit workers for their own purposes, and the film illustrates how difficult it is for workers to organize unions and fight for their rights. But the workers in the film also clearly state that there is no alternative to globalization, and that they will have to organize globally to fight for their rights.

Another prolific director in this investigation into global realities of working conditions and exploitation is Austrian Michael Glawogger. In his film from 2005, *Workingman's Death,* he looks into what is happening to the hard physical work that we in the West tend to see as disappearing because of technological developments. But what Glawogger shows us with often shocking cruelty is that this work is still there, but more invisible and, to a large degree, outsourced to developing countries or to migration workers in our own backyard. The film also, with the use of visual archive material, compares the way this kind of work was celebrated, for instance in the early film tradition, where physical work and workers were almost heroes. Here a more mundane and down-to-earth attitude is taken – this work is better than no work. In the five parts of the film we visit meat workers in Port Harcourt Nigeria, ship-breaking yard workers in Pakistan, sulphur workers in East Java, Indonesia, freelance miners in Ukraine and steel workers in China.

Glawogger's documentary shows the cruel realities of hard work on a global scale, and the film contributes to a strong tendency in modern documentaries to document the impact of globalization on the lives of workers and ordinary people around the world. In a way these documentaries are doing the same to global work and realities as the early documentary movement did on a national basis: they open the eyes of the public to a reality unknown to most, and they thereby contribute to a critical, democratic global dialogue, and they certainly have the potential to expand the global imagination of audiences around the world. Michael Glawogger's *Megacities* (1998) is an example of this. Like *Workingman's Death*, this is not about a particular national context, but about life in a transnational era, where work, economy, politics and everyday life in one part of the world is directly linked to, and dependent on, conditions in other parts of the world. *Megacities* could be called global, urban anthropology because the film tells stories about work and everyday life in twelve episodes shot in the slum areas of Mumbai, Mexico City, New York and Moscow. It is a film about the global proletariat and their fight to survive and rise above the hardest and must humble conditions.

Megacities is a truly global documentary, with a multi-plot structure taking us to Mumbai, New York, Mexico City and Moscow and telling stories about people living on the edge of society or under appalling work and life circumstances. Glawogger himself has called it a film about how to survive in a global reality, but he has also pointed to the fact that even though the film shows people living a terrible life in sometimes very gloomy parts of the world, it is also a film that wants to change our attitude and image of 'the rest of the world'. Behind the 'mostly bad news as observed from our colonial touristic perspective, we do not see the reality, the real people living here, and we do not see them having the same struggles and dreams that we all have' (Glawogger, in press release for film, my translation). The subtitle of the film is therefore 'Twelve stories about surviving'.

The structure and visual form of the film is lively, almost chaotic and far from just gloomy realism. The Mumbai sequences, for instance, move us through neighbourhoods, places and different activities – music performances, family life, street scenes, train rides full of people – and finally focus on a man living by showing film on a very primitive hand-driven film machine. Where the rest of the world live in an advanced, digital media culture, here we are way back in history, with the side street shopkeepers representing a very non-modern way of life and work. Work is done manually with ancient tools and machines. The images from Mexico City are just as chaotic and bustling, with forms of life and work that are quite different from modern Western societies and big cities. But the basic intention of the film also rings through clearly, because we see people under different conditions but with the same activities and hopes as the rest of us.

Part of the work shown in the film is hard, dangerous and dirty, it is work with a classical physical, human dimension. The value produced is directly related to a physical activity. It is, among other things, the sheer physicality of the work, the dirt and lack of regulated working conditions that is striking in the film's portrait of the global realities. This is also the case with the Moscow sequences, which confront people living under normal circumstances, their voices heard reading in trains and waiting at the station, and those living on the street. Work is not central here, although we see the cleaning ladies; the sequences deal with dreams and hopes, just as other sequences from other megacities actually focus on aspects of everyday life connected to love, happiness and joy. One of the Mexico sequences is a strong and revealing portrait of the work of female prostitutes, another critical look into a global reality, but shown without moral overtones.

The form used in the different stories varies. In the Moscow sequence called 'The fairytale', focus is on dreams of another life, illustrated by the reading of a story during work at an assembly line, music contrasting heavy industrial work, or family scenes with television images. Glawogger is a master in making contrasting layers in his film. Another example is the hectic New York sequence called 'The Hustler' about hustlers on the street, shot almost as a rap tune and performance. Extreme realism is often combined with creative and expressive dimensions, even though the basic feeling is that of living under hard conditions. In one of the Moscow sequences dealing with alcoholic men, Glawogger makes women sing out their disappointment with men and husbands, while we see the men being taken to prison or medical treatment.

The mediatization of global politics

Just as the national media have developed a much closer look at politics and politicians backstage, so has the coverage of international news and the links between media across borders, in the existing national media, the new global 24-hour media and internet-based media. But covering global news and affairs in general puts a high demand on resources of individual broadcasters or publishers, which do not nearly match what is available for global players and governments. The amount of spin and use of strategic, political communication has been on the rise in modern democracies, because the media have penetrated our daily lives much more than previously. In documentary film and television this merging of spin in a more complicated, global information network, and the rise of a stronger and more diverse global media coverage, has given rise to an often critical and self-reflexive form of documentary dealing with the role of media in global politics. The dramatic case of Wikileaks also indicates what is at stake in a new media order where the control of the flow of information seem to be slipping from the usual political or journalistic gatekeepers. But in this form of documentary we also find very critical reporting on corporate media and their potentially corrupt alliances with the political or business power elite.

In the four-part PBS series *News Wars* (2007) this self-reflexive criticism takes its starting point in the first year after 9/11 and the fact that the spin on Iraq before the invasion was largely supported by even the most independent media like the *New York Times*. This indicates the difficulty of even large, national media to see through stories planted carefully by the government, simply because the power to break and see through intelligence fabricated by big government institutions is difficult – especially in a national atmosphere of patriotism. As researchers have demonstrated, the global collaboration between security agencies was growing (Svendsen 2010), a collaboration that was not matched by collaboration between news media. It became even more important that the media performed the role as global watchdog, but the conditions for doing that were not improved fast enough, although the access to internet information greatly enhanced work done in the global media environment. *News Wars* gives evidence of this development and talks to key figures inside the media, politics and the intelligence community. The programme also gives a rather detailed, historical analysis of how the relation between media and politics has developed since the 1960's, it looks into both network news, for instance ABC and CBS, and other media, and notices the decline of longer slots for critical, investigative journalism and documentary – like *CBS Reports, 60 Minutes, Dateline* etc. The commercial development and competition has taken a large toll on critical, independent reporting.

Figures 7e and f: John Pilger's *The War You Don't See* (2010). John Pilger talking about government influence on the media, but the film also deals with the power of media to expose misuse of power. Frame grab. Cinematography: Rupert Binsley.

A similar British film by John Pilger with both historical and contemporary dimensions is *The War You Don't See* (2010), but here the cases analyzed are mostly to do with war reporting. The film starts with startling images of the killing of civilians in Baghdad and jumps directly to equally candid images of soldiers killed during the First World War, the link being that the media did not report it and thus it was unknown to the public. The film looks mainly at how the media report wars, along with the decisions to go to war, and how the connections have been between governments, the military and the media. It also points to similarities between the selling of cigarettes and other goods, and the selling of war. For instance, experts explain how the Pentagon works to sell their politics and how they influence and address the media, something that for instance Dan Rather from CBS acknowledges as a problem in connection with the war in Iraq. The programme also goes into the problems of embedded journalism in modern media and journalism, and we get very strong and emotional clips of war episodes, mainly dealing with civilian casualties that were not reported at the time. The historical sequences that link the present with the past are equally disturbing. The programme is also interesting by taking us all the way up to our internet age, featuring an interview with Wikileaks founder Julian Assange, and a description of their project of uncovering the unseen and untold.

One of the most interesting documentaries about global news is the independent, American film by Jehane Noujaim, *Control Room* (2004). It is one of the few films that manages to get inside a major non-Western news broadcaster, Al Jazeera, before and during the invasion of Iraq. The film throws new light on the global media sphere by letting us follow how Al Jazeera handles the balance between its 20 million Arab viewers and viewers in the rest of the world, and also how the station operates and gets its sources from around the world, not least among them the US Central Command (CENTCOM). Views from CNN, NBC and Al Jazeera reporters are mixed in the film in connection with the war reporting, but we also learn about the channel's history and the fact that it is controversial in many Arab countries, although widely watched, because many Arab regimes consider it too independent and critical.

The film is also a dramatic, unfolding story of news coverage just before the Iraq War breaks out. One of the controversial issues in Al Jazeera's coverage is that they show pictures of both civilian casualties – including dead women and children – and at one point also dead American soldiers. Seen from the American point of view this is propaganda, and showing dead soldiers is even a violation of the Geneva Convention. But the discussions with US journalists and the CENTCOM military representative develop into an interesting intercultural dialogue where both sides change their positions, or at least, learn to understand and tolerate each other. The film is particularly dramatic during the American bombing of Al Jazeera's office in Baghdad, a bombing seen by many as a direct attempt to intimidate the station. This belief in the Al Jazeera newsroom is, of course, greatly influenced by the well-documented public attacks by Rumsfeld and others on the station for being a propaganda station for terrorism.

Control Room thus demonstrates interesting and deep divisions in global media culture between the traditionally completely dominant Western media, and the upcoming new global players from the Arab world. Al Jazeera's position is clearly illustrated by the fact that the station is declared propagandistic in their reporting by both the American government and by Arab governments, but for completely different reasons. The programme also shows how representatives of CENTCOM complain over bias, and try to change their coverage, but how a new growing feeling of the need for diversity in global reporting is also developing. The fact that the film is made by Jehane Noujaim, an American but with an Arab background, furthermore points in the direction of a pluralization of global media. It is not just the rise of new media with global reach in other regions of the world, it is also about Western media getting more and more journalists with different regional and cultural backgrounds that make it possible for them to report with an increasing 'inside' understanding from different regions.

Old media empires and the new digital media culture

The interest in the role of the media on a more global scale is of course also very much oriented towards the role of global media corporations, and here the empire of Rupert Murdoch has been in focus. The BBC has made *Murdoch – Breaking the Spell* (2011), a very critical, investigative film about Murdoch's empire following the UK scandal at his newspaper *News of the World*. A similar American film is Robert Greenwald's *Outfoxed: Rupert Murdoch's War on Journalism* (2004), which deals with Murdoch's American media empire, especially Fox News. The BBC programme is a classical, journalistic portrait of Murdoch's rise to become the most powerful media mogul in the UK – with a wide global reach – through his newspaper empire, News International, and the television station Sky News. The programme documents his deep connections to, among other things, the political and cultural elite, the police, and not least, the illegal and corrupt working methods employed in order to gain influence and find news. The focus is, of course, on the 2011 hacking scandal that brought down the newspaper *News of the World*, which was closed, but which, as the programme clearly demonstrates, only temporarily hurt Murdoch's British and global empire. Despite the critical hearings following the scandal, and the widespread disgust over the methods of *News of the World*, not least the hacking of a dead girl's phone during the police investigation of the case and the phone hacking of members of the royal family, Murdoch has come back.

Robert Greenwald's film *Outfoxed* is perhaps even more aggressive and profound in its criticism, and one of the important strategies of the film is going backstage in Fox News concepts, working procedures, and through in-depth interviews with several former employees at the television station. At the beginning of the film Bob McChesney, a media expert, uses a scene from *Godfather* to talk about US media politics as dominated by lobbyists going for the biggest slice of the cake, behind closed doors and outside the eyes of the public. Murdoch's US and global empire is a rime example of this, and between interviews with people describing his empire we get cartoon-like sequences with data and images of the reach of his global empire. Former employees talk openly about news production as a kind of propaganda for points of views and people that Murdoch wanted promoted, quite contrary to the official statements of the CEO and Murdoch himself. Some of the former employees speak anonymously because they are afraid that open statements might hurt their career. Interviewees talk about a 'culture of fear' where you were monitored and under surveillance. The allegations are substantiated by quotes from internal memos and other documents that define in some detail how stories should be made, and what kind of discourse and direction they should have. But the film also gives many examples of actual news items from Fox News where the principles and editing techniques are seen in practice. So in many ways this film is more about the Murdoch empire's degradation of journalism and direct harm to democracy, than about the Murdoch empire as a global institution and the collaboration with certain power elites. However, the film demonstrates a station supporting and promoting patriotic right-wing ideology; it is simply partisan politics disguised as journalism.

But in the age of global Internet – at least to most parts of the world – stories on what this Internet can do to improve democracy and enhance transparency in global reporting are beginning to emerge. The fact that numerous websites are beginning to appear as part of the global news feed is a challenge to the way the traditional media work, and at the same time the Internet in itself has become an important part of how journalists work and get their information and sources. The case of Julian Assange and Wikileaks seems to be the symptomatic and dramatic story of conflicts and possibilities contained within the Internet in the hands of information activists, and the often complicated alliances hackers and information activists make with mainstream media. One of the first longer documentary programmes on Wikileaks was made by Swedish SVT, *Wikileaks – med läcken som vapen/ Wikirebels – the Documentary* (2010), a programme made just after the Swedish rape case against Assange started and Wikileaks ended in serious problems after the arrest of the American informer Bradley Manning. Still, the programme depicts Wikileaks as the leading global power in a new world of digital activists, and the portrait of Assange is as 'the scarlet pimpernel of the digital age', even though this role has become tainted, and Wikileaks' role as defender of freedom of information is problematized. But the programme also gives us the story of the collaboration between this scarlet pimpernel and some of the most prestigious quality newspapers in the world: the *Guardian*, the *New York Times* and *Der Spiegel*.

This theme is given more critical focus in British director and BAFTA winner Patrick Forbes' Channel 4 documentary *Wikileaks: Secrets and Lies* (2011). Here we get a first hand backstage story not just from the perspective of Assange and other Wikileaks representatives, but even more from the newspaper journalists they cooperated with on the launching of the three packages of documents in 2010: The Afghan warlogs, The Iraq Warlogs and the US diplomacy cables. PBS also made *Wikisecrets* (2011), where the story of the American soldier Bradley Manning is naturally more in focus and we get the story from an American perspective. Forbes' Channel 4 documentary clearly wants to unfold the whole story of Wikileaks from its beginning in 2006 until its downfall in 2011. Assange himself and one of his former right-hand men, Domscheit-Berg, are interviewed throughout the film and the project is seen as a project born out of idealism. It is in Assange's own words a project of empowerment through information, it is about abolishing censorship, which reveals the fear of reform by knowledge.

But both the Channel 4 and PBS films are also rather critical towards the way the Wikileaks project develops. The journalists at the *Guardian*, the *New York Times* and *Der Spiegel*, who first express admiration and fascination for Assange and his project, gradually start seeing him as rather self-promoting, and even as untruthful. Both the Channel 4 and PBS documentary pay tribute to the fact that the publication of the very first video on YouTube showing American forces killing innocent people, among them two Reuters journalists, was an important act of counter-information. The video was seen by 11 million people in a very short time and has certainly contributed to a global knowledge of how US troops have violated basic principles of warfare. In the same way, the spreading of the Afghanistan and Iraq warlogs have lead to the revealing of massive violations of human rights and killing of innocents in both wars to a degree not documented by the mainstream press. There is also no doubt that the publishing of the Documentary Cables has played a role in the Arab Spring uprisings, because the documents revealed how the corrupt power elite actually behaved and used their power.

However, neither of the two programmes want to paint an uncritical, heroic image of an internet rebel and idealist. The position of the political systems and the military against Assange, and especially Bradley Manning, for espionage and treason is not supported by any of the programmes, although spokesmen for those positions are interviewed and quoted in the films. But both films raise the question of how to get more information, transparency and accountability into global politics, and point to the important role to be played in accomplishing this goal by IT grassroots and activists in some kind of collaboration with professional media institutions and journalists used to working with critical, investigative journalism. Both films go into details with how this collaboration between Wikileaks and quality newspapers like the *Guardian*, the *New York Times*, *Der Spiegel*, *Le Monde* and *El País* is established, organized and developed. The programmes also show how the political and military system work to try to prevent the leaks, how a whole department in CIA is dedicated to Wikileaks and the like, and how one of the things that caused Manning to be discovered and arrested was his very 'open' use of, and communication through, social media. One of the problems with Wikileaks' sometimes completely unedited versions of leaks was furthermore that some of the information could be dangerous for innocent persons and civilians. So the films point to the dilemma facing a policy of complete transparency and openness in the global information society: who can decide where the limits of openness and transparency are? Nevertheless, the case of Wikileaks illustrates the mediation of politics in a more and more global world, where the spreading of information can happen with a speed and outreach unprecedented in history. The traditional media have not lost their importance in the global media sphere, but the conditions have changed and the balance between non-professional actors and media institutions and media professionals has shifted.

Chapter 8

A multicultural world: migration, culture and everyday life

That we live in a multicultural world cannot be contested, but this empirical fact of modern, global life creates tensions and even violent conflicts, and it raises the question of the relation between basic, universal norms and rights, cultural differences and tolerance. Multiculturalism is a complex and contested concept in philosophy, anthropology and politics, and generally attempts to develop *normative* theories of multiculturalism can create serious problems. In the book *Adskillelsens politik: Multikulturalisme – ideologi og virkelighed* (2008; English edition, *The Democratic Contradictions of Multiculturalism* 2012) – written partly in response to the Danish cartoon crisis in 2005 – the Danish cultural historian Frederik Stjernfelt, and his co-author Martin Eriksen, search for the roots of the modern concepts of multiculturalism. They find some of those roots in the concept of culture as expounded by the founding texts of anthropology, and they point to a problematic tendency to understand cultures as more self-contained and closed towards other cultures than is often the case. Referring to Ruth Benedict's influential book in anthropology, *Patterns of Culture* (1934), they uncover an understanding that leads not only to seeing cultures as closed homogenous units, but also a cultural relativism where they all have an equal value and status. But as they point out, such a concept could undermine the ability to see universal elements across all cultures and the openness of, and interaction between, them. Behind normative concepts of multiculturalism, claiming to defend the diversity of cultures, we may find a very strong cultural essentialism. Contrary to what is indicated in Stjernfelt and Eriksens's book, the anthropological concept of culturalism is not necessarily relevant for more philosophical theories on multiculturalism. In the liberal tradition of multiculturalism, for instance Kymlicka (see below), the arguments for some kind of support for minority cultures are not based on culturalism but are derived from the liberal principle of equal opportunities and thus based on universalism.

Pragmatic approaches to our multicultural reality

In the Danish documentary anthology film *Mit Danmark* ('My Denmark', 2007) – introduced as a documentary response to the cartoon crisis in Denmark in 2005, where drawings of the prophet Mohammed in the Danish newspaper Jyllands-Posten incited an attack on Denmark in a number of Arab countries and media – we find both a pragmatic portrait and defence of a multicultural reality, and a problematization of essentialism. The film was launched as an initiative to bring together Danish and Arab voices, and Danish directors have created ten portraits of foreigners in Denmark in collaboration with those portrayed. It is a story of different Danes living in the same reality but with different norms and lifestyles. As a film project of cultural understanding and tolerance, it presents stories of a multicultural Denmark by diving into everyday life and trying to get behind the ideological conflicts and cultural 'iron curtains'. It is somewhat of a paradox that Denmark, being one of the countries in Europe with the lowest percentage of non-Western immigrants and foreigners in general, became the site of the cartoon crisis. But on the other hand Denmark, like other European countries, has gone through a period with a strong anti-immigrant policy, with strong demands for assimilation and a re-nationalization of cultural values and norms among the liberal-conservative parties.

The ten short films in the anthology film *My Denmark* are different in form and subject, and they portray both quite ordinary Danes with a different ethnic background along with well known public figures. Some of the films deal with experiences of conflict and racism, but others show that in normal everyday life Danes and people with foreign backgrounds live together quite peacefully, despite the cultural and religious differences sometimes involved. In the second film, Birgitte Stærmose makes a portrait of Janus Nabil Bakrawi, a well-known and popular Danish actor, born in Denmark to a mother with Polish background and a Palestinian father. His story is probably typical: he grew up and felt completely like a Dane, and he did not believe himself to be different. But in the film he speaks about the growing feeling that he was different in other people's eyes: an immigrant, a stranger. 'It was very strange,' he says, 'suddenly to get another identity created from the outside.' Around the age of 18 this resulted in a temporary attempt to actually connect with the Arab-Muslim identity, but with the result that he became strange both in the eyes of his Danish and Arab friends. He seemed caught in between two identities that were not his, so in an ironic final statement he says: 'I am not Danish in the cultural sense often identified with that. My name is Janus, I live in Copenhagen, that is my home, my Denmark.'

What the story clearly illustrates is Denmark as a multicultural society in a sociological, descriptive sense of the word. Danes – whether ethnic Danes, Danes with another ethnic background, or immigrants and foreigners living in Denmark – have different backgrounds and stories. There is no essential Danishness that all share, and probably class differences, regional differences and differences in education and mode of life are more important than cultural and ethnic differences in a more narrow sense. *My Denmark* deals with new ethnic Danes, but many documentaries dealing with Danes show big differences in Danish culture between other groups of Danes. If we go further into the sociology of everyday life and culture among Danes, even without taking foreigners and immigrants into consideration, Danish culture is not a homogeneous culture.

Much of what we may consider to be indigenous culture has roots in our interaction with other cultures and nations. A given national culture can of course be homogeneous, although based on imports and interactions with other cultures over a long historical period. But what national conservatives refer to as national culture is very often seen as based on a language and a culture developed as part of a natural, home-grown tradition. But even

Figures 8a and b: Birgitte Stærmose's contribution to the anthology film *My Denmark* (2007). A portrait of the well-known Danish actor Janus Nabil Bakrawi with Palestinian-Polish parents and his confusions about who he is. Frame grab. Cinematography: Birgitte Stærmose.

before the intense, modern globalization of societies and cultures we had slower, though not less important, forms of globalization. Even though cultures cannot be seen in theory as 'closed worlds', the reality of our modern societies and the global world represents many examples of conflicts and wars based on what people see as basic cultural differences, and norms that cannot be reconciled.

A film like *My Denmark* clearly demonstrates that there are different cultural norms and traditions, but that they do not only follow ethnic lines and that behind cultural differences we are all very much alike. We are individuals with much the same universal aspirations and feelings *before* we are human beings belonging to a specific culture and a specific ethnic group. Collective attachments, social networks and cultural orientations are important for all humans, but we are not essentially tied to one culture, and cultural orientation and social networks may vary and change over time. But at the same time no human can only live in a universal culture, we are linked to our origins and our experiences in specific locations and parts of the world.

Concepts and politics of multiculturalism

A documentary collection of films like *My Denmark* points to everyday experiences and mental reactions to living in modern, globalized societies in which ethnic and cultural differences have become 'normal'. The fact that Western European societies are democracies, based on universal principles of equality and right, does not in itself secure tolerance and a cosmopolitan attitude towards people with different ethnic, cultural and religious backgrounds. Therefore the mere sociological fact of a multicultural reality in modern societies has given rise to numerous political and theoretical debates on multiculturalism.

In her book *The Claims of Culture: Equality and Diversity in the Global Era* (2002) the American political scientist and philosopher Seyla Benhabib defines a new and problematic use of culture which:

> risks essentializing the idea of culture as the property of an ethnic group or race; it risks reifying cultures as separate entities by overemphasizing their boundedness and distinctness; it risks overemphasizing the internal homogeneity of cultures in terms that legitimize repressive demands for communal conformity (p. 4)

Benhabib also points to the political consequences of this type of multiculturalism and culture concept, where the state keeps getting drawn into culture wars, because different cultural groups demand recognition and support to develop and protect their culture (p. 1). The criticism of the essentialist culture concept has much in common with the already mentioned criticism of the anthropological culture concept in Stjernfelt and Eriksen's book, and they acknowledge that in a footnote (Stjernfelt and Eriksen 2008: 466, note 43).

Benhabib tries to construct a position in which she accepts that cultural differences may seem very real and deep when viewed from the inside of a culture trying to define its boundaries versus other cultures, but at the same time, she sees all cultures as based on the same universal principles and types of narratives and actions. 'Cultures are formed through binaries because human beings live in an evaluative universe (...) human cultures are constant creations, recreations and negotiations of imaginary boundaries between 'we' and 'the others' (p. 7–8). Rather than the support and protection of cultures in order to preserve them as they are – either from a conservative or a progressive point of view – Benhabib talks about 'norms of universal respect and egalitarian reciprocity' (p. 11). Basically she sees cultures as expressions of fragile and open interactive processes, although in reality, cultures may seem to fence themselves off against others. A politics of multiculturalism in modern, global societies can therefore not be based on strategies to preserve group identities and collective cultures, although pragmatic political initiatives to secure democracy and equality can take forms of affirmative actions towards group cultures into consideration.

Benhabib's position seems to go against culture-based group support by the state and is very critical towards cultural essentialism. But the debate on multiculturalism is at the same time often very influenced by policies aimed at changing dominant patterns of what seems to be systematic marginalization or suppression of minorities, and certain underrepresented and unprivileged groups in society. In the thinking of Canadian philosophers Charles Taylor and Will Kymlicka, this position is developed to a politics of recognition towards certain group cultures, a politics developed in practice in Canadian law and politics since 1971, and further developed in *The Canadian Multicultural Act* (1988). Here the politics of multiculturalism is understood as a policy to sustain cultural and racial diversity as part of the Canadian cultural heritage through the elimination of barriers for equal rights and the recognition and support for different group cultures. This policy involves active support for different languages and multicultural products related to the different cultural groups (see www.immigrantwelcome.ca/Canada-multiculturalism-act).

This act has, as already mentioned, a philosophical background in thoughts that were later formulated in Charles Taylor's famous article 'The politics of recognition' (1992). Taylor goes against individualism and classical liberalism in the sense that he argues for the importance of cultural recognition as a basis for a good society and a well functioning democracy. If individual rights are not supported by the feeling that the culture one belongs to is recognized, democracy will lose value, according to Taylor. Cultural recognition of different groups is part of democracy. Will Kymlicka, another influential Canadian philosopher, also argues for a politics of multiculturalism, especially in *Multicultural Citizenship* (1995). Kymlicka makes a distinction between multiculturalism as an empirical, social reality and the politics and ethics of multiculturalism. What he tries to do is to bridge the gap between the liberal idea of individual freedom and rights, and instances where a politics of multiculturalism might be necessary in order to secure this individual freedom and right further. This line of thinking clearly has similarities with Taylor's politics of recognition, but Kymlicka stresses the liberal, individual dimensions more strongly (see also Stjernfelt and Eriksen 2008: 204ff).

As pointed out by Stjernfelt and Eriksen, it is not just the Canadian policy of multiculturalism that runs the danger of creating fixed and closed cultural spaces. This does not exclude the possibility of pragmatic use of cultural exemptions for certain groups, for instance the Danish exemption from the general law of wearing safety helmets when driving a motor bike, thus allowing Sikhs to drive with their turban. But on a general level this dilemma between universalism and multiculturalism can create serious conflicts between universal and cultural principles. This is clearly seen in the UN system, especially in the conflict between the UN and UNESCO. On the other hand the UN's General Assembly in 1948 passed the 'Universal Declaration of Human Rights', which clearly defines the rights of any individual regardless of age, sex, class, nationality etc. Articles 18 and 19 deal with freedom of thought, conscience, religion, opinion and expression and protect the individual's right to manifest but also to change religion and belief. As a whole, this declaration expresses the classical ideas and norms of liberal democracy and the tradition of the Enlightenment. But this declaration does not talk specifically about culture, multiculturalism or group rights other than in connection with the individual's right to manifest itself. In contrast to this, UNESCO has followed a more developed politics of multiculturalism to a degree that is potentially in conflict with the universal declaration.

Based on recommendations by the French anthropologist, Claude Lévi-Strauss (Stjernfelt and Eriksen 2008: 172), UNESCO in 1952 launched a global culturalism in which the global culture is seen as a coalition and collaboration between essentially different regional cultures. A consequence of this way of thinking is a kind of proactive support for a diversity of cultures, a global plurality of essentially distinct and different cultures. But behind this positive principle of cultural tolerance and understanding one can also see a potential undermining of a more universalist, cosmopolitan concept of globalization, where the same principles of freedom, democracy and rights apply to all humans, despite national and cultural affiliation. In the UNESCO declaration 174/EX 46 (2006), freedom of expression is suddenly linked to respect for cultural and religious values and symbols. This protection of cultural and religious values and symbols potentially indicates an essentialist culturalist position and a protection of cultural diversity that can also result in the suppression of freedom of speech and criticism of cultural and religious positions. Although it is important to protect people's right to their religion, it must never be a right that undermines the freedom of speech and the right to criticize religion. The concept of multicultural diversity hidden behind this discourse of global tolerance and understanding, seems at odds with modern global societies where individuals, ideas, communication, cultural forms and products are merging and interacting all the time.

Images and realities of a multicultural world

In a large-scale survey of how people all over the world think of immigration and what the truth is concerning the actual number of immigrants, the German Marshall Fund clearly demonstrates that people think there are more foreigners and immigrants in their country than is actually the case. In countries like the US and UK, who have a long tradition of being multicultural nations, the difference between what people think and imagine is the percentage of immigrants and what the reality is, is particularly big: in the US, immigrants only count for 12.5 per cent but people think it is 37.8 per cent, in the UK, it is 11.3 per cent vs 31.8 per cent. But the difference is also quite big in Germany, France, Italy and Spain, who take the majority of immigrants in the EU. In a small country like Denmark, the difference is much smaller: the actual number of immigrants is 7.9 per cent and people estimate that it is 8.9 per cent (German Marshall Fund 2011).

The fact that people exaggerate the number of immigrants may indicate that the public discourse on migration, and foreigners in general, has been high in both the media and global political agenda, especially after 2001 and the rise of the war against terrorism. The debate on our multicultural society is especially influenced by the Muslim and Arab immigrants and the images of this particular group, almost to the degree of a 'clash of civilizations', between the Muslim East and the Christian West. The worries expressed in a survey like this, where imagined immigration is much bigger than real immigration, are probably not just tied to security anxieties or cultural anxieties ('they are terrorists and they want to change our culture') but also to questions of threat to social welfare. As pointed out by the Danish philosopher Nils Holtug in an analysis of the Danish discussion on multiculturalism, 'Danish Multiculturalism, Where Art Thou?' (2012), 'In Denmark and many European countries, the immigration of non-Westerners primarily increases competition amongst relatively poor, low-skilled workers, who are also threatened by other effects of globalization such as outsourcing' (p. 204). These people are the core groups in the support for the xenophobic parties on the rise in Europe, whereas Eurobarometer statistics, generally, do not show an alarming rise in such anti-global and anti-immigrant attitudes.

If we take a broader historical look at immigration and multicultural issues in Europe and the US, it must be said that immigration and multicultural societies are not only a result of recent developments and modern forms of globalization. On the contrary: US history and self-image as the ethnic and cultural melting pot of the world, as the home of all those fleeing from tyranny and oppression dates way back. European history is somewhat different, but for centuries the inclusion of immigrants into the European nations has been quite significant, just as the relation between former nations under European empires have given rise to an influx from these former colonies. As Stephen Castles has pointed out in his analysis of European postwar immigration, immigrant groups, the markets and populations in the European colonies played an important role in the creation of the modern, European nation states (Castles 2012: 203). The role of immigration in European nation states developed in different ways, but perhaps the UK with its wide former empire can be considered the most advanced example of a multi-ethnic nation state.

Castles points out that the early strategies in Europe concerning the management of cultural and religious diversity fall into different categories: some countries have 'pillarized' structures with widespread support and autonomy for different religious and cultural groups (Netherlands, Belgium), others have had a stronger focus on assimilation and alignment of minority cultures with a dominant culture (Germany, Denmark, France for instance). The UK was the only nation where, the fact that it was an empire covering very wide and different areas, resulted in a strategy for assimilation of a rather large variety of ethnic, cultural and religious groups. But the new waves of migration after 1945 put a strain on all forms of management of cultural diversity that had worked during the formation of the modern nation states in the eighteenth and nineteenth century. But it is worth noting that the multicultural reality and political issue has been around for centuries in some form or other in both Europe and the US. The modern forms of globalization and multicultural challenges have a longer history in all nation states, and the conflicts and discourses connected with the modern politics of multiculturalism can often be explained with reference to a historical context and background.

The story of modern migration has some clear stages, as Castles points out: in the 1960s many Western countries were short of labour and invited guest workers or workers from their former colonies. By around 1973, when the crisis stopped this trend, there were already around 12 million guest workers in Western Europe. But on top of that there were refugees from Eastern Europe or from areas with war and famine. Added to this was the family reunion of guest workers and other immigrants and refugees. But even though we have seen an increase in the number of 'foreigners' in Western Europe and include the figure of what Castles calls 'the foreign born population' (that is those with an actual foreign nationality or born with one, even though now they have the nationality of their new country of residence), the figure from 2005 only comes to 39 million people in the OECD area, or 8 per cent of the total population (Castles 2012: 215). Even though we could also start talking about the children of former immigrants and refugees now naturally born and living in Europe and thus increase the number we are talking about, this is hardly a figure that can be characterized as a 'flood' of foreigners into Europe. Nevertheless this is sometimes what the political and cultural debate seems to indicate, and as we have already seen, people tend to exaggerate the actual number of foreigners in their country.

But the different forms of immigration and global movements have clearly led to a change in discourses over culture. The fact that new groups with other religions, cultural preferences, languages etc. enter has certainly put pressure on notions of national identity and culture as a given and homogeneous reality. As Castles points out:

> In a situation of insecurity, inequality and individualization, the assertion of national identity has taken on a new significance. It appears as a form of resistance against globalization, but is in fact impotent against the economic and political processes that have brought rapid change. Yet the nostalgia for myths of homogeneity can act as a powerful force of exclusion against immigrants and ethnic minorities. The latter are not only visible signs of globalization, but are also vulnerable to populist sentiments and actions (Castles 2012: 216).

This development creates a political paradox for European nations. On the one hand there seems to be a certain backlash in the acceptance of globalization and the fact that we live in a multicultural world. On the other hand Europe is facing a demographic crisis, with dropping birth rates that make immigration necessary if we want to preserve our welfare. The backlash also has cultural dimensions, for cultures thrive on interaction and exchange. If people start barricading themselves in closed cultures, traditional, national or new ethnic cultures, we kill the dynamic of modern culture and communication. We should not essentialize differences and create stereotypes of others: behind cultural differences lies a large common ground, universal principles and realities uniting us as human beings.

Cosmopolitanism and the understanding of diversity

The idea of cosmopolitanism, in its most general and abstract form, means looking at our global world with the focus on all the things that unite us and all the universal aspects of human society. Cosmopolitanism, as an idea, stresses the fact that we all, despite cultural and national differences, belong to a universal world community. But since we all belong to or have a background in some particular society or culture, or even several cultures and societies, cosmopolitanism and multiculturalism are both linked to the same global reality that we live in. In order to take a cosmopolitan stance to globalization we also need to acknowledge that we live in a multicultural reality, and that freedom and equality on a global scale may include elements of a multicultural policy. One of the strongest modern voices in favour of cosmopolitanism is the sociologist Ulrick Beck. In his book, *The Cosmopolitan Vision* (2006) he links the increased globalization to the necessity of developing a cosmopolitan vision for both politics and culture, a cosmopolitan outlook that is 'a global sense, a sense of boundarylessness. An everyday, historically alert, reflexive awareness of ambivalences in a milieu of blurring differentiations and contradictions' (Beck 2006: 3). In Beck's concept of cosmopolitanism he includes references to the fact that sociologically we do live in a multicultural world, but he rejects the notion of a world based on separate, nationally organized societies and exclusively different cultures. We need to realize that in the globalization of the present, further developed modernity, multicultural dimensions of our reality become natural. We need to realize that empathy and recognition of difference is not incompatible with a universal cosmopolitan position and that indeed – as always, but today even more – local, ethnic, national, religious, cultural and cosmopolitan cultures interact and mingle in many ways.

Many of the documentaries dealing with our multicultural world after 2000 move into different ethnic groups and cultures in a particular national space, but by doing that they contribute to a broader understanding and feeling of cosmopolitanism. They become a kind of ethnographic tale of a cosmopolitan world, seeking out the more invisible dimensions of everyday life in different ethnic and cultural groups. In this way they can give insights into 'otherness' but at the same time point to similarities between different cultures, the fact that we have much in common beneath a surface of difference. In Alexandra Pelosi's HBO-documentary, *Citizen USA: A 50 State Road Trip* (2011), she gives us what the Los Angeles Times called 'a joyful movie about America'. The film is based on a very simple idea and structure: we witness naturalization ceremonies around the US, we witness new Americans getting their US citizenship, and we hear them talk about why they chose the US as their new country. The film is a celebration of the US as a melting pot, of the success of integration and tolerance, acceptance and respect for others. The film manages to give snapshots of people and ceremonies in all 50 states, portraying people from more than 100 different nations, and illustrating that at least for all these immigrants, the American dream is true, and the road to freedom and a new life came through. On top of the many short life stories we get, the film also includes portraits of famous American immigrants and a short introduction to their story of becoming citizens, for instance, Madeleine Albright and Henry Kissinger.

In many ways Pelosi's film is an illustration of the American myth of a true multicultural society, and a portrait of a nation of colourful difference. It is an expression of the famous inscription on the Statue of Liberty of Emma Lazarus' poem: 'Give me your tired, your poor. Your huddled masses yearning to breathe free. The wretched refuse of your teeming shore. Send these the homeless, tempest-tossed to me. I lift my lamp beside the golden door.' The Statue of Liberty and the American dream is a powerful immigration myth of an open, multicultural society, and in many ways the huge number of successfully integrated people from all over the world points to a true reality. But behind this lies a different and much more complex reality, with ethnic, cultural, social and religious conflicts, just like in the European case. Both in American and European documentary traditions, the more cosmopolitan approach to the understanding of the multicultural reality therefore has forms and faces other than the celebratory.

US documentaries with a multicultural dimension have not been very high on the documentary agenda, although illegal immigration has been a political issue and the multicultural question has certainly surfaced in relation to the War on Terror as already pointed out. This might seem a paradox, given the fact that the US is one of the world's most multicultural countries. But recent developments have resulted in some documentaries trying to enter and explain other cultural groups after 2001. PBS's *Muslims* (2002) is such a programme with direct reference to 9/11, asking the question what a Muslim culture is. The programme was announced on PBS with the following text:

> Muslims make up one fifth of the world's population. But to most Americans they are a mystery. Islam shares its origins and principles with Judaism and Christianity, but still Islam is seen as a threat. Patriarchal, hostile to the West, militant Muslims stand accused of jeopardizing liberal values and Western democracy. The fears exist but are they justified? Tonight on Frontline, the many faces of Islam – a journey to the Middle East, to Africa and Asia, to Europe and America (PBS 2012b).

In the American context, this two hour programme is a very rare example of a documentary going deep into Arab and Muslim culture in several countries, including Iran, that will be viewed by other media and many Americans as simply the modern enemy of all that America stands for. But here, the image of the Muslim world is clearly shown as a rather heterogeneous culture with huge differences from country to country. Modern Muslim culture is shown in the programme through different experts in those countries, but also via interviews with ordinary citizens. PBS was also the only television station to launch an even broader series of documentaries under the general title *America at a Crossroads* (2007–2009), presenting the challenges facing America following 9/11. Twenty programmes were made, many of them focusing on American–Muslim issues, and in particular one of them, *The Muslim Americans* (2007), followed up on the programme on Muslims abroad, mentioned above, by looking inward.

The film shows how Muslims in America have reacted to 9/11 and the following War on Terror. It gives examples of Muslim Americans being discriminated against or even persecuted for just being Muslims, but it also shows that extremism and radicalism is not widespread in the Muslim American population and that the younger generation especially, are very engaged politically and otherwise in their local communities. By focusing on Muslims in America, this documentary does what is rarely done in mainstream media, it looks into the diversity of America's own culture, and confronts some of the crude stereotypes of Muslims both abroad and at home. It is a documentary clearly contributing to a cosmopolitan and nuanced understanding of our multicultural reality, a programme that gives a perceived 'enemy' a human face and character. But programmes in this series also include a critical looks at parts of the Muslim culture in the US. In *The Mosque in Morgantown* (2009) for instance, Asra Nomani takes us into a community in West Virginia where extreme forms of Islam and intolerance against others seem to flourish. This rather strong and confrontational documentary, that also created widespread debate, is an example of taking the universal principles of a cosmopolitan position seriously, and not falling into the trap of a cultural relativism and laissez-faire multiculturalism.

Ways of living – close encounters with 'the other'

The rather slim tradition of multicultural documentaries in the US is in contrast to the steady flow of programmes in Europe on these matters since the 1980s. Quite early on, for instance, the British Channel 4 defined itself as a channel devoted to exploring the multicultural and regional UK. A series of documentary programmes from the 1980s dealt with different ethnic groups and how their original culture and lifestyle mingled with the British, for instance, *Banding File* 1985–1991, *Eastern Eye* 1982–1985 and *Black on Black* 1982–1985. This tradition has also been strongly present in fiction dramas, some of them by directors with a mixed ethnic background, such as Gurinder Chadha with *Bend it like Beckham* (2002), but also with British directors focusing on the multicultural issue, sometimes very close to a political, documentary reality, like in Kenneth Gleenan's *Yasmin* (2009) on how the War on Terror affects a British-Pakistani family. Also the Channel 4 documentary series *Dispatches*, bringing both British and foreign programmes to the screen, developed a strand of programmes called *Unreported Worlds*.

The idea behind these programmes, starting in 2006, is simply to report on ways of living in remote parts of the world that are often not reported on. It becomes a multicultural and cosmopolitan counterpart to most foreign affairs programming and news reporting, where the focus is almost always on the same regions and places, and usually the more official, institutional aspects of politics and conflicts. In 2006, for instance, we witnessed life in West Papua, Guatemala, Lebanon, Pakistan and India, and the programmes focused on unusual aspects that shed new light on those parts of the world. It is generally about how people live with the conflicts and problems there. The focus is clearly on everyday life, but often with a clear relevance for understanding the more political dimensions of global conflicts, like for instance in the 2006 episode called *Afghanistan: Never Mind the Taliban*. Another, different kind of Channel 4 documentary looking at cultural diversity, this time just around the corner, is Sue Bourne's documentary *My Street* (2008). Here the director discovers the diversity of people in the neighbourhood she lives in, just 300 people living in 116 houses. Multicultural Britain is more than just foreigners and immigrants – we are always surrounded by people that live different lives, have different backgrounds and stories.

My Street is a fascinating look behind the surface of the ordinary, everyday UK in a mainstream middle- and upper-class neighbourhood that turns out to have completely different kinds of people living there, including people with immigrant backgrounds. Looking at the familiar, national reality like this sheds light on the broader and more confrontational discussion of the multicultural reality. We all seem to be somehow different and strange to each other. Another way of confronting the 'normal' British way of living is by exposing it to completely foreign eyes, which happens in *Meet the Natives* (2009), a staged documentary series made originally in the UK and then remade in the US. Here a group of tribesmen from the South Pacific Island, Tanna, go to both the UK and US to report on life as they find it. Here documentary anthropology is so to speak reversed: the natives are looking at the 'civilized' white culture, and the fun and exposure goes both ways. Another innovative documentary strategy is presented in Danish Eva Mulvad and Judith Lansade's portrait of Danish immigrants in Argentina, *Kolonien/The Colony* (2006). What the film shows is how Danes abroad, as immigrants, do exactly what they often criticize foreigners in Denmark for doing: they continue living in their own little Danish ghetto culture. In many ways they behave more traditionally Danish than the Danes at home, and they are very slow to mix with and get integrated into Argentinian culture.

Cultural diversity and different forms of living are increasingly common in modern societies, and many documentaries deal with the fact that we do not live in homogeneous societies. But documentaries dealing with ethnic others are still in a category of their own, and they often deal with much more complex problems and conflicts of multiculturalism. What many of these documentaries try to do is to show the universal and very familiar patterns behind different ethnic 'skins', the fact that what seems so strange to us at first is really not that strange. Stereotypes and prejudices are often based on lack of knowledge and personal contact, and documentaries dealing with ethnic groups and cultures can get us closer to an experience and understanding of differences and similarities. In Janus Metz's Danish and international prize-winning films *Love on Delivery* and *Ticket to Paradise* (2008) we follow

Danish-Thai marriages and relationships in Northern Jutland in Denmark. It is probably fair to say that many consider such relations with scepticism, almost like a kind of legalized prostitution, where Danish men go down to Thailand and buy poor woman. What these films show is that this, of course, is based on some truth, there is a lot of prostitution in Thailand, and European men do travel there to buy local women. But the film also tells the story of women from Thailand that are clearly not suppressed but have a very clear

Figures 8c and d: Janus Metz' *Love on Delivery* (2008). The strong Thai women in Denmark, a film changing cultural stereotypes. Frame grab. Cinematography: Lars Skree.

social agenda for a marriage with a Danish man. The film tells their story, lets us experience how they live – much like the rest of us – and also gives a broader story and context in which to understand these women, their past in Thailand and their present much better life in Denmark. It is a story of an ethnic meeting, a cultural and social exchange between two different 'cultures' that makes sense, and it is therefore a balanced story about the positive and negative sides of globalization.

A very fine documentary dealing with cultural diversity in a Danish context is Jens Loftager, Erlend E. Mo and Sami Saif's *Paradis/Paradise* (2008), a group portrait of very different people living in Denmark. We follow a soldier and his family as he prepares to go off to war in Iraq, we follow a very young girl and her family living in an asylum centre, waiting continuously without knowing what will happen to them, and we meet a young middle-class couple having their first child. Around these main characters we follow an old woman's burial, people from a drug culture, a lonely man longing for a woman and an old lonely man just commenting on life. Despite the film's low-key, observational form, it has a kind of existential blues character, a commentary on how differently we live on the one hand, but also how we all have the same dreams and hopes.

Multicultural conflicts – and the political game of integration

Ethnographic studies of ways of living and multicultural dimensions of Western societies are only one part of multicultural documentaries. The other part deals with conflicts and political dimensions of how to deal with immigration and the challenges it raises. The BBC in particular has produced many critical documentary programmes on asylum seekers, the British system on asylum seekers, and the various social and cultural conflicts arising from the increase in immigrants. Also, Channel 4 has dealt directly with open and hidden forms of racism and multicultural conflicts. One of the most inventive BBC programmes was Mike Robinson's *Panorama* report *The Asylum Game* (2003), in which a female reporter pretended to be, and lived as, an asylum seeker under false identity for six months. The programme clearly demonstrated how confusing and accidental the system seemed to be. The programme was part of a whole BBC theme day on the asylum issue, a day in which debates, documentaries, reports, news and more interactive programmes caused quite a debate and also criticism from politicians. Part of the day's programme was a broadcast in which viewers could make decisions in stories taken from real asylum cases on whether to give asylum seekers access to the UK or not, thus comparing popular decisions with the professional system.

According to the BBC web page on the programme (BBC News 2003b), the immigration minister Beverly Hughes reacted strongly against the programme, calling it a 'game show (…) trivializing the real consequences of "life and death" decisions'. She continued:

Asylum raises many complex and emotive issues and we always welcome debate on them – it is important, however, that the debate is rational and measured. The BBC has often covered these issues in a considered manner, but we have some serious concerns about some of the content of the BBC's 'asylum day'.

The BBC has made a number of other, all very different, but critical, investigative programmes on asylum seekers and immigration policy, both in the UK and in a broader European context. In the *Panorama* documentary *Destination Europe* (2007) the focus is on those that organize and make a profit on bringing illegal immigrants to Europe, especially African asylum seekers. The programme shows terrible conditions for the refugees and links to, among other things, the Russian mafia. It is also a dramatic human story where we meet and hear the stories of several of the refugees and we follow a dramatic near drowning of 27 asylum seekers. The programme was followed up later in *Destination UK*, dealing with the UK policy towards these people, where reporters talked to the asylum seekers from the 2007 broadcast on what had later happened to them.

But BBC programmes on migration also include Paul Kenyon following in the footsteps of Africans on the move towards Europe. *Migrants, Go Home* (2009) deals with the harsh and tough policy of France, working with Libyan dictator Muhammed Gaddafi on sending people back immediately. In *Europe Or Die Trying* (2009) we follow hopeful African asylum seekers from Sub-Saharan Africa to Southern Europe. Many do not make it even to the sea, but one of the main characters did and we get his story just as we get in contact with his native village, three years after his escape. The programme is a powerful illustration of some of the most brutal aspects of globalization and the clash between realities and dreams of people for whom Europe seems to be a paradise. Some BBC programmes like, for instance, *Immigration – Time for an Amnesty?* (2009) deal with those who have made it into the UK and are now living as illegal immigrants. The programme talks to experts and politicians, and also portrays illegal immigrants that are doing pretty well and asks whether it is time to give these immigrants a permanent residence. One particular case in the programme deals with 28-year-old Farhan Zakaria from Bangladesh who has managed to get an education, has a good job and is paying his taxes, but is now threatened with deportation. The programme exposes the dilemmas of immigration, seen by some as a threat to the welfare society but by others as a necessary openness towards a global world with much to offer Western societies with a declining population.

Critical programmes like the BBC programmes on broader aspects of immigration, looking both outward and into the specific national reality can be found also in Danish documentaries. Early documentaries like Frantz Ernst's *Flygtning/Refugee* (1963) or Werner Hedman's *Flygtning I Danmark/Refugee in Denmark* (1969) or Mette Knudsen and Rachid Mehailias' *Fremmed/Stranger* (1971) deal with the first wave of immigration to Denmark, the 'guest workers' that ended up staying on and laid the foundation for a new group of Danes with different ethnic and cultural backgrounds. But from the 1990s, documentaries start dealing with immigrants and the multicultural society on a much broader scale. Films following the dangerous routes of immigrants from Africa are for instance Janus Metz' *Eventyrerne/The Adventurers* (2007) whereas Niels Boel's *Migranterne/The Migrants* (2009) deals with poor South American farmers migrating towards the big cities in their own region, but as part of a bigger, global migration pattern.

An early, very strong TV documentary dealing with the darker sides of clashes between different cultures and norms is Poul Martinsen's *Den sagtmodige morder/The Gentle Murderer* (1989), dealing with a brother's killing of his own sister based on Turkish family honour concepts. The programme is a dramatic reconstruction of the events and the trial against the murderer and his family, but it is also a programme using a lot of time to go back to the roots of this kind of killing. The programme takes us back to the family in Turkey and anthropologists and sociologists try to explain how this kinship culture and code of honour works. The programme also deals with the difference between a more modern Turkish culture in the bigger cities and the still very traditional culture in the countryside. In the same league, but with a much more political agenda, we find Alex Frank Larsen's investigative TV documentary *Blodets bånd/The Ties of Blood* (1990), which eventually caused the fall of the liberal-conservative government, for violating human rights and UN conventions in connection with a large group of refugees in Denmark. The programme is both a human interest programme portraying the refugees and the country and culture they come from, and a sharp and critical, investigative programme showing how the Danish political system systematically mistreated them and also covered up the mistreatment.

Similar to the critical BBC programmes on refugees and immigrants, Poul Erik Heilbuth from the Danish public service station DR, from the early 1990s made a whole series of programmes on the migration towards Europe and the political problems this created. Programmes like *Flugten til Europa/The Flight to Europe* (1992) about the many waves of migration towards Europe and *Det andet Europa/The Other Europe* (2006) about the illegal immigrants in Europe, much needed by European companies, but working under terrible conditions, clearly unfold the social and political dilemmas of national and European policies. An equivalent to the BBC's critical investigation of the asylum seeker process is found in DR's, Thomas Gade and Nils Giversen's *Det store asyllotteri/The Big Asylum Lottery* (2003). It is a programme pointing out that the system seems to reach random decisions and work under a rather unclear political and legal mandate, maybe because the decisions reflect a political division between hardliners and more soft decision-makers. Other programmes use a human case story approach to tell stories about people caught inbetween systems. Line Fabricius and Hussein Ferdowsipour's *Udvist til tortur/Sent Back to Torture* (2003) deals with a young Iranian man who fled to Denmark but in 1999 was sent back and since then has been in and out of Iranian prisons and exposed to torture. Other programmes show hidden racism, even against highly educated immigrants, like Poul Erik Heilbuth's *For klog til Danmark/Too Clever for Denmark* (2003), but there are also programmes dealing with fraud in connection with foreigners seeking family reunion, like Jacob Adrian Mikkelsen's *De falske børn/The False Children* (2005), about parents trying to get children to Denmark by pretending to be their parents.

The everyday life dimensions of a multicultural reality

The difficulties of integrating large groups of foreigners or naturalized immigrants has created political and social tensions in many European countries, but gradually the existence of new groups in society and everyday life also creates new cultural dynamics. Documentaries have dealt with this in many ways, and the conflicts and dynamics both create new dimensions in the way we perceive our own national culture and everyday life, and the way we perceive those regions where refugees and immigrants come from. This is one important dimension of globalization and the multicultural reality, that no matter what our basic attitudes are, many of us get acquainted with other cultures, religions and nationalities in our own everyday culture. This can cause both increased understanding and a cosmopolitan outlook, but it can also create stronger tensions and conflicts, at least in the short term.

The question of integration into Danish culture can be addressed in a very polemic, personal way, as done by the Danish director Fenar Ahmad, who has an Arab background. In his film *Den perfekte muslim/The Perfect Muslim* (2009) he raises the question of when a foreigner is Danish enough to be called a Dane, and what defines Danish culture. In the film he hires a specialist in advertising, and he wants to use a focus group method along with a survey to define what Danes see as Danish and what they think about integration of foreigners. The result is a rather fuzzy and individual picture of Danish culture and also what it takes to be a fully integrated immigrant. The film focuses rather intensely on both Fenar's background and family history and what a very diverse focus group of 'Danes' can come up with when asked to define Danishness. Culture, it seems, is a very fluffy concept, and even though we may experience some kind of cultural difference when we encounter other nationalities and cultures, it is hard to define and pinpoint. The same point is clearly made in another ironic, personal documentary by Ziska Szemes, *Mig og min næse/Me and my Nose* (2009). Ziska is born in Sweden and has a father with Hungarian background and a mother with English-Indian background. She is a Swedish citizen now living in Denmark and married to a Danish man. So who is she, what are her cultural and biological genes, and is it her nose that prevents other people from seeing her as a true Scandinavian? The nose and the question of whether she can get a new, more Scandinavian nose, is the comic entry point for a documentary on cultural identity and our perception of it.

Cultural differences are clearly difficult to define precisely, and we are probably basically more alike than we want to admit. This also means that even though cultural differences are difficult to define, we are sociologically programmed to create and bond in networks with people we see as like ourselves. But many conflicts also arise from lack of concrete knowledge and experience with 'others'. Documentaries are particularly good at giving us first hand experience of a 'reality of otherness'. Newer Danish documentaries that have done just that, for instance, by going close to 'ghetto areas', have been very popular with a large audience. Anja Dalhoff's TV documentary, *Babylon i Brøndby/Babylon in Brøndby* (1996) was seen by almost one million Danes. It is an ethnographic everyday life study of one of the biggest multicultural residential areas, Brøndby Stand, south of Copenhagen. Among the 7,800 people living there, 40 per cent are immigrants, and people come from 66 different countries. We go behind the façade of both Danish and foreign families and we meet people in schools, childcare institutions and in connection with different social and cultural activities. We follow a caretaker and a group of workers with different backgrounds around the area, and the film on the one hand shows that cooperation and peaceful living together is possible, despite ethnic and cultural differences, and on the other hand shows that both foreigners and Danes clearly express prejudices and stereotypes towards each other. We define ourselves through cultural differences. There may not be strong and clear cultural distinctions in reality, but nevertheless these differences have a strong and clear social and mental function. Dynamic processes of social and cultural relations are both related to what we do and what we think, and sometimes the two are not completely compatible.

Two other Danish TV documentaries use the ethnographic, collective approach to multicultural everyday life in Denmark. Poul Martinsen and Anders Riis-Hansen's *Høje historier/Tall Stories* (1–4, 1999) deals with life in a typical high-rise building complex in Copenhagen's rather dreary Northwest neighbourhood. With its observational, multiplot narrative we get inside the life of a colourful selection of immigrants and Danes, old and young, drug addicts, alcoholics, maniacs and nerds, but also stories of meetings across divides, romance and people trying to develop a community and a sense of being together. It is social documentary realism at its best. So is Jørgen Flindt Pedersen's outstanding and prize-winning series *Drengene fra Vollsmose/The Boys From Vollsmose* (1–3, 2002), made for TV2, a portrait of a group of young and very socially challenged Palestinian boys at one of the schools in Denmark's largest immigrant neighbourhood, Vollsmose, near Odense on Fewnen. It is a strong and dramatic story of a school, and in particular one teacher, trying to develop social and psychological skills that can make these rather dysfunctional kids active members of society. Large parts of the series are shot with tiny digital cameras, giving the story a very intense and intimate character, where we get close to the main characters, often only described in the news media as criminals and troublemakers. Here a seemingly lost generation is changing in front of our eyes, and we get behind the stereotypes and conflicts into individuals and human beings like the rest of us.

Under the skin – national culture contested and challenged

In Denmark and Danish documentaries there is a clear tendency to challenge and question norms and forms of national culture as conditions for integration of foreigners, and the toughening of integration policy is often seen as an expression of a nationalist demarcation against globalization. In Erland E. Mo's film, with the ironic title *Velkommen til Danmark/Welcome to Denmark* (2003), we follow three refugees from ex-Yugoslavia, Afghanistan and Cameroon during one year. Their background and story before they came to Denmark is dramatic and traumatic, but so is the story of a frustrating integration that takes new turns all the time and keeps them locked up in uncertainty. It is a human story but also a story about immigration policy under pressure. Such stories run through many British documentaries as well, but here the question of racism and extreme nationalism is also raised, even in connection with official political discourse and government initiatives.

In Denmark, the then liberal-conservative government started a project to define a national, cultural canon, defining the official version of our national culture. In the UK, the BBC's *Panorama* dealt with similar policies by the Labour government in *True Brits* (2008). A starting point for the programme was the Minister for Borders and Immigration, Liam Byrne's, idea to make an official Britishness day in line with the US's 4th of July. Faced with this suggestion, Prime Minister Gordon Brown defined Britishness as all about 'shared values', and he defined these as liberty, democracy and social cohesion, thus proving that these values are in fact not very British but belong to our common European, American, universal ideas of enlightenment. If Britishness suddenly becomes a politically defined set of norms and values, they can be seen as policies which exclude others or claim a set of national values and identity markers that are not at all culturally specific. Also in the UK, national culture seems to be something nobody can really define. National culture, it turns out, is not really a national culture as such, but often a mix of universal, global and local and national traditions. Universal norms and rights can be part of a national culture, but can never be a unique definition of it. In the BBC programme, the reporter asks the question of Britishness to a large group of people, very much like in the Danish programme *The Perfect Muslim* (see above), and the answers are scattered in the wind. As one of the young immigrants in the programme says: 'The government should not be asking what Britishness is at all, because a British citizen will be different everywhere you look.'

A rather interesting programme investigating 'Britishness' from a very diverse, ethnic perspective is Channel 4's two-part series *Make Bradford British* (2012). In the opening sequences of part one we witness several groups, some with a Muslim origin and others with a British origin, taking the official test to become citizens, both groups failing with more than 90 per cent. Neither the foreigners nor the natives seem aware of what Britishness is. But starting from this point the programme takes a reality programme turn, and in the rest of the two programmes we get a kind of staged, social experiment. Representatives with a different ethnic, social and cultural background are brought together to discuss and try to develop new forms of collaborative community activities in a town often torn by ethnic conflicts. The programme is a kind of bottom-up experiment in integration.

Nationalism – extreme nationalism – is, however, strongly present in most European countries, and nationalist and xenophobic political parties have a certain success, although never gaining power or majority. The *Panorama* programme *Under the Skin* (2001) deals with the British National Party, which represents such tendencies, although never directly represented in parliament. The programme is a clear revealing of the true racial separatism behind this political party that is in contrast with the often disguised rhetoric they parade in public. The programme partly uses undercover techniques, techniques also used in the very revealing BBC programme *Undercover – Hate on the Doorstep* (2009). It is an outrageous and shocking documentation of how two Arab BBC journalists – taking on a traditional Muslim identity – were harassed and beaten during the eight weeks they went undercover. What the programme documents is the really ugly side of globalization and the multicultural reality, the fact that aggressive racism is in fact a more widespread part of British everyday life than surveys and polls reveal.

Racist, white and nationalist extremism is only one side of the more negative aspects of living together in a democratic and multicultural society, the other side is Muslim extremism and terrorism. In the BBC's programme *Muslim First, British Second* (2009) this side of the coin is dealt with in a way that actually focuses on cooperation instead of confrontation. The programme reports on a contested but efficient strategy followed by the British anti-terror police in the years after the 2005 London terror bombing. They cooperate with rather extreme groups among Muslims in order to make them fence in even more radical groups. So the philosophy is that it is better preventing development of militant radicalism by communicating with those groups, but without supporting and condoning actual acts of terror and violence. The background for such an initiative is also clearly demonstrated in *British Schools, Islamic Rules* (2010), which uses partly undercover techniques to document how teachers and priests in Islamic schools are preaching hate and extremism, although officially acting under the British school system and British law.

Unity and diversity – the challenges of a multicultural reality

The official, cultural motto of the EU is 'unity in diversity', indicating a transnational collaboration between nation states with a different culture and history, but also united by strong universal ideals and norms of democracy and individual freedom rights. Each of these nation states also has different multicultural stories and developments, neither Europe as such, nor the individual nations forming the alliance, represent homogeneous ethnic cultures. The US was originally formed by immigrants from a Europe that did not seem to respect them and give them possibilities, and this made the US the imaginary symbol of unity in diversity. As demonstrated, both European and US documentaries have been deeply engaged in the documentation of multicultural realities and dilemmas of unity and diversity. They have tried to demonstrate how diversity often creates the opposite of unity. They deal with migration and the existence of different ethnic groups and cultures in the same national and everyday life space, and how this can often lead to conflict and more aggressive forms of radicalism and terrorism. But they have also worked to give people a first hand experience and understanding of the fact that, behind the colour of the skin or the different ways of living, we are all human beings and pretty much alike. Prejudices and stereotypes are often caused by lack of knowledge, contact and personal experience. People that have regular contact with foreigners and groups with another culture or religion often change their attitudes. But these documentaries have also dealt with the difficulties of a politics of multiculturalism when politicians are faced with popular sentiments and attitudes towards immigrants, refugees and foreigners in general.

Politics and discourses of multiculturalism are many, and the British sociologist Gerard Delanty has defined four main positions or traditions in his book *The Cosmopolitan Imagination* (2009: 133): egalitarian multiculturalism, liberal multiculturalism, ethnopluralism and radical multiculturalism. Delanty sees *egalitarian multiculturalism* as the classic form, especially clear in American history, where many different groups where accepted without recognition of their particular rights as minority cultures and ethnic groups but based on their status as equal citizens in the public domain. Culture and their private matters were of no concern to the US nation state under construction. Unlike Europe, where assimilation into a firmly established national culture was the case, it was and is quite common in the US to define oneself as Irish-American for instance, or any other kind of hyphenated national identity. Whereas this is not common in many European countries, it is probably a possible way of defining oneself as a EU citizen to be for instance, Danish-European. At least Eurobarometer data shows Europeans accept such a double identity (*New Europeans* 2011). The other forms of multiculturalism are variations of *liberal multiculturalism*, as already indicated with the Canadian philosophers Will Kymlicka and Charles Taylor (see p. 203f), where a combination of the liberal, individual rights and some sort of state acceptance and support to national minorities, indigenous people or other cultural groups is developed. In the case of actual Canadian law and politics, the politics of multicultural recognition has a strong influence from the communitarian version of liberal multiculturalism in Charles Taylor's writings.

As many of the documentaries demonstrate, the balance between universal human rights and specific cultures is not an easy one, neither in everyday discourse nor in political discourse. What defines a particular culture, in what ways ethnic cultures are different from each other, and in what ways they require intervention and state support, can be difficult to decide. To give support to a specific cultural group, thus giving special treatment beyond the freedom and rights we all have, may prove complicated. Concepts to the extreme right in strong nationalistic or religious groups, both among white national groups and other ethnic groups, seem to identify themselves as very much defined by their religion and culture, and do not seem to recognize that all cultures are strongly mixed and influenced by interaction. Concepts to the left, on the other hand, develop positions that Delanty defines as *radical multiculturalism* or forms of *communitarian ethnopluralism* (Delanty 2009: 139f). Here cultural relativism and postmodernism undermines the liberal, universal dimensions of democracy and human rights. Diversity almost becomes a 'religious' concept as all cultures seem entitled to be understood only on their own terms: we become defined by a particular culture. But a concept like this is on a collision course with the mixing of, and interactions between cultures, nations, social groups and products in the accelerating global media sphere. Delanty's own position, defined as a modern and open form of cosmopolitanism, is much more in tune with this development, even though his insistence on 'unity *through* diversity' (Delanty 2009: 133) remains a bit theoretically unclear. What he seems to suggest is that diversity is not a problem for unity, and that *cultural diversity* is not the biggest problem, as long as one creates a strong public space for debate and communication and does not enter a radical policy of cultural differentiation. We are human beings first of all, under universal norms and principles, and in our basic ways of living we are very much alike. Only secondly are we defined by culture, social belonging, religion etc.

Chapter 9

Risk society: the environmental challenge

A	nthony Giddens introduces his book *The Politics of Climate Change* as being about 'nightmares, catastrophes – and dreams' (2011: 1) and he makes two further important observations on these global issues. The consensus among most scientists is that climate change and the consequences of our modern way of life, the heritage of the industrial age, is a global problem. But even though we may all realize this and the media may report on it, it still seems to be at the back of our minds. It seems hard to bring something mentally to the fore that is future-oriented, unless it becomes somehow more tangible and concrete for us in our day-to-day lives (Giddens 2011: 2–3). Compared with the other global challenges dealt with already in this book, this may be an issue which calls for global multilayered governance, and a change in our mentality from local to global (Giddens 2011: 5).

In his book, Gidden spends a lot of time on giving scientific evidence to back up the climate change threat, and to argue for the necessity of global governance of a completely new nature. But he also uses the climate challenge to point to a broader need for a global political perspective, which climate change is perhaps the ultimate test of:

> Our civilization is truly global in scope; and it couldn't exist without the inanimate energy sources that fuel it. For better or worse, modern industry has unleashed a sheer volume of *power* into the world vastly beyond anything witnessed before. I mean here inanimate power, but also the power of human organization – the complex social, economic and political systems upon which our lives now depend (Giddens 2011: 229).

Giddens also notes that this global challenge, more than any other, requires a political balancing between the developed industrial countries and the new developing regions.

This is also a theme in Ulrick Beck's book *Risk Society: Towards a New Modernity* (1992): the industrial society is changing and moving towards a whole new form of modernity that will need new global policies. Beck also uses metaphors taken from disaster movies to describe this new modernity and risk society: 'living on the volcano of civilization' (p. 17f). The logic of growth and wealth distribution within an industrial nation-state-defined society seems to have reached a turning point, and we are faced with global challenges that threaten to undermine our whole way of life. Beck's argument for a new global, cosmopolitan politics in his latest work is clearly introduced in this book, in which he points to the uncontrolled development of industrial society, where it is beginning to overrun and overcome its own coordinate system: 'This coordinate system had fixed understandings about the separation of nature and society' (Beck 1992: 87).

Documentary narratives of climate change and the risk society

We may still debate the nature and scope of the global climate challenge, and maybe Al Gore and director Davis Guggenheim painted too dark a picture of some of the trends on our way to disaster in *An Inconvenient Truth* (2006). But Franny Armstrong probably raised a very important issue when she made her film *The Age of Stupid* (2009), which looks back from a future where the disaster has happened: 'Why didn't we save ourselves when we had the chance?' Both films were major global successes and Franny Armstrong even financed her film on the Internet, indicating the birth of a new global, political factor in documentary production. Perhaps it is not quite a coincidence that it was a film about global climate change and the ecological threats to our planet and way of life that became the first crowdfunded film success. But another major indication of changes in the global mentality concerning our planet is clearly the American Warner Brothers independent film production *The 11th Hour* (2007), directed by Leila Conners Petersen and Nadia Conners. It is a strong follow-up to *An Inconvenient Truth,* and it is a film that defines the greatest global challenge right now as the balance between human society and the global environment.

Nature documentaries have been part of the documentary film tradition for decades, and apart from the strong British BBC tradition for long series, for example the amazing series *Planet Earth* (10 parts, 2006, David Attenborough) ending with 'Planet Earth – The Future', we now have whole channels dedicated to scientific and nature material, for instance, Discovery (see Mjos 2010) or National Geographic. For a broader audience the image of the globe, the mental ability to see our world and universe as a whole has changed dramatically – and this is perhaps seen most clearly and symbolically in the Google Earth app, which is now giving us instant access on our mobile phones to a picture of our earth and its different parts seen from space. Images of the blue planet and the potential threats to it, with changes visible in terms of ice caps melting and forest areas disappearing, is part of all climate-oriented documentaries. Images like this are changing our ability to imagine and almost feel a global crisis. News broadcasts of extreme weather and catastrophes that may be related to climate change come to us with increased speed, and add to this potential imagination of a global crisis.

The last part of the BBC series *Planet Earth* shows some of the most stunning images of the global environment and climate, images of the diversity of species, but we also listen to the voices of the BBC team that have mixed feelings after finishing the series because they have encountered signs of a threat to the global environment. We also listen to representatives of the scientific community, NGOs and people in the threatened areas as they express the need for a change in our way of life to save the diversity and balance of the blue planet. A series like *Planet Earth* and other similar series on the BBC have no doubt created an important mental and emotional framework for a new kind of feeling for the global, for how the global actually looks, when the best nature photographers put all their skills and megabudgets into recreating it in front of our eyes. Man has never before had this kind of view of the globe and the nature which inhabits it, and by creating this new, global imaginary nature, documentaries contribute to the more concrete basis of global challenges that can otherwise often appear as part of a more abstract scientific and political agenda.

But still the magnitude and causes of climate change are under debate, and some scientists tend to reduce the role of society and humans in the environmental changes, pointing instead towards natural causes and cyclical changes, for instance, in the atmosphere of the sun. Does the increase in CO_2 change the atmosphere to such a degree that we have to change our way of life and consumption drastically, or do the larger part of the changes come from changes in the solar system we cannot influence? After all, we have had warm and cold periods before in the history of the earth and mankind. Such discussions can create passionate scientific and political disagreements, and ordinary citizens are left in doubt and confusion.

Putting the climate issue on the global agenda

Even though global warming and the whole idea of a greener way of living, both at a society level and in your private and personal life, began to emerge in the 1980s and influenced the media agenda in numerous ways, it is probably not an exaggeration to say that Al Gore's intervention in 2006 in Davis Guggenheim's documentary *An Inconvenient Truth*, had a global impact. It does matter in a global context if a former vice-president of the US becomes active and takes a stand on a scientific and political issue that is already supported by global NGO movements. According to IMDb Pro data on box office popularity, this film has by now been launched all over the world on both TV channels and internet sites, and as of July 2012 the global box office was approximately 42 million dollars. If we estimate the total amount of viewers of this film, we are talking several hundred million, although such figures are hard to prove, since nobody is really counting all platforms. *An Inconvenient Truth* is made by the independent US production company Participant Productions, a company with a strong profile in socially engaged films, both fiction and non-fiction, and as an American production it is situated between mainstream and alternative productions. This is also underlined by the fact that Paramount is the distributor.

But as in the area of many other global issues, mainstream media and the more established independent production companies are supplemented by quite active digital activist film sites, either facilitating access to a large number of independent and alternative films or even producing films. Examples are sites like Top Documentary Films (TDF), which in August 2012 listed 79 documentaries on 'environment', and Free Documentaries, which only listed about 20 in this category. But sites like this work by connecting independents, activists and

NGO groups to niche audiences around the world, and thus expanding the global audience and discussions on these matters. An extraordinary example of the documentaries that can come out of these platforms and the YouTube community, which is often linked to it, can be found on TDF: the documentary series *Climate Change* (see http://topdocumentaryfilms. com/climate-change/). This series of films, trying to seriously explain the different scientific schools within climate change research, is made by the YouTube activist known as potholer54 (see www.youtube.com/user/potholer54) and his videos have, according to YouTube statistics, been seen by a total of 8 million viewers. In 2010 he revealed his true identity as British journalist Peter Hadfield. This activist was thus in fact a professional using a different outlet.

Peter Hadfield's YouTube documentaries on climate change, posted also on TDF, are in no way alternative, political activist documentaries. The format is the classical science documentary with an authoritative voiceover explaining scientific facts, using visual, graphic and written documentation, and talking to different experts. So the classical, authoritative science documentary has been extended to digital platforms, but enters into a dialogue with other more traditionally produced documentaries. Documentaries on climate change do come in aesthetically very different forms, there is a very strong tradition for authoritative documentaries, but even though this more informational and journalistic format dominates, we do see other genres, and in most of the films a variety of aesthetic and rhetorical forms are used. *An Inconvenient Truth* is so authoritative in form, that it has basic elements of a lecture, a lecture that was followed up by both a book on how to solve the climate crisis, *Our Choice – A Plan to Solve the Climate Crisis* (Gore 2009) and a global slide show tour for Al Gore. In *An Inconvenient Truth* the science arguments in the authoritative documentary are combined with a global, political agenda addressed to the global policy makers.

The film clearly follows the form of a lecture with slideshows and inserted sequences of films that fill the whole screen, and with Gore as lecturer and reaction shots from audiences around the world. But it also has a classical, rhetorical structure; it speaks to our experiences of nature and to our emotional layers where nature becomes the threatened other, mistreated systematically by us and by big corporations. So the film speaks to both our rational and emotional sides. It is based on tons of data, graphic representations and arguments, but it puts Gore as a person and politician at the centre, combining these two dimensions using humour and irony. The film starts with Apollo 8 pictures of the globe, the first ever from space, and they are followed up with the Apollo 17 and Galileo pictures of the same earth much later. As Gore's comments make clear, these are landmark pictures in the human minds image of the globe, because they visualize globalization in ways never seen before, and because they demonstrate ecological changes.

Part of the emotional rhetoric, supplementing the scientific data and political arguments, are the images of catastrophe, images of melting ice, flooding and storms creating enormous destruction. There is a clear connection between this and the catastrophe narrative of the Hollywood blockbuster. Our sense of disaster, our ability to imagine consequences, is called upon by both the scientific documentation and visual data, and a broader narrative framework. But in the film there are other narrative, visual layers tied to emotions. We do not just see the public figure Gore, we are also confronted with his family background and his childhood experiences, where things looked different. The change demonstrated through personal memories and narrative sequences from the past is a part of the rhetoric which makes us believe in the narrator, but which also anchors the abstract in our mind and body in a more emotional and experiental way.

An Inconvenient Truth is a political one man show building on the work and arguments from a large number of scientists, but very much working rhetorically and emotionally through Gore's character and charisma, and also the fact that he shows a very personal side of himself with his story as a child, as a father, and as a politician. As communicative strategy this places a macro, global problem in the sphere of personal memory and everyday life; abstract data and scientific arguments are combined with experiental and emotionally loaded images that everybody can relate to. There is also a clear activist agenda when we see Gore talking to politicians around the world, and at the end of the film where we are all addressed: 'Are you ready to change lifestyle? Here is what you can do.' In Lelia Conners Petersen and Nadia Conners' *The 11th Hour* we find another authoritative documentary strategy, but with some of the same rhetorical elements at play. But even though a Hollywood star like Leonardo DiCaprio is used as narrator and the film follows a very authoritative and scientific approach, it also uses a much more interview-based structure, with many characters discussing and presenting facts and views. The opening of *The 11th Hour* uses the same emotional rhetoric and catastrophe pictures as Guggenheim and Gore, but there is not the same kind of personal subjective dimension as in *An Inconvenient Truth*.

In the beginning of *The 11th Hour* different people talk about the earth as an infected organism going out of balance, and DiCaprio's voiceover and speeches to the camera sum up that we are close to an ecological disaster, and that we need to act now. Where *An Inconvenient Truth* has the character of an advanced lecture with inserted narratives, strong images and other visual data, *The 11th Hour* looks and sounds much more like a traditional TV science programme. We are not bombarded with graphs and data, although they are present, but with arguments by many scientists and other people illustrated by images related to the climate and our environment. Those images draw on the same emotional dimensions as Gore and Guggenheim, and the pictures of natural catastrophes certainly do bring the more abstract questions and arguments raised closer to the viewer's everyday life. The film is also more critical and political in the sense that it raises the question of corporate responsibility in a much sharper and more direct way than Gore and Guggenheim, who mostly address the political system. At the end of the film, a variety of people also talk rather concretely about how we can develop sustainable forms of production and lifestyle, again bringing the global macro problem down to the individual and more concrete level.

Figures 9a and b: Lelia Conners Petersen and Nadia Conners' *The 11th Hour* (2007). Leonardo DiCaprio as narrator in a film with striking images and arguments of the suffering planet and global warming. Frame grab. Cinematography: Jean-Pascal Beintus.

A very different kind of documentary raising fundamental scientific and political questions about climate change is Franny Armstrong's *The Age of Stupid*. It is dramatized and experimental in form and genre, and it was made through crowdfunding on the Internet, thus representing a new sort of collective documentary activism, or at least a cooperation between a professional director and the NGO and digital network of climate activists.

The official world premiere of the film was also quite extraordinary and spectacular, as it was broadcast simultaneously in 60 different countries. On top of that, people can get a licence to put on independent screenings of the film and keep the profit for themselves. Seen just from the point of production and distribution, the film is thus a good example of a new type of global documentary using the new digital media culture. *The Age of Stupid* has a dramatized framework, in which a curator of The Global Archive (played by Pete Postlethwaite), placed at the North Pole, is looking back from an almost dead world in 2005 and comments on what led to this catastrophe. The film thus has the most fantastic and imaginary construction of this devastated world, but as pointed out from the start, all the evidence put forward is based on scientific data, and all the visual material from present and past times is based on actual footage from media and film. The film is therefore a clear example of a dramatized documentary where the created 'fictional' world of the future is based on 'factual' data, and where documentary footage is inserted into the dramatized framework.

The archivist shows us round the archive, but on his magic screen he can also call to life media sequences from the past. The kind of media content he calls forth can mainly be divided into two types: on the one hand factual and scientific clips that illustrate how the media have reported on climate change and what scientist observers said, on the other hand individual stories of different types of people, that directly or indirectly illustrate the development that led to the catastrophe, and the kind of everyday life people led before things went wrong. The stories are about an Indian businessman and his plans for a really low cost airline company for everybody; a French glacier guide who has observed the development of climate change in the alps all his life; a resident in New Orleans who has worked in the oil industry whom we follow after Hurricane Katrina, a story getting us very close to a natural disaster but also to the corporate dimension of climate change; two Iraqi children who fled to Jordan illustrating global war and divides; a wind farmer working for sustainable energy and a Nigerian woman struggling to survive, again a story connected to global divides.

The dramatized framework and structure of the film, and the way the documentary footage is used, clearly gives the film a strong reflexive dimension. This reflexive dimension, in which we are forced to look back on ourselves from at point in time where the catastrophe has become reality, is strongly underlined by the very different documentary forms we encounter. We move from typical newscasts to scientific statements, from observational human stories and narratives to satirical, creative and poetic illustrations (cartoons for instance) of human development and ways of behaving in the past. The film creates a patchwork of not only documentary forms but also stories from a global world of social and cultural differences, but all linked by the fact that we face a global challenge. The archivist is a disillusioned witness speaking to us from a not so distant future, in order to convince us to act from our present position while there is still a chance. The strength of the film is also the dimension of global dialogue involved in bringing stories from all over the world together, and letting people comment on the same global situation and challenges, but from their very different backgrounds.

Climate wars – the scientific and political dimension

In July 2012, the well known climate change sceptic Richard Muller, professor of physics, University of California, Berkeley changed his concept of the climate crisis and the factors behind global warming (Muller 2012). He called himself a converted climate change sceptic, and based on data coming out of his Berkeley Earth Surface Project, measuring average earth temperatures over the last 250 years, he concludes that man-made changes have increased the average temperature dramatically, and that this rise follows the development of industrialization and global growth in the use of fossil energy. So the CO_2 outlet into the atmosphere is a very important factor in the changes. Having been financed by the Koch Charitable Foundation, owned by a family having made their fortune in coal, Muller's research might have looked as if it was directly connected to another political agenda, one dependent on the energy that is part of the problem. But Muller's scientific conscience and independence was stronger than ideology and politics. However – as with all major, global agendas – the climate change question is heavily burdened by interest groups and ideology, more than facts.

The American public and political system is generally considered rather reluctant and sceptical towards theories on global warming and the greenhouse effect. The UN system and the global Earth Meetings in Kyoto, leading to the Kyoto protocol (1997) on climate goals, followed by a number of later meetings, was neither received warmly nor strongly supported by the US governments during the 1980s and onwards. But even here the attitudes were changing, and when PBS on their Frontline programme *Hot Politics* (2007) drew up the history of American climate politics, they pointed to a change on the way just before the election of Obama as president. The starting point was around 1998, when a senate hearing and testimony from the scientist James Hansen of the NASA Hoddard Institute, for the first time *inside* the US policy establishment, put forward arguments and data that were heard. As the programme argues, until then the debate seemed similar to the debate on smoke and cancer: scientist paid by the tobacco companies argued against, and independent researchers were often not heard. The sceptics talked about the 'gloom and doom scenario', but gradually both the Clinton administration and the Bush administration were forced to take climate change and the human factor more serious. Both media images of climate disasters, and not least Hurricane Katrina's deadly flooding of New Orleans in 2005, brought the problem into people's backyard. What this classical, journalistic documentary shows is that global issues on the political agenda are dominated by strong ideological, political and corporate interests, but also that the agenda can change when both data, arguments and emotional embedding take hold through the media or in our everyday life.

Hot Politics is dominated by talking heads, and by scientific and political arguments, but the programme also uses global images of climate change as emotional documentation and signifiers, and thus embeds a complex and difficult issue in our imagination. This strategy is much more evident in *Too Hot Not To Handle* (HBO 2006, directed by Maryann DeLeo), a programme that gives a systematic explanation of global warming, the reasons for it and the effects on our societies and lives, and the actions we need to take to fight it. But it uses a much more visual, rhetorical strategy, because the talking heads are mostly shown for a shorter period, and visual sequences are used to illustrate their points of view or make their statements comment on visual documentation. For instance, the programme shows images from Alaska and other places taken from back in time until now, images that show incredible changes in ice, water and coastline. Not only does this strategy make climate changes visually close up and concrete, but the arguments and the images also anchor the global developments in direct relation to people's own lives and local environment. When we hear that the oceans are rising this may seem difficult to understand and relate to, but when you learn that people living within 50 miles of the ocean can be affected, things become very tangible. The programme also makes an effort to get changes in our way of living down to practicalities: 'live smart and save the planet' is the motto and principle.

The covering of scientific and political climate wars can be found in numerous documentary films also in the UK and Denmark. One of the most innovative documentaries is the BBC 2 series *Earth: The Climate Wars* (1–3, 2008, episodes available on YouTube). It is a visually rich documentary, using montage and music in a creative way. As a serious science documentary it is unusual in its combination of a very personal, subjective narrative and perspective by the director and narrator Ian Stewart, a geologist from Plymouth University. As a child of the roaring 1960s, and the more crisis-ridden 1970s, he uses his own experience and story of growing up in those days in comparison with his life now as a father and scientist. Music and images of everyday life, images of his childhood and youth are combined in a very illustrative way with images of the broader social, cultural and political history, and these layers of personal and socio-cultural history are again combined with a narrative of our concepts of climate and climate change. Although the series is highly informational and fact-driven, it is also able to combine the factual and the emotional, the more objective and the more subjective.

In part one of the series, *The Battle Begins*, we focus on the 1970s and 1980s, but the programme also paints a much broader, historical picture of how climate changes have taken place for millions of years – sometimes quickly and with rather drastic consequences. As such, the programme sets the broader framework for a discussion of natural and human factors in climate change. The programme also demonstrates how influential scientists in the 1970s were convinced that we were not facing global warming but a new ice age. So scientific disagreement and scientific and ideological wars on what is happening, and the causes of it, go back a long time. The programme also clearly points – often with use of satire and irony – to the links between politicians, big business and science. When Reagan became president in 1981, the science had moved more in the direction of global warming and was beginning to look at the role of carbon dioxide and the greenhouse effect. But as the programme indicates, Reagan – being president of the country with the largest production of greenhouse gasses – wanted this agenda to go away. He appointed a scientific committee which came up with a report largely diminishing the global warming theory to speculation and fiction.

Earth: The Climate Wars does not use many graphs or quantitative visuals to document the arguments behind the scientific wars, it takes a more visual, rhetorical and narrative approach. It is a documentary dealing with deep science agendas but communicating them by oral, visual and narrative strategies. In the second part, *The Fightbacks*, the focus is on the present day sceptics, those questioning the importance of human factors in climate changes. The approach is very much 'seeing is believing', as for instance, when we see and hear about how the instruments actually measuring global warming or other changes in the climate. This doesn't mean that images of the globe and striking graphics are never used in order to create this sense of experiencing climate science at work, but as a whole the series relies much more on visual narrative, personal presence and experience. For example, in a particular sequence Stewart goes to Las Vegas to illustrate some of the main aspects of the sceptics' arguments. So instead of primarily interviewing them and showing us data, he creates a visual narrative and through this, and his own presence and narration, he makes the abstract problems extremely present and concrete. When the programme uses data directly, they become very crucial and almost dramatic. This is the case with the famous Michael Mann temperature graph showing the average earth temperature all the way back from 1000 A.D. till today, a graph since supported by other forms of measurements of ice, trees etc. What it shows is, that even though the earth has gone through some dramatic variations of temperature, the last part of 1900 and beginning of 2000 is by far the hottest period ever in the history of earth. But as Stewart points out, this graph of course doesn't tell us the reason for the increase, whether it is man-made or whether other factors are important.

Stewart's three-part documentary series treats most of the arguments and theories on global warming with great clarity, but he also takes a clear stand. This is highlighted for instance in the final part of the second programme, where he deals with the alternative solar theory on global warming. He concludes that the arguments do not hold up, and he also goes against the high-profile Channel 4 documentary, *The Great Global Warming Swindle* (2007), which supports the solar theory of climate change. But the disagreements in science and politics over climate change, and how to understand it and act on the knowledge, continue. In the last part of the series, *Fight for the Future*, he deals with predictions of the future: how will global warming affect us, how bad is it going to get and how drastically do we have to react and change our way of life? The programme is not a doomsday warning, but Stewart again shows very concrete examples around the world where things have changed and nature and man are starting to adapt to this.

There are not many Danish documentaries on climate science and political climate wars, but Lars Mortensen, an independent documentary director with previous experience in the DR-documentary group in the 1990s, has made two documentaries on the Danish scientist Henrik Svensmark, one of the scientists involved in studying the sun and its effect on clouds and the climate. In *The Cloud Mystery* (2008, available on YouTube) the focus is on his theory claiming that variations in solar energy is the most important factor in climate change. In the film, Svensmark takes the role of a scientist going against the dominant paradigm, and being rejected by journals and funding agencies. So the film is mostly about science wars, but it is also a science documentary explaining and demonstrating an alternative climate theory. In the second of the films, *Doomsday Called Off* (2004), the focus is much more on the political and social aspects of the theories on climate change. The focus is on the fact that the two competing scientific discourses, the theory supported by the UN Climate Change Panel and the solar theory, have very different consequences for costs and the nature of actions taken. It is a sign of a healthy diversity in the global documentary, that programmes like Mortensen's are made and widely distributed, although some find them controversial because they diverge from what now seems to be the dominant position in climate change. Disagreement and dialogue, however, are vital for global democracy and discussion.

Nature gone wild – images of catastrophes

Catastrophes are not just the stuff blockbuster Hollywood movies are made of; they are also a very present part of modern documentaries and the daily news. Catastrophes such as the Haiti earthquake in 2010, or Hurricane Katrina in 2005, combine elements of natural disasters that have always been part of life on earth with discussions on how much some of the catastrophes may be influenced by man-made climate change. Catastrophe narratives deal with human suffering on a large scale and they give rise, at least temporarily, to human empathy and actions to help out on an often global scale. Images of nature gone wild, and the enormous powers unleashed on society, show how fragile humans are, how quickly life can be taken and your whole existence can be washed away. Catastrophes are a dramatic and emotional entrance to the big questions and anxieties that lie at the bottom of the climate change debate, and the whole question of whether we have a lifestyle that is part of the problem.

Catastrophes as such are, as already indicated, not directly and primarily linked to present day climate change. The spectacular five-part documentary series *Catastrophe* (Tony Robinson, Channel 4 2008) demonstrates this by taking us back to the birth of the earth and into the present situation. In the final part, *Survival Earth*, the focus is on the last 75,000 years, and man is presented here as a species that has not yet been hit by such forces of nature that have made other species extinct. At the same time, the last part indicates that we may be facing such a challenge. As Tony Robinson says in his opening speech, spoken in a modern railway station:

It is easy to forget, when you are somewhere like this, that the world has suffered from a series of global catastrophes, disasters that have wiped out 99 per cent of all the species that have ever lived. But the forces that wiped out many of our ancestors are still at work today. All we have to protect us is a thin shield between us and the universe, and a thin crust of ground. We humans have been lucky so far, we haven't been threatened by a truly global crisis yet. But history reveals that we are much more at risk than we might think, the big one could be just around the corner.

Robinson's documentary is the story of how vulnerable we are, and this is visually and dramatically underlined by the transformation of the landscape of modernity he is standing in, into a site of dust and fire – the earth after the final disaster.

But how close are we to disaster in our own backyard? That is a question which a number of contemporary documentaries have started asking. In 2010 Channel 4 broadcast *Britain's Big Freeze*, looking at periods of big freeze incidents in the UK in 1947, 1963 and 2009 and asking whether there was a pattern towards more extreme weather due to climate change. The programme combined interviews with experts and eyewitnesses, but also used dramatic visual and narrative documentation. This tendency is further developed in the Channel 4 series of programmes *Britain's Worst Weather* (1–4, 2008), where Nick Middleton from Oxford University guides us through floods, storms, lightning and freezing cold, miniature catastrophe narratives all leading on to the overall question whether this is part of a bigger pattern of climate change. The programme combines clear-cut scientific information and demonstration of the basic phenomenon of nature's forces with a quite performative host, and rather dramatic images and stories of man's meetings with natural forces.

Polluting for profit: corporate dimensions of the ecological crisis

In 2004 Hupert Sauper wrote and directed the Austrian, French and Belgian co-production *Darwin's Nightmare*, a classical documentary dealing with the corporate and political dimensions of our present ecological crisis in many parts of the developing world. The film won the European Film Award for best documentary in 2004. The ecological catastrophe described in the film is, on the one hand, about the destruction of the lake ecosystem in Lake Victoria, Tanzania, where the aggressive Nile Perch was released in the 1960s to secure processed fillets for Russia and other countries, resulting in the extinction of a huge number of endemic species. On the other hand, it is about Western aid to Africa creating imbalances and conflicts created by export and the flow of weapons back into Africa. Since everything is produced for and exported abroad, the local population is paradoxically living in poverty and lack of proper local food.

The film of course has a very local story and context; it is about one particular place in an African nation and the connections between this specific place, Russia and parts of the Western world. But in the opening presentation of the film, Hauber gives the story a broader, more general and mythological meaning. On the screen we read: 'Lake Victoria, the heart of Africa, said to be the birth place of mankind', and thus this particular story is turned into a narrative illustrating the broader ecological crisis of our planet and mankind. As a documentary this is not a classical, journalistic and investigative documentary, although elements of that are certainly present, for example when the director walks around talking to people and asking questions about connections to arms arriving in the same planes that take the fish back to Russia and Europe. The film also takes on a wider political dimension when we listen in on the talks and debates at an international conference dealing with the ecological catastrophe around Lake Victoria.

But *Darwin's Nightmare* is also very much an observational story of a culture and a lifeform in decay. It is a series of human stories, bleak and miserable lives set against magnificent natural landscapes and a potentially rich and happy life that's gone wrong. The film also signals this tragedy by very symbolic, emotional pictures of a landscape in decay and by heartbreaking pictures of starving, sick and deformed children playing among ruins and garbage. We follow the Russian airplane crews with local prostitutes and we learn about the devastating effects of HIV. We experience the perverted economy, where the money from the fishing industry goes into the wrong pockets, and the local fishermen and the workers at the fish factory get next to nothing. We witness how, despite all the fish in Lake Victoria, the local population cannot afford to buy fresh food but live on fish carcasses left over from the production of fish fillets. So in the film, the birthplace of mankind is rotten to the core and an ecological disaster is taking place, destroying the very foundation of local life. This is a symbolic, documentary representation of a broader crisis, and it links the development to corporate interests and to the lack of a global political force that can change the route towards disaster. The UN and Western aid seem to be either inadequate, useless or undermined by corruption.

Throughout the history of modern industrialization, headed by the US and Western Europe, but also involving the big Asian economies, the balance between getting access to oil, coal and other basic resources, and taking the environment and human costs into consideration, has always been precarious. Political control has often failed and only after disasters have demonstrated the potential magnitude of the possible consequences has political action been taken. When, on 24 March 1989, the American oil tanker Exxon Valdez hit a reef and spilled between 11 and 32 million gallons of crude oil off the coast of Alaska, this was called the most devastating man-made environmental disaster ever. But in 2010, a disaster of an even bigger magnitude took place in the Gulf of Mexico, when a BP-owned oil rig exploded and resulted in a massive oil spill, threatening both the general environment and the local fishing industry.

A film clearly illustrating this basic problem and the consequences for the environment, people and animals, is Joe Berlinger's *Crude* (2009). The film deals with the legal action against one of the world's biggest oil companies, Chevron, taken by 30,000 inhabitants of a severely polluted area of the Amazon forest in Ecuador in 1993 and 2001. The film is an intense and complex observational documentary where we follow all groups and parties from the opening of the case and during inspections of the site. We meet and follow the indigenous people, we follow lawyers, activists and politicians, we follow a conflict unfolding with many complex issues representing problems not just in this particular case, but globally. It is not just a film about the clash between corporate interests and the global environment, it is a clash between developed and developing countries, between the needs of Western high modernity and nature and natural resources. The people from Ecuador meet their adversary on their home ground, an alienating experience, but the corporate city people are also brought to Ecuador and the Amazon rain forest. The film focuses on human interactions, confrontations and discussions, but we also witness aspects of media coverage of the case, and of corporate communication and propaganda from Chevron corporate films.

The film is not just an illustrative confrontation between corporate power and populations exposed to the consequences of this power, it is not just a story about different life worlds and about our natural resources and our overexploitation of them, it is also a film with direct journalistic dimensions. On the one hand, we have the chief environmental scientist of Chevron denying any connection between the environmental pollution, damage and sickness of the local people due to their drilling, and on the other hand, we have numerous cases to the contrary documented by both independent scientists and local people that have witnessed the historical development from before Chevron started work there. It seems a clear case of corporate cynicism and indirectly an accusation of the whole political system that has allowed corporate interests to act the way they have done. The strength of the film, compared to news journalism, is the intense human and political drama it unfolds. We go way beyond the courtroom case and into the real life of all the actors and people involved. We witness the result on people and nature directly and can judge for ourselves, and we see how proofs and arguments depend on which side you belong to. The truth in this film is human and concrete, it doesn't just rely on data presented by experts and arguments by lawyers, although these are also important in the film. The film presents us with a case that represents thousands of others around the world, cases where big corporate and political powers have gambled with our future.

The case, which started first against Texaco and since then Chevron, which took over Texaco, was not finished in 2009 when Joe Berlinger's film came out. It took him three years to document the case, and shoot and edit the film, and by the time it was finished Chevron seemed to have a very weak case. However, the final text on the film screen estimates that it could take another ten years to actually sentence Chevron and make them pay compensation to the area and its people. The complexity of these types of cases and the long time it takes to bring them to an end is very visible in many other documentaries dealing with corporate or political liability.

American PBS in 2010 made *Poisoned Waters*, a programme dealing with the long-term pollution of one of the biggest and richest water areas, Puget Sounds/Chesapeake Bay, around Seattle and Tacoma in the state of Washington. For decades companies here have let out toxic waste that now threatens the water, the wildlife and the people living in the area, for instance by polluting the drinking water with cancer-causing PCBs. As the journalist behind the programme states in the presentation, this is a pollution case where there is no single company or actor to blame, it is a question of everyone polluting, and of farmers, industries and the political system allowing this to happen. As he says at the end of the programme:

(...) the condition of the Chesapeake Bay is like the canary in the coal mine. It is a symbol. It is an indicator of what we are now learning to expect in any body of water nationwide and across the planet. Water pollution has slipped off our radar screen in the face of other, seemingly more urgent, crises. But water pollution is a ticking time bomb. It's a chronic cancer that is slowly eating away natural resources that are vital to our very survival (PBS 2012c).

Whereas *Poisoned Waters* clearly points to a broader liability and negligence when it comes to water pollution, the PBS programme *The Spill* (2010) deals with the Mexican Gulf oil catastrophe in 2010, and clearly talks about BP's corporate liability based on countless documented safety violations, and a general corporate culture where high risks were taken to secure large profits for the shareholders. Compared to Berlinger's *Crude*, this PBS programme takes a much more classical, journalistic road. It is a critical, investigative documentary, where the journalist is documenting how BP as a company has for decades developed a very aggressive, profit-seeking global strategy with numerous incidents already that have harmed both workers and the environment.

The Mexico Gulf spill is thus just the biggest incident among many, and a sign of deeper problems in global corporate culture. What also comes out is that BP paid off victims and their families to keep quiet when incidents happened, a strategy also followed in the big Mexican Gulf Spill, but with no great success. This is documented by a classic voiceover narrator and numerous testimonies from outside experts and inside voices from former BP employees. But it is also documented that we are not just talking about corporate responsibility. The Bush administration was also very interested in the deep water drilling in the Gulf of Mexico and encouraged the risky project, promising among other things very low penalties if something should go wrong. The Obama administration also supported deep water drilling, although it enforced tougher measures to control corporations acting in risky areas. The half-hour *Panorama* documentary *BP In Deep Waters* (2010) tells the same story about BP's corporate culture, but at the same time it delivers a much more minute-by-minute account, based on eyewitnesses and experts, of the explosion at the rig that started the whole catastrophe, and the consequences for the locals.

The way we think and live our lives: civic dimensions

Corporate greed, negligence, and lack of political control and interference are a big part of the global challenge we are now facing in terms of the environment and our relation with natural resources. It is also a challenge for each of us as citizens and human beings, it's a challenge that has to do with the way we live our lives and how we think about change. Are we ready to change our consumer habits? Are we willing to think about the products we buy and how they may affect the environment? Are we ready to recycle and buy more expensive but organic products? Are we willing to change the cars we drive or select alternative public transport? These are some of the questions relating to choices each of us will have to make, because in the end consumer choice may also change corporate culture and bad products.

In 2004 the American documentary filmmaker Morgan Spurlock, in the film *Super Size Me*, put his own health at risk by going on a fast food diet, much like the one that numerous Americans live on, and one of the causes not just of a big obesity problem, but also of the serious health problems related to that. It is estimated that more than 100 million Americans have trouble with obesity and the inspiration for Spurlock's film was a failed attempt by two teenage girls to sue McDonald's for having ruined their health. The question Spurlock wants to ask with his film is: 'where does personal responsibility end, and corporate responsibility begin?' The film combines a performative, subjective dimension with all the classical dimensions of the authoritative documentary. On the one hand Spurlock puts himself on a controlled, fast food diet, to document how it affects his body and health, on the other hand he feeds us with information on the fast food culture in America, and how it works and affects us. We hear independent experts, consumers, representatives of the food industry, and we visit schools and talk to both teachers, children and parents, just as we see some of the more drastic effects of obesity and fast food in people that have had to undergo surgery.

Spurlock won the prize for best director at the Sundance Festival in 2004, and the film is a strong mix of satirical entertainment and hugely informative. Instead of preaching or moralizing, the director demonstrates by putting himself at risk, to show what your lifestyle can do to you. You literally experience how to a large degree we are what we eat. The projects is launched with all the elements in place for a real scientific experiment: Spurlock is checked medically before, during and after the 30-day McDonald's diet by no less than three doctors, a nutritionist and a physiologist. But despite the healthy starting point for our hero, the effect on his body is quite shocking, and we witness how he almost cannot swallow the food and vomits. The programme does not only deal with the reality of eating in fast food restaurants and what it does to us. It also deals with how the fast food companies invest in advertising and merchandise and how this creates images present everywhere in our everyday life to such a degree that even small children can immediately recognize the signs and the culture it belongs to. The point made in the film is that the fast food culture has spread from being a corporate culture to also being a culture of school food, and even more importantly, the family eating culture. The line between corporate and personal responsibility is thus paper-thin, and public, regional policies clearly reflect a nation on fast food.

The part of the film where Spurlock engages with children and the school system brings us into the true critical and informational activist side of his project. When he asks children in school, or grown-ups on the street, what a calorie is, for instance, he becomes a popular educator. He wants to change our mental attitudes, our knowledge of food and health, so it's not just about attacking corporate culture, but also about pointing out that consumers can actually change things. But what his personal experiment demonstrates is that a perfectly healthy man can in fact bring his health to the brink of disaster, and even develop an addiction for the kind of food that he actually disgusts. So your own decisions on how you eat and live have a great importance, but addiction is developed, and corporate and political responsibility is obvious too. Spurlock's many calls to the McDonald headquarters have no effect and nobody responds or wants to talk to him about the facts he can present.

A number of PBS programmes deal with the same problem that Spurlock is addressing so vigorously. In Jon Palfrenan's *Diet Wars* (2004) there seems to be some inspiration from Spurlock, but concerning a narrower issue, which is how to get rid of excess weight and obesity. Starting with a visit to an upbeat Weight Watcher's meeting, the journalist puts himself in line for getting rid of his excess weight, a fact he had not earlier focused on. The programme takes a historical look at how American food culture has developed since the 1950s and from there his own route back from being overweight is used as a way to inform viewers on better forms of living and eating. The programme has a clear and pedagogical subjective dimension, and it is also highly informational when it comes to dealing critically with the many types of advice on how to live healthily. So the corporate and political dimension of the food and health issue is far less present in this PBS documentary than in Spurlock's. But the programme ends by pointing to the need for corporate and political responses to this problem.

Other PBS programmes focus more on the corporate and political dimension, and this is also the case with British documentaries. In *Modern Meat* (2002) PBS asks very critical questions about the meat industry, and how they have developed the food we eat, and they also ask questions about the strong connection between the industry and the political system. In *Is Walmart Good for America?* (2004) PBS asks even more critical questions and confronts the biggest and most powerful company in the US. It is not just about their products, but more about how the relentless fight for lower prices and higher profits is harming both product quality and jobs. In the UK the BBC has made similar programmes dealing with both consumer behaviour and choice, and the lack of political control of product quality and information. In *What's Really in Our Kids' Food* (2010) for instance, the BBC addresses the same problem that Spurlock takes up, and with a clear political message. In *Coming Clean* (2001) they attack both the meat industry and the government for negligence, and in *May Contain Nuts* (2009) the critical eye is on the fact that the food declarations are not to be trusted. In *Tax the Fat* (2010) the BBC on the other hand deals with a need for political action to get rid of what Channel 4 in 2003 called the *Fat Plague*. Channel 4 also dealt with the British obesity problem in a much-watched programme called *Generation XXL* (1–2, 2010) where we follow a group of children and youngsters clearly addicted to fast food.

But perhaps one of the most seen and influential documentary films on health and food is the American Robert Kenner's *Food, Inc.* (2008). The film is about how American agricultural production has developed into an unsustainable and unhealthy corporate culture, producing food that is endangering our health but is also polluting our whole environment. The film opens with a sweeping flight over mythological, American rural landscapes, and then a voice

Figures 9c and d: Robert Kenner's Oscar winner *Food, Inc.* (2008) is a strong and very graphic tale of the difference between the image and the reality of modern food culture. Frame grab. Cinematography: Mark Adler.

tells us: the way we produce our food has changed more in the last 50 years than in the previous 10,000, and yet the imagery used to see the food remains the same. The film then zooms back from a picture of a traditional farm and the words 'All Natural – Farm Fresh' in a big supermarket. What the film does is to deconstruct this pastoral fantasy. Talking to images of fruits, vegetables and meat in the supermarket we are told that the way it's sold and packaged is all a fiction that has very little to do with how the products are made. It is a big corporate, industrial system producing food for profit, food that is poor in quality. The link to the development of the fast food concept is shown with a historical perspective. For example, McDonald's is the largest purchaser of beef in America, and other fast food chains dominate other areas: the modern food industry is controlled by a few major corporations.

The film takes us through the real farmlands and behind the scenes of modern food production. Animals are kept in large industrial places and treated and developed according to preset corporate standards. If farmers want to change their production culture they are aggressively attacked and threatened by the big companies. The film is full of facts and arguments, but it also has a strong emotional dimension, not just through the images of inhuman treatment of animals, but also in drawing attention to some of the dire consequences of the industrial production. There is, for instance, the story of a small boy, Kevin, dying of food poisoning, from an E. coli infection, in 10 days. In the film we follow his mother as she turns into an activist, talking to politicians to make them take action to change the food industry. But as the film shows, it's a huge integrated and powerful system, and they lobby heavily to prevent political intervention and regulation. The film also clearly focuses on consumer behaviour and the fact that consumer choices can also change the industry. As is illustrated with one particular family as an example, this choice is mostly virtual, because the bad food is cheap. So, as an expert explains, the cheap food is also an industrial choice, it could be done differently. We are back to the difficult question of personal and corporate responsibility. But the farmers are also key persons, they too can change the system. This is shown in the last part of the film, where we get the story of an organic farmer going back to basics. The film raises some very fundamental questions about our way of life, our food production and the corporate culture that goes with it.

Megacities – mega problems

The problem with finding and using enough energy to sustain a rapidly growing world population is often touched upon in documentaries dealing with both global warming and sustainable growth, and the environment in general. Oil and coal have been in focus, but nuclear power has also been a major issue, and especially the radioactive waste problem. The Three Mile Island accident in the US in 1979 was the first major warning, and since then the Chernobyl disaster in Ukraine in 1986 has been a landmark warning on the safety problems with nuclear power, and the long-term effects on humans and the environment. A bigger population on our globe, and the growing number of big cities, demand high levels of energy, but at the same time those energy sources threaten to cause damage in densely populated areas. There are numerous documentaries on nuclear energy and environmental problems, as demonstrated by the Chernobyl documentaries, for example. Right after the incident the heavy news coverage turned into more background, investigative documentaries and soon also dramatic human stories. One example is *Black Wind, White Land* (1993), initiated and partly financed by The Chernobyl Children Project and directed

Figures 9e and f: Michael Madsen's *Into Eternity* (2010). The problem with getting rid of harmful nuclear waste. Frame grab. Cinematography: Heikki Färm.

by Gene Hoban. As the title and the production background indicates, this is a film about the dire human consequences and especially the consequences for the young and future generations. A similar, human story approach was taken in American Maryan DeLeo's two documentaries, *Chernobyl's Heart* (2003), supported and broadcast by HBO, and the follow-up *White Horse* (2008). We get close to especially children, but also other Ukranians that have serious diseases following the Chernobyl accident, and DeLeo takes us round the area, talking to people and measuring the level of radiation and its impact on the environment.

But environmental documentaries come in many aesthetic forms, and in 2010 Danish director Michael Madsen won the IFDA Green Screen Award with his documentary, *Into Eternity*, a very factual and very poetic documentary about the dilemmas of nuclear waste. In his declaration of what the film is about, Michael Madsen clearly states his creative intentions: 'I am interested in the areas of documentary filmmaking where additional reality is created. By this I mean, that I do not think reality constitutes a fixed entity, which accordingly can be documented, revealed. I suspect reality to be dependent on and susceptible to the nature of its interpretation' (DVD cover). The film is a typical modern, European co-production, with the Danish Magic Hour film as production company, and the British-based Dogwoof Film as distributor. The film was supported by the Danish, Finnish and Swedish Film Institutes, by Nordic Film and TV Fund and also by Eurimages. So it is an independent documentary with a clear independent, creative status, and distributed by a company whose motto is that 'films can change the world'.

The topic of the film is prosaic and scientific: it is about the building of the world's first gigantic underground compound for nuclear waste, Oncala in Finland, a facility constructed to last for the 100,000 years that it is estimated to take for nuclear waste to disintegrate. But as the film progresses, it becomes clear that this is also about the monstrosity of man's endeavour to control nature, the present and the future. It becomes an almost science fiction kind of documentary, with an existential and philosophical approach to civilization, technology and the way in which man has created civilization on this planet. The film uses slow zoom motion pictures, mysterious nature imagery and turns the technological universe we are confronted with into high tech surrealism, and it combines the universe of this underground bunker with montage sequences of natural and man-made disasters and time-lapse sequences of big city images. The specific story of a nuclear waste bunker and the fancy technology and thoughts behind it is combined with a highly symbolic and poetic depiction of a broader reality, of our civilization at the point it has reached after thousands of years. In this way the film raises question about our civilization, about the way we live and the way in which we have treated the natural environment we are placed in.

Michael Madsen situates his film on nuclear waste in a broader context involving man's relation to nature, technology and the development of civilization, and among the contexts indicated we find processes of urbanization and concentration of many people in big cities. In 2010 the Danish Film Institute and DR (the main public service broadcaster in Denmark) launched a series of four remarkable films under the title *Cities on Speed*. Again, this is a clearly socially engaged documentary project, dealing with very concrete global problems, but at the same time the four films represent very different creative and aesthetic strategies. The individual films were produced by some of the best independent documentary production companies (Upfront Film, Bastard Film, Nimbus Film and Danish Documentary Production) and it was distributed through the international festival system, and on European, American and Asian channels. In his introduction to the films, in the booklet accompanying the DVD versions, the project coordinator Kristoffer Horn points to the factual background. Around 1900 about 10 per cent of the worlds population lived in cities. Around the year 2000 this figure had risen to 50 per cent, and future forecasts indicate that by 2050 the number will be 80 per cent. So we are moving to cities all over the globe, and cities are becoming bigger and bigger.

The incentive for making these films, focusing on the four biggest megacities (Shanghai, Mumbai, Cairo and Bogotá) was the combination of fear and fascination connected with big cities as a life form, in Kristoffer Horn's words: 'If the 20th century saw the city as a utopian space – a dream place where everything was possible – the megacities of the 21st century may well turn out to be our nightmare, our nemesis.' What megacities also bring, besides hope to all the different groups of people migrating to them, are also enormous challenges caused by slums, huge inequalities and huge problems with infrastructure, traffic and basic energy supply. Megacities in a way are mirrors enlarging the problems haunting the globe in general.

This is clearly demonstrated in the first of the films, Nana Frank Møller's *Shanghai Space*, characterized by using different types of citizens as identification figures and entry points to the understanding and experience of Shanghai as an urban space. On the one hand we have the amateur photographer Xixian Xu, who is himself threatened by the development of the city, in this case the building of yet another tunnel that will remove his house in one of the older and more traditional parts of the city; on the other hand we have the urban planner and professor Yu Shu, who has utopian, futuristic ideas of developing an underground city where a new kind of environment can be recreated. With his camera Xu is trying to capture and preserve the old parts of town, on the other a completely new town structure is being developed, but in both cases the actual city as it is developed is seen as rather dysfunctional. The film has many layers and forms of factual information, and we get a clear feeling of what kinds of problems and challenges are facing a city of 18 million inhabitants in rapid expansion. But the use of a subjective perspective from two very different vantage points gives the film a more concrete, human dimension, and at the same time the visual and narrative structure of the film creates an extra dimension. In the film we see a combination of horizontal, panoramic views of the city, and more vertical camera movements taking us down to levels below the modern city structure, to the forgotten or dying places or to nature spots. The surface-depth structure of the film illustrates how modern cities have developed as layers on top of older structures, some of which are still there. The director and photographer have deliberately chosen what one might call a very tranquil cinematic language, the narrative and visual rhythm of the film is partly in contrast to the hectic megacity they are portraying, but this form is also chosen to match the mind and personality of the two main characters.

In Camilla Nielsson's and Frederik Jacobi's *Mumbai Disconnected* we also have a character-driven documentary, where three very different people lead us into an exploration of the complex problems related to megacity transport and traffic. Veena Singhai represents the more educated and socially well-to-do activists, she is chairman of the local citizens organization, she knows how to speak up and communicate. Yasin, on the other hand, is an immigrant and one of the city's countless street traders. And finally we have Mr Das, caught up among piles of papers in one of the many public offices that are supposed to solve the complete transport chaos, a chaos with a life of its own that nobody seems to be able to tackle. The directors have called their documentary 'a comedy of infrastructure' and they point to the fact that all Mumbai inhabitants are well aware of the grotesque nature of the chaos they live in, where only miracles and patience seem to make it work. So in a way the characters play out their roles in this comedy, based on their real situation and background and the fact that reality is absurd and grotesque. Singhai is fighting in vain probably, and is on her eighth year against a new highway bridge that will completely destroy their neighbourhood, Das is fighting chaos in his office, in his mind and in the reality of the city, with very little success, and Yasin is just going through with his daily business to survive, in reality hoping to be a Bollywood star and showing his skills in front of the camera. In the meantime the city is growing completely unchecked, with roads and new structures being added on top of old ones, Mumbai is like a cancer cell, only it is not dying. The visual and narrative style in this film is influenced by the frenzy of Mumbai as a city: the shots are often taken on the move, from the backseat of a car, and the rhythm is much more hectic, the montage is rougher and sharper, and both the images and sound give a much stronger experience of this smelly, chaotic and noisy city.

The two last films in the series are formally very different in both style and sub-genre. Mikala Krogh's *Cairo Carbage*, has no main characters, but is a more collective portrait of a city about to drown in its own garbage. We do meet a lot of different people, but no characters become central to the story. The film is also much more classical, authoritative with loads of information and a continued male voiceover guiding us through the film. There is a certain irony and satirical tone, which tells us yet another story of collective megacity chaos against which all good forces fight in vain. People from the municipal authorities, cleaning companies, citizen groups and many more try to contribute to the solution, but the city just seems to live on amidst the garbage, as illustrated in a disgusting fast-motion sequence where we see how the garbage grows and rots. Contrary to the message in the three films mentioned so far, Andreas Dalsgaard's *Bogotá Change*, leaves some hope of change, as the title also indicates. This film is at the same time the most traditional of the films, a portrait of two charismatic mayors, Antanas Mockus and Enrique Penalos, who made a difference. Bogotá was a typical South American nightmare megacity with crime, violence, huge infrastructure problems and very big social differences. But after a strong political effort the city changed and became a model for urban planning and democracy.

Global challenges – global dialogues

Documentaries from both the US and Europe have again and again dealt with global challenges in politics, in migration and in social, cultural and religious conflicts following globalization, and in issues related to global warming and environmental problems. But it is, at the same time, very clear from these documentaries that we do not have the platforms, tools and democratic instruments to properly deal with these global challenges. As citizens of the globe we now have more of a feeling of being part of a global world than ever before, and new social media and digital platforms – and the fact that traditional mass media have a broader global reach – have increased global information and dialogue. But each of us still very much lives in our national, regional and local worlds, and when action is needed, the dialogue much too often becomes an endless debate and fight. Despite that, documentaries seem to converge towards global themes in ways that create a fruitful, global dialogue.

Documentaries in the three countries covered in this part of the book, in many ways, tell the same story of the global challenges in the political system in general, and in relation to the multicultural challenge and the global environmental challenge. Although they vary in form and themes, they raise the same fundamental questions and point to the common need for change and a solution. In the chapter dealing with politicians and the political system there is a general focus on the consequences of the heavy mediatization of politics, but also on the complex relations between corporate power on a global scale and politics, often only on a national and regional scale. The chapter also points to the fact, that although a new digital landscape and many social networks have challenged the traditional media power and political system, it is still very much the more traditional institutions that have the upper hand. In the chapter on the multicultural challenge, the focus is very much on how difficult it is in practice to stick to the universal norms for freedom of speech and human rights when facing cultural and religious groups that do not honour these rights as universal. The global dialogue is often turned into bloody conflict, but many documentaries have tried to show how cultural and religious differences should not in themselves be in conflict with universal norms. By entering a project of trying to portray a multicultural reality in all societies, they invite us to see the world of 'the others' without prejudice, but also without yielding principles of universalism and tolerance. We are all the same under the skin and besides our different beliefs and attitudes – that is the message of the documentaries dealt with here that go behind and beneath multicultural conflicts.

The global climate challenge is perhaps even more visible to us all. The assumption by many experts is that in this area we cannot just continue to discuss, here we need coordinated global action. The documentaries almost all tell that story about different areas within the overall problem – although fundamental disagreement about causes and solutions can also be found. But they also demonstrate how actions must rest on changes on the corporate, political and citizen levels, and how these different actors are more often in confrontation than acting together. If this is true on a national, regional level, it is even more true on the global level. The UN climate conferences indicate this: a lot of confrontational discussion, but very little global action. As the documentary films in all these areas in global politics and challenges show, globalization is very far from resulting in anything remotely like a global public sphere. But they are contributions to a global dialogue that is growing, and is increasingly necessary and important.

Conclusion

Cosmopolitan narratives: documentary in
the new digital media culture

The documentary film and television programmes analyzed in this book could all be called cosmopolitan narratives in the sense that they deal with global challenges, and try to develop narratives based on reality that address us cognitively and emotionally as global citizens. They are also part of a mediatized reality that stretches beyond the nation state and, in different ways, enters into a communicative space of a more global nature than ever before in history. Although we cannot in any way talk about a global public sphere, the new digital media culture and the many new media platforms clearly make transnational communication easier. Studying world television news, Alexa Robertson (2010) has pointed to a clear shift in communicative frames over the last decades. Television news is still very much linked to local and national culture, along with social imaginaries, but has also developed a broader global dimension, 'facilitating encounters with various global others' (Robertson 2010: 9) and thus also the forming of a more cosmopolitan mentality. Global news channels such as BBC World, CNN and Al Jazeera have shifted the balance between traditional national news reporting and news with a more global reach. At the same time, this shift has also influenced national news channels and brought new ways of reporting. With the rise of online digital news platforms this means that the linking of national citizenship and global dimensions has been brought closer together in our everyday culture and daily communicative rituals. Although documentaries are not a normal part of news reporting, the fact that documentaries also take up global issues and challenges points in the same direction to a much larger degree.

Building on arguments formulated by Nick Stevenson in *Cultural Citizenship: Cosmopolitan Questions* (2003), Robertson argues that if culture and citizenship are linked, globalization will clearly influence both dimensions:

> If cultures are no longer assumed to be homogenous and national by definition – a not unreasonable assumption in the twenty-first century – then it no longer makes sense to prioritize the link between the nation and the citizen (…) to talk of cultural citizenship in a cosmopolitan context (…) means developing and appreciation of the ways in which 'ordinary' understandings become constructed (Robertson 2010: 13).

The documentaries analyzed in this book all contribute to the development of a new cosmopolitan narrative and citizenship, to forms of social imagination that transcend the traditional national space. They are part of the new global imaginary Arjun Appadurai talks about (Appadurai 1996) when he points to the global mediatization of cultures, the development of a new global mediascape through which audiences globally are more strongly linked together. Despite asymmetric power structures in the global media industry, this global mediascape nonetheless offers new dynamic ways of cultural exchange and images of what previously were the distant others.

Cosmopolitan realities – cosmopolitan politics

As already remarked on, sociological thinkers like Ulrich Beck, Anthony Giddens and Gerard Delanty have also pointed to the need for cosmopolitan visions in a more concrete political sense. The lesson of phenomenons like the present financial crisis, or climate change and the ecological challenge, is that we are globally in it together and that national solutions have no real value in themselves. This may seem abstract to ordinary people still living and experiencing life from a national and local perspective. But documentaries like those analyzed here bring the global challenges and the global reality much closer to us all. The dominant theme after 2001 of war and terror is also a theme of globalization and how to develop a cosmopolitan understanding. American, British and Danish documentaries have not just told stories about terrorist activity, and nations and soldiers going to war. They have also told stories and created intimate portraits of what we may conceive as the enemy, and as a very different and distant culture and society. As cosmopolitan narratives they have brought the other closer to us, and stressed our common status as global citizens.

These new documentaries have illustrated how global politics is a necessity, no matter how difficult it is, and they have brought the multicultural challenge into our different kinds of national spaces and realities, and our living rooms and daily life, in a very direct way. They have illustrated that handling migration is not just a small and local matter, but part of a global challenge that affects us all, and has to do with global divisions, power structures, and huge differences in conditions of working and living. Documentaries have also demonstrated that the climate challenge is not just a future and distant problem – or an illusion – but very important for our everyday life here and now. By drawing on both cognitive, informative and emotional strategies, by combining rhetoric, narrative and visual forms, documentaries impact our social imaginary and our ability to develop cosmopolitan understandings and visions. They become symbolic and communicative elements for the new cosmopolitan imagination Delanty talks about:

> … the global public impinges upon political communication and other kinds of public discourse creating as a result new visions of social order. To speak of cosmopolitanism as real (…) is thus to refer to these situations, which we may term as the cosmopolitan imagination, where the constitution of the social world is articulated through cultural models in which codifications of both Self and Other undergo transformation (Delanty 2006: 37).

That the global agenda is important, and not just visible in political sociology and documentary film production, can be seen in the EU's cultural policy on globalization, for instance the Commission document *On a European Agenda for Culture in a Globalizing World* (Commission of the European Communities, COM (2007) 242 final). The general aim here is to develop ways in which to contribute to the 'world-wide cultural diversity and intercultural dialogue' and to support the development of a global order 'based on peace, mutual understanding and respect for shared values'. Cultural and communication policy is thus seen as a direct and active part of a global strategy, and the policies for transnational exchange and collaboration within the EU are combined with initiatives for global, external partnerships and forms of cultural collaboration. The challenge of globalization, as many of the documentaries analyzed show, is just as much about dealing with a national reality where a global agenda is present in many forms in both culture, communication and politics, as it is dealing with the national space and culture in a broader regional and global context.

New digital communicative platforms

In May 2013 Danish DR documentary producer Mette Hoffmann Meyer, and the BBC's documentary producer Nick Fraser, received the prestigious Peabody Award for outstanding contributions to public service broadcasting. The main reasons for this prize were their common initiatives *Why Democracy?* (2007) and *Why Poverty?* (2012) (see p. 5f), two unusual examples of a global, collaborative film and media project setting a clear global and cosmopolitan agenda. While the first series focused on culture, democracy and freedom of speech with documentary films from very different parts of the world, the second series focused on the relationship between developed and developing countries, exploitation, conditions of life and poverty. Twenty documentary films from all over the world and a series of short films together with other forms of information were used to establish a global platform for transnational debate and dialogue.

The initiative is impressive as an example of collaboration between established public service broadcasters and national film funding bodies in the making of the films. But the initiative is also impressive as an experiment in global dialogue and distribution, using both traditional platforms and new digital platforms. The films were shown on as many as 70 TV stations in 180 countries, and thus are estimated to have reached about half a billion viewers. But mobile cinemas were also used to reach low-tech parts of the world, and all films and additional material were made available online on the two websites of the two series. The global digital communication and debate on the series is estimated to have generated 33 million tweets and listings on Facebook, and other social sites must be added to that. Even in China the series were seen by 2.7 million people, although in a censored version and with government-monitored access for audiences. The two series, and the project as a whole, clearly illustrates the potentials for a global public sphere and debate in collaborative, international documentary projects, and the cosmopolitan dimension in our modern, digital media culture.

Our use of media is not primarily technology-driven, but it is quite obvious that new technologies can enhance and develop forms of media use that have a clear personal and social function, and new media can make the performing of these functions faster and easier. *Why Democracy?* and *Why Poverty?* are also interesting because they combine different media and communication forms and platforms, and because they represent a collaborative project between well-established media institutions, new grassroots movements and independent individuals and groups on a global level. In the discussion on the new digital media culture, one of the main themes has been the relation between user-driven content and the future role of traditional media. Utopian positions pointing towards a new media democracy based on easy accessible mobile technologies have sometimes clashed with more dystopian positions, for instance in Andrew Keene's *The Cult of the Amateur* (2007). Keen sees the digital development and possibility of very individualized publishing and communication as an undermining of the quality control represented by cultural institutions and the media. Keen puts it very directly:

> In the digital world's never-ending stream of unfiltered, user-driven content, things are indeed not what they seem. Without editors, fact-checkers, administrators, or regulators to monitor what is being posted, we have no one to vouch for the reliability or credibility of the content we read and see on sites like Xanga, Six Apart, Veoh, Yelp, Odeo and countless others. There are no gatekeepers to filter truth from fiction, genuine content from advertising (Keen 2008: 64–65).

Keen illustrates his point with a number of examples of fraud, fiction posted as fact and hoaxes: examples of political slander of candidates during election by people with false identities putting lies on the Internet. One example is the infamous conspiracy movie *Loose Change*, accusing the Bush administration of orchestrating the 9/11 attack themselves, which went to the top 100 of Google video in 2006, and was seen by more than 10 million people.

But even though user-driven content can lead to an overflow of unedited communication and the downfall of some of the gatekeeping and quality control functions of the existing media culture, Keene's pessimism seems unfounded. A counter-example to Keene's understanding of the new user-driven, digital media culture is one of the many new, journalistic internet sites, Paul Thompson's *9/11 Complete Timeline Project*. This is the story of organized grassroots journalism online, supported by a group of creative commons journalists and historians, the Centre for Cooperative Research (see www.historycommons. org/project.jsp?project=911_project). Paul Thomson is an independent investigator who in the months after 9/11 started wondering why some of the news stories about this event and the politics behind it did not add up. For the next three years he started stitching together more than 7000 news stories from mainstream media, simply putting them up for comparison on a timeline. Incredible patterns of contradictions came up, very revealing for top politicians and administrators in the Bush administration. In 2004 his book based on the online timeline, *The Terror Timeline* (Thompson 2004) was published by HarperCollins. What we see here is actually the power of persistent, systematic journalism and research on and through the Internet, and also an example of how online journalism succeeds in setting an agenda in the mainstream media. The publication of the book is the final proof of that, but more important is the fact that the timeline became a major source of information for journalists in the established media, whether network TV or newspapers. The timeline also became a major resource behind the independent documentary film *Press 9/11 for Truth*, which deals with the famous Jersey girls, widows of 9/11 victims, and their search for answers.

So even though blogs and other features of personal communication through the Internet have challenged gatekeepers and traditional mass media, professional media have also taken up the new form of blogs as part of their daily routine and established media often call upon 'citizen journalism' and inputs from ordinary readers and viewers, for instance in the form of video reports from global incidents. With mobile media, local and global community functions have transcended the former restrictions of distance communication. Mobile phones, mobile computers, video-skypeing and sites like Facebook, Twitter and YouTube have made it easier to bond with family, friends and business partners, but also professional media institutions have benefited from this. The decentralization of these easy-to-use technologies is an increase of communicative democracy, and recent global events in both China, Iran, Libya and Egypt show that authoritarian regimes have a hard time keeping the flow of visual information from on-the-spot users out of global media. But although the new mobile technologies can enhance information and the fight for democracy, the new media is also characterized by the ability of established media to develop multimedia strategies.

Converging media – online realities

In 1939, long before the digital revolution, Jorge Luis Borges wrote an essay called 'The Total Library' where he described a chaotic network of all the texts in the world assembled and joined in one system (Keene 2008: 86). Borges' vision is now becoming reality, and one of the truly democratic, social and cultural benefits of the internet revolution is the open access to all sorts of media material that could often be difficult to get, and in the old media culture was often spread among many institutions. Searching, for instance, for documentary material on a specific subject is now often only one click away from wherever you are in the world. Where broadcast media used to exist in linear time, publish and disappear or go into archives, most media today move towards total digital online existence, with all output accessible with or without a certain control. Our public debate can now benefit from a vast digital memory bank that can easily be activated and used at any given moment. So besides giving the ordinary citizen a potential new voice in the public sphere, the new media also gives access to an almost endless pile of information and documentation. There are still national content access barriers for film and television programmes, we are still far from the total, global archive, but the opening up of a global film and television archive is gradually moving forward.

The truly revolutionary dimension of the new digital media culture is no doubt interactivity and convergence, the fact that you can respond and link to all forms of media output and that you can link between different platforms and types of media. This gives room for non-professional and non-profit organizations or individuals to get their stuff out there, and to enter into different forms of dialogue with a potential audience. But even though this can clearly have a democratizing effect on global communication and shift the balance between established players and institutions, the chance of this completely changing the game for documentary film production is slim. As Inge E. Sørensen has demonstrated in her doctoral dissertation *Documentary in a Multiplatform Context* (2013), based on a study of the development of British television, the big stations, BBC and Channel 4, still very much dominate the funding, commissioning and distribution of documentaries. Their monopoly has to some degree been challenged by online funding and distribution, but at the same time the traditional broadcasters have been very good at adapting to the new digital media culture and to integrating online strategies and digital broadcasting in their strategy.

In her article on documentary viewing platforms, Ana Vicente (2008) deals with the relation between television, theatrical distribution and alternative online distribution platforms. Her conclusion is that television so far is the best platform for most documentaries, that a few documentaries have in the recent years made it to some form of theatrical success, giving documentary a status in line with independent feature films, but that the range of new digital distribution platforms (VOD, free online viewing platforms etc.) hold a new promise for broader distribution not yet fulfilled. But even though there are problems to be solved to bring the new digital distribution platforms to their full potential for documentaries, Vicente sees this as part of the future of a much more global documentary. She also points to already known examples, for instance Franny Armstrong's very critical film about McDonald's *McLibel – Two Worlds Collide* (1998), which was broadcast globally by many TV stations but was also distributed as streaming video on the Internet, and which managed to get an audience of 26 million (Vicente 2008: 275f). So here the lesson is exactly the combination of many platforms, both more traditional and more alternative digital forms.

What seems to be happening is not that new, alternative digital forms take over, and that documentary becomes user-driven and user-funded. The situation is rather that old and new technologies merge and converge, they actually supplement each other. Even though user-driven projects and user-driven funding and distribution is also on the rise, creating a greater interactivity of many levels, the collaboration and convergence between users and professionals, either on the creative level or in a broader, institutional sense, seems to be the trend. One example of this is the YouTube platform, where professional content is clearly mixing with more established media institutions and professional output (Burgess and

Green 2009). It is therefore rather typical that YouTube was the site for one of the most global, collaborative documentary projects ever made, *Life in a Day* (2011). This project was a joint venture of Hollywood producer and director Ridley Scott and his Free Scott Production, the YouTube channel and community and National Geographic film. The film was directed by the established British director Kevin MacDonald, but the material for the film consisted of about 4500 hours of footage from people from 192 nations. In total 80,000 short videos were submitted to the YouTube site of the film project, all shot on one day, 24 July 2010.

The film could be called the first truly global and cosmopolitan observational documentary, a snapshot of life on earth in all its forms, all its diversity, but also with pictures of universal structures and feelings that we all share as human beings. The editor of the film, Joe Walker, has said: 'We always wanted to have a number of structures, so it's not just midnight to midnight, but it's also from light to dark and from birth to death … bashing things together and making them resonate against each other and provoking thought' (Walker 2011). The film is a kind of ethnographic essay of cosmopolitanism, on the way in which we see ourselves and thus how different people in different places on our globe choose to present themselves to what they know is a truly global audience. The film demonstrates the power of user-driven content and the Internet as distribution channel: as of June 2013 the film had been seen by 34 million people on YouTube alone, but to that we will have to add the global television audience and the film's presence on other, digital, documentary platforms such as TopDocumentary. The new digital platforms, at least potentially, create global communities, both in terms of production and distribution, and the interactive debate in the form of blogs, comments and links to social networks.

The Internet and digital media in general have given rise to many utopian ideas about the development of a new, active democracy by the people and for the people. But all too often overly high expectations have been put on the technological platform itself, and the infrastructure of it, and too little on the social and cultural context of the citizens and users. Communities basically cannot be created with technology if the social and cultural networks are not there, and if users do not see the benefits or are not motivated to use the technology. However, even though many of these sites and utopian ideas have not proven very successful, there is no need to underestimate the potentials of interactivity and engagement through digital media. After all, a project like *Life in a Day* could never have been made without the existence of open networks and platforms like YouTube and the Internet, and cheap digital cameras that can be used by people outside the developed, high-tech world.

However, aside from the very interesting and important collaborative projects we have looked at involving both ordinary citizens and users and professionals, there is also on the other hand, the ability of the established media to adapt to the new media culture and the more organized grassroots political movements to take advantage of the situation. The US-based *Democracy.now* (see www.democracynow.org) uses the Internet, podcast and web-TV, as well as more traditional media. Their website is also an example of a very developed alternative online journalism. Their daily news show is shown on the web and

Figures 10a and b: Kevin MacDonald's collective YouTube project *Life in a Day* (2010). Local stories from all over the world, in this case Kabul, Afghanistan. Frame grab. Cinematography: Jane Haubrich – and the YouTube contributors.

on independent channels across the US and constitutes one of the very few dissident voices on national television. The *Democracy.now* website is highly professional and diverse in genres and formats, and it shows how media genres and technologies for production and distribution are being developed beyond their original form. Another, somewhat different, US initiative is *MediaChannel* (www.mediachannel.org), founded by Danny Schechter and Rory O'Connor:

MediaChannel exists to provide information and diverse perspectives and inspire debate, collaboration, action and citizen engagement. (...) The vitality of our political and cultural discourse relies on a free and diverse media that offers access to everybody. Journalists and media professionals, organizations and activists, scholars and citizens all need improved access to information, resources and opportunities to reach out and build connections. MediaChannel has been created to meet this need at the dawn of the new millennium (www.mediachannel.org, accessed 1 October 2008).

So what we see here is a movement of critical journalists and political activists trying to create an alternative to the dominant news agenda, and mobilizing people by creating a higher media awareness. The new media environment is used for very well-known critical, political and educational purposes.

Global documentaries – cosmopolitan dialogues

Documentary films were once locked into a few production and distribution forms: cinema, schools, libraries, along with different public and private associations. In many ways, documentary before the arrival of TV had an impressive audience. After the breakthrough of television, documentary film and documentary programmes made for TV got an even broader social platform. But with the arrival of widespread and often transnational digital platforms, as well as TV stations sometimes being given access to already broadcast programmes, with VOD, streaming and different forms of download, the technology has created a potential global network for the distribution of documentary film. There are still national barriers, and other problems in creating this global documentary archive, but at least technologically the potential is there. But this does not in itself create a global public sphere, where documentaries can speak to a wide global audience on the kinds of global problems dealt with in this book. As already said, technology in itself is not enough; there needs to be public demand and a widespread public interest in transnational dialogues.

But despite the fact that we do not yet have a functioning global public sphere, and we have great difficulties in dealing politically with global issues, the documentary agenda since 2000 shows a growing awareness of global challenges and issues. The best proof of this is not just the fact that many documentary directors take up global issues in single documentaries, but that broadcasters such as HBO, PBS, the BBC, Channel 4 and Danish DR have developed strands and thematic focus on some of the big global issues. But another important element in this global development for documentaries is the increase in online platforms that are accessible globally. *Freedocumentaries.org*, for instance, is a site dedicated to bringing socially engaged, independent documentaries out to a broader, global audience. They have, and they carry full documentaries for free from all regions of the world, including Africa and Asia. Other documentary platforms are *Top Documentary Films* (http://topdocumentaryfilms.com) and *All Documentaries* (www.alldocumentaries.org).

There are numerous other sites and also video on demand sites for various purposes. There is a new structuring of the documentary universe of distribution under way, created by the new digital platforms, and on these platforms new and old players are given further possibilities. The new digital media culture, even with all its many defects as a global platform, has certainly increased the possibilities of a global dialogue. It used to be rather difficult to get hold of documentary film and television outside your own national space, but this situation is dramatically changing now. The first condition for these documentary films to act as part of a global and cosmopolitan dialogue is thus being secured. Globalization has moved up the agenda in documentary films since 2000. As this book has demonstrated, they may not change the world, but they are certainly engaging with reality on a global scale.

References

Aitken, Ian (1990), *Film and Reform: John Grierson and the Documentary Film Movement*, London: Routledge.

——— (ed.) (1998), *The Documentary Film Movement: An Anthology*, Edinburgh: Edinburgh University Press.

Anderson, Benedict (1983), *Imagined Communities: Reflections on the Origin and Spread of Nationalism*, London: Verso.

Anderson, Joseph (1996), *The Reality of Illusion: An Ecological Approach to Cognitive Film Theory*, Carbondale: Southern Illinois University Press.

Anderson, Joseph and Barbara Anderson (eds.) (2005), *Motion Picture Theory: Ecological Considerations*, Carbondale: Southern Illinois University Press.

Appadurai, Arjun (1996), *Modernity at Large: Cultural Dimensions of Globalization*, Minneapolis: University of Minnesota Press.

Arthur, Paul (2008), 'The Horror: Paul Arthur on Errol Morris's *Standing Operating Procedure*', *Artforum International*, 46: 8.

Austin, Thomas and Jong, Wilma de (eds.) (2008), *Rethinking Documentary: New Perspectives, New Practices*, New York: McGraw Hill.

Barnouw, Eric (1992), *Tube of Plenty: The Evolution of American Television*, 2nd edn, New York & Oxford: Oxford University Press.

BBC News (2003a) http://news.bbc.co.uk/2/hi/programmes/panorama/3097864.stm. Accessed 7 January 2012.

BBC News (2003b) http://news.bbc.co.uk/2/hi/uk_news/politics/3089999.stm. Accessed 25 July 2012.

BBC News (2012a) http://news.bbc.co.uk/2/hi/programmes/panorama/2858047.stm. Accessed 19 January 2012.

BBC News (2012b) http://news.bbc.co.uk/2/hi/programmes/panorama/4311768.stm. Accessed 19 January 2012.

BBC Panorama (2012) www.bbc.co.uk/programmes/b00yk329. Accessed 8 February 2012.

Beattie, Keith (2004), *Documentary Screens: Nonfiction Film and Television*, New York: Palgrave.

Beck, Ulrich (1992), *Risk Society: Towards a New Modernity*, London: Sage.

——— (2006), *Cosmopolitan Vision*, London: Polity.

Benedict, Ruth (1934/and later editions), *Patterns of Culture*, London: Taylor and Francis.

Benhabib, Seyla (2002), *The Claims of Culture: Equality and Diversity in the Global Era*, Princeton & Oxford: Princeton University Press.

Benkler, Yochai (2006), *The Wealth of Networks: How Social Production Transforms Markets and Freedoms*, New Haven: Yale University Press.

Bennett, W. Lance and Robert M. Entman (eds) (2001), *Mediated Politics: Communication in the Future of Democracy*, Cambridge: Cambridge University Press.

Berger, Peter and Luckmann, Thomas (1966), *The Social Construction of Reality: A Treatise in the Sociology of Knowledge*, New York: Anchor Books.

Billig, Michael (1995), *Banal Nationalism*, London: Sage.

Blogcritics (2012), http://blogcritics.org/video/article/interview-with-phil-grabsky-director-of/. Accessed 26 September 2012.

Bondebjerg, Ib (2012), *Virkelighedsbilleder: Den moderne danske dokumentarfilm*, Frederiksberg: Samfundslitteratur.

——— (2009c), 'Behind the Headlines: Documentaries, the War on Terror and Everyday Life', *Studies in Documentary Film* 3(3): 219–31.

——— (2009b), 'War on Terror – War on Democracy? The Post 9/11 Investigative Documentary', *Northern Lights: Film and Media Studies Yearbook*. 7: September, Bristol/Chicago: Intellect Books.

Bondebjerg, Ib and Jensen, Klaus Bruhn (2009), *Clips – et medieeksperiment*, Report, University of Copenhagen.

Bondebjerg, Ib (2008c), 'Danmarkshistorie – mens den bliver til.' Interview med Christoffer Guldbrandsen', *Ekko*, 43: 50–56.

——— (2008b), 'Dokumentarister på krigstien: militæret i dansk film- og tv-dokumentarisme', *Kosmorama*, 242, pp. 7–25.

——— (2008a), *Virkelighedens fortællinger: Den danske tv-dokumentarismes historie*, Frederiksberg: Samfundslitteratur.

Bordwell, David (1985), *Narration in the Fiction Film*, Madison, Wisconsin: University of Wisconsin Press.

Bovard, James (2003), *Terrorism and Tyranny: Trampling Freedom, Justice and Peace to Rid the World of Evil*, New York: Palgrave Macmillan.

Brannigan, Edward (1992), *Narrative Comprehension and Film*, London: Routledge.

Bruzzi, Stella (2000), *New Documentary: A Critical Introduction*, London: Routledge.

Bullert, B.J. (1997), *Public Television: Politics and the Battle over Documentary Film*, New Brunswick, N.J.: Rutgers.

Burgess, Jean and Joshua Green (2009), *YouTube: Online Video and Participatory Culture*, London: Polity.

Byrd, Robert C. (2004), *Losing America*, New York: Norton & Co.

Canadian Multicultural Act, The (1988).

Carroll, Noël (1983), 'From Real to Reel: Entangled in the Nonfiction Film', *Philosophic Exchange*, 14, pp. 5–45.

Castells, Manuel (1996–2000), *The Network Society: 1–3*, London: Blackwell.

——— (2001), *The Internet Galaxy: Reflections on the Internet, Business and Society*, Oxford: Oxford University Press.

Castles, Stephen (2012), 'Immigration and Asylum: Challenges to European Identities and Citizenship', in Dan Stone (ed.) *The Oxford Handbook of Postwar European History*, Oxford: Oxford University Press, pp. 201–220.

Chandrasekaran, Rajiv (2006), *Imperial Life in the Emerald City: Inside Iraq's Green Zone*, New York: Vintage Books.

Channel 4 (2012) www.channel4.com/news/articles/dispatches/afghanistan+unveiled/514247. html. Accessed 10 February 2012.

Christakis, Nicholas and James Fowler (2010), *Connected: The Amazing Power of Social Networks and How They Shape our Lives*, London: Harper Press.

Christensen, Christian (2009), 'Political documentary, online organization and activist synergies', *Studies in Documentary Film*, 3: 2, pp. 77–94.

Commission of the European Communities, COM (2007) 242 (final), *On a European Agenda for Culture in and Globalizing World*.

Cook, David (ed.) (2000), *Lost Illusions: American Cinema in the Shadow of Watergate and Vietnam, 1970–1979*, New York: Scribner & Sons.

Corner, John and Dick Pels (eds) (2003), *Media and the Restyling of Politics*, London: Sage.

Corner, John (1995), *Television Form and Public Address*, London: Edward Arnold.

———— (1996), *The Art of Record: A Critical Introduction to Documentary*, Manchester: Manchester University Press.

Cowie, Elizabeth (2011), *Recording Reality, Desiring The Real*, Minneapolis: University of Minnesota Press.

Croft, Stuart (2006), *Culture, Crisis and America's War on Terror*, Cambridge: Cambridge University Press.

Damasio, Antonio (1991), *Descartes' Error: Emotion, Reason and the Human Brain*, New York: Avon Books.

———— (1999/2000), *The Feeling of What Happens: Body, Emotion and the Making of Consciousness*, London: Vintage Books.

Delanty, Gerard (2009), *The Cosmopolitan Imagination*, Cambridge: Cambridge University Press.

Dickenson, Ben (2006), *Hollywood's New Radicalism: War Globalisation and the Movies from Reagan to George W. Bush*, London: I.B. Tauris.

Diesen, Jan Anders (2005), *Fakta i forandring: Fjernsynsdokumentaren I NRK 1960–2000*, Oslo: IJ forlaget.

Dovey, Jon (2000), *Freakshow: First Person Media and Factual Television*, London: Pluto.

Doyle, Gillian (2002), *Media Ownership*, London: Sage.

DR-Web (2010), www.dr.dk/OmDR/Nyt_fra_DR/Nyt_fra_DR/2010/08/27105914.htm. Accessed 3 September 2010.

Durham, Chris (2008), 'The Road to Guantanamo: A Commentary', *Communication, Culture & Critique*, 1: 2, pp. 222–6.

Ellis, Jack C. and Betsy A. McLane (2006), *A New History of Documentary Film*, New York: Continuum Books.

Esping, Ingrid (2007), *Dokumentärfilmen som tidsresa – Modstrilogin*, PhD dissertation, University of Lund.

Evans, Rob and Chris Tryhorn (2006), 'Public has a right to know why BBC apologized after Hutton, Dyke says', *The Guardian*, 21 December.

Faludi, Susan (2007), *The Terror Dream: Fear and Fantasy in Post 9/11 America*, New York: Metropolitan.

Fassihi, Farnaz (2008), *Waiting for an Ordinary Day: The Unraveling of Life in Iraq*, New York: Public Affairs.

Ferguson, Charles (2008a), *No End in Sight: Iraq's Descent into Chaos*, New York: Public Affairs.

———— (2008b), *Interview by Ib Bondebjerg*, New York, August, 2008.

Fiske, Susan T. and Shelley E. Taylor (1991), *Social Cognition*, New York: McGraw Hill.

Free Cinema Manifesto (1956).

Furuhammer, Leif (1995), *Med TV i verkligheten*, Borås: Stiftelsen etermedier i Sverige.

Gellner, Ernest (1983), *Nations and Nationalism*, London: Blackwell.

German Marshall Fund (2011), *Transatlantic Trends: Immigration 2011*, see: www.gmfus.org/archives/transatlantic-trends-immigration-2011. Accessed 20 August 2012.

Giddens, Anthony (2011), *The Politics of Climate Change*, 2nd edn, London: Polity.

Goddard, Peter, John Corner and Kay Richardson (2007), *Public Issue Television: World in Action, 1963–98*, Manchester: Manchester University Press.

Goffman, Erwin (1959), *The Presentation of the Self in Everyday Life*, New York: Anchor Books.

Goldie, Grace Wyndham (1977), *Facing the Nation: Television and Politics 1936–1976*, London: Bodley Head.

Goldschmidt, Jack (2007), *The Terror Presidency: Law and Judgment Inside the Bush Administration*, New York: W.W. Norton & Co.

Goodman, Ellen (1998), 'A Jefferson for Our Times', *Boston Globe*, Column, 5 November.

Gore, Al (2009), *Our Choice – A Plan to Solve the Climate Crisis*, New York: Rodale Inc.

Gottschall, Jonathan (2012), *The Storytelling Animal: How Stories Make Us Human*, Boston: Houghton, Miffin, Harcourt.

Grant, Barry S (ed.) (2006), *Five Films by Frederic Wiseman*, Berkeley and Los Angeles: University of California Press.

Green, Felix (1964), *A Curtain of Ignorance*, New York: Doubleday.

Grodal, Torben (1997), *Moving Pictures: A New Theory of Film, Genres, Feelings and Cognition*, Oxford: Oxford University Press.

———— (2009), *Embodied Visions: Evolution, Emotion, Culture and Film*, Oxford: Oxford University Press.

Habermas, Jürgen (1989), *The Structural Transformation of the Public Sphere*, Cambridge: Polity.

Hannerz, Ulf (1996), *Transnational Connections: Culture, People, Places*, London: Routledge.

HBO (2009), www.hbo.com/docs/programmes/baghdadhospital/interview.html. Accessed 13 May 2009.

HBO (2012a), www.hbo.com/documentaries/section-60-arlington-national-cemetery/index.html#/documentaries/section-60-arlington-national-cemetery/interview/jon-alpert-and-matthew-oneill.html. Accessed 9 February 2012.

HBO (2012b), www.hbo.com/documentaries/love-crimes-of-kabul/index.html#/documentaries/love-crimes-of-kabul/interview/tanaz-eshaghian.html. Accessed 10 February 2012.

Held, David, Anthony McGrew, David Goldblatt, and Jonathan Paerraton (1999), *Global Transformations: Politics, Economics and Culture*, Stanford: Stanford University Press.

Held, David and Anthony McGrew (2000), *The Global Transformation Reader: An Introduction to the Globalization Debate*, London: Polity.

Herman, Edward S. and Robert W. McChesney (1997), *The Global Media: The New Missionaries of Corporate Capitalism*, London & Washington: Cassell.

Highmore, Ben (2002), *Everyday Life and Cultural Theory: An Introduction*, London: Routledge.

Hitchens, Christoffer (2001), *The Trials of Henry Kissinger*, London: Verso.

Hill, Annette (2007), *Restyling Factual TV: Audiences, News, Documentary and Reality Genres*, London: Routledge.

Hjarvard, Stig (2013), *The Mediatization of Culture and Society*, London: Routledge.

Hjarvard, Stig, Nete Nørgaard Kristensen and Mark Ørsten (2003), *Mediernes dækning af invasionen af Irak 2003*. Working Paper no. 13. Center for Media and Democracy in the Network Society, University of Copenhagen.

Hjarvard, Stig (1999), *TV-nyheder i konkurrence*, Frederiksberg: Samfundslitteratur.

Hjort, Mette (2009), 'Living with diversity: What difference can film-making make', *Northern Lights*, 7, pp. 9–27.

Hjort, Mette, Ib Bondebjerg and Eva Novrup Redvall (2013), *The Danish Directors 3: Dialogues on the New Danish Documentary Cinema*, Bristol/Chicago: Intellect.

Holland, Patricia (2006), *The Angry Buzz: This Week and Current Affairs Television*, London: I.B. Taurus.

Holtug, Nils (2012), 'Danish Multiculturalism, Where Art Thou?', in Raymond Taras (ed.), *Challenging Multiculturalism: European Models of Diversity*, Edinburgh: Edinburgh University Press, pp. 190–215.

Höijer, Birgitta (1992a), 'Reception of Television Narration as a Socio-cognitive Process: A Schema-theoretical Outline', *Poetics* 2, pp. 283–304.

—— (1992b), 'Socio-cognitive Structures and Television Reception', *Media, Culture and Society*, 14, pp. 583–603.

Jaramillo, Deborah (2009), *Ugly War – Pretty Package*, Bloomington, Indiana: Indiana University Press.

Kahana, Jonathan (2008), *Intelligence Work: The Politics of American Documentary*, New York: Columbia University Press.

Katz, Elihu and Liebes, Tamar (1990), *The Export of Meaning: Cross-cultural Readings of Dallas*, London: Wiley Blackwell.

Katovsky, Bill and Carlsson, Timothy (2003), *Embedded: The Media and the War In Iraq*, Lyons Press.

Keen, Andrew (2007/2008), *The Cult of the Amateur*, New York: Doubleday.

Kellner, Douglas (2010), *Cinema Wars: Hollywood Film and Politics in the Bush-Cheney Era*, London: Wiley Blackwell.

Krugman, Paul (2003),' New Year's Resolutions'. *New York Times*, December 26, 2003.

Kymlicka, Will (1995), *Multicultural Citizenship: A Liberal Theory of Minority Rights*, Oxford: Oxford University Press.

Lakoff, George and Mark Johnson (1980), *Metaphors We Live By*, Chicago & London: University of Chicago Press.

Lakoff, George (2008), *The Political Mind*, New York: Tantor Media.

Margulies, Joseph (2006), *Guantanamo and the Abuse of Presidential Power*, New York: Simon & Schuster.

Mayer, Jane (2008), *The Dark Side: The Inside Story of How the War on Terror Turned into a War on American Ideals*, New York: Doubleday.

McEnteer, James (2006), *Shooting the Truth: The Rise of American Political Documentaries*, Westport: Praeger.

McNair, Brian (2006), *Cultural Chaos: Journalism, News and Power in a Globalized World*, London: Routledge.

Meyrowitz, Joshua (1985), *No Sense of Place: The Impact of Electronic Media on Social Behavior*, Oxford: Oxford University Press.

Miller, Toby (2005), *Global Hollywood*, London: BFI.

Mjos, Ole J. (2010), *Media Globalization and the Discovery Channel Networks*, London: Routledge.

Morrison, David E. (1992), *Television and the Gulf War*, London: John Libbey.

Muller, Richard A. (2012) 'The Conversion of a Climate-Change Skeptic', www.nytimes.com/2012/07/30/opinion/the-conversion-of-a-climate-change-skeptic.html?pagewanted=all. Accessed 16 August 2012.

New Europeans (2011), European Commission. Special Eurobarometer Report.

Nichols, Bill (2001), *Introduction to Documentary*, Bloomington: Indiana University Press.

Nørgaard Kristensen, Nete and Mark Ørsten (eds. 2006), *Krigen i medierne, mediernes krig*. Frederiksberg: Forlaget Samfundslitteratur.

PBS (2012a) www.pbs.org/wgbh/pages/frontline/choice2008/view/. Accessed 23 February 2012.

PBS (2012b) www.pbs.org/wgbh/pages/frontline/shows/muslims/etc/script.html. Accessed 24 July 2012.

PBS (2012c) www.pbs.org/wgbh/pages/frontline/poisonedwaters/etc/script.html. Accessed 17 September 2012.

Pilger, John (2012a) 'The New Rulers of the World', www.johnpilger.com/videos/the-new-rulers-of-the-world. Accessed 23 April 2012.

—— (2012b) 'The War on Democracy', www.johnpilger.com/videos/the-war-on-democracy. Accessed 23 April 2012.

Pilkington Report (1962), *Report of the Committee on Broadcasting 1960*, London: HSMO.

Plantinga, Carl (1997), *Rhetoric and Representation in Nonfiction Film*, Cambridge: Cambridge University Press.

—— (2009), *Moving Viewers: American Film and the Spectator's Experience*, Berkeley: University of California Press.

Power, Samantha (2002), *A Problem from Hell*, New York: Basic Books.

Priest, Dana (2003), *The Mission: Waging War and Keeping Peace with America's Military*, New York: W.W. Norton.

Priest, Dana and William Arkin (2011), *Top Secret America: The Rise of the New American Security State*, New York: Litte Brown and Company.

Primeur, Francois (2007), *American Dissident: The Political Art of Michael Moore*, Napa: Lulu Press.

Prince, Stephen (2009), *Firestorm: American Film in the Age of Terrorism*, New York: Columbia University Press.

Reeves, Byron and Clifford Nass (1996), *The Media Equation: How People Treat Computers, Television and New Media Like Real People and Places*, Cambridge: Cambridge University Press.

Renov, Michael (2004), *The Subject of Documentary*, Minneapolis: University of Minnesota Press.

Roscoe, Jane and Craig Hight (2001), *Faking It: Mock-documentary and the Subversion of Factuality*, Manchester: Manchester University Press.

Robertson, Alexa (2010), *Mediated Cosmopolitanism*, Cambridge: Polity.

Rumelhart, David (1980), 'Schemata: The Building Blocks of Cognition', in Bertram Bruce, Rand Spiro and William Brewer (eds), *Theoretical Issues in Reading and Comprehension*, Hillsdale: N.J. Erlbaum, p. 99–135.

Saunders, Dave (2007), *Direct Cinema: Observational Documentary and the Politics of the Sixties*, London: Wallflower Press.

Scannel, Paddy (1996), *Radio, Television & Modern Life*, London: Blackwell.

Schechter, Danny (2008), *Interview by Ib Bondebjerg*, New York, August 2008.

—— (2006a), *When News Lies: Media Complicity and the Iraq War*, New York: Select Books.

—— (2006b), 'Countering Journalistic Jingoism', www-forusa.org. Accessed October15 2008.

—— (2004), *Weapons of Mass Deception*, New York: Cinema Libre.

Schlesinger Jr, Arthur (2004), *War and the American Presidency*, New York: Norton & Co.

Shudson, Michael (1998), *The Good Citizen: A History of American Civic Life*, New York: The Free Press.

Schutz, Alfred (1932/eng. Version 1967), *Phenomenology of the Social World*, Evanston, Illinois: Northwestern University Press.

Smaill, Belinda (2010), *The Documentary: Politics, Emotion, Culture*, London: PalgraveMacMillan.

Smith, Anthony D. (1998), *Nationalism and Modernism*, London: Routledge.

Stevenson, Nick (2003), *Cultural Citizenship: Cosmopolitan Questions*, Maidenhead: Open University Press.

Stjernfelt, Frederik and Martin Eriksen (2012, Danish edition 2008), *The Democratic Contradictions of Multiculturalism*, London: Telos.

Svendsen, Adam (2010), *Intelligence Cooperation and the War on Terror: Anglo-American Security Relations after 9/11*, London: Routledge/Studies in Intelligence Series.

Swinson, Arthur (1955), *Writing for Television*, London: Adam & Charles Black.

Swann, Paul (1989), *The British Documentary Film Movement 1926–1946*, Cambridge: Cambridge University Press.

Sørensen, Inge Ejby (2013), *Documentary in a Multiplatform Context*, PhD dissertation, University of Copenhagen.

—— (2012), 'Crowdsourcing and Outsourcing: The Impact of Online Funding and Distribution on the Documentary Film Industry in the UK', *Media Culture & Society*, 34(6), pp. 726–43.

—— (2012), 'Newsjacking the Media: Video Ambushing and AV Astroturfing', in Kevin Howley (ed.), *Media Interventions*, London: Peter Lang.

Taylor, Charles (2004), *Modern Social Imaginairies*, Durham and London: Duke University Press.

—— (1992, original, republished 1994), 'The Politics of Recognition', in Amy Gutmann (ed.) *Multiculturalism: Examining the Politics of Recognition*, Princeton: Princeton University Press. 1994: 25–73.

Thompson, John. B. (2000), *Political Scandal: Power and Visibility in the Media Age*, London: Polity.

Thompson, Paul (2004), *The Terror Timeline*, New York: HarperCollins.

Thussu, Daya T. (2006), *Media on the Move: Global Flow and Contra-Flow*, London: Routledge.

Tomlinson, John (1999), *Globalization and Culture*, London: Polity Press.

Toplin, Brent (2006), *Michael Moore's Fahrenheit 9/11: How one Film Divided a Nation*, Kansas: University of Kansas Press.

TV2 (2009) http://omtv2.tv2.dk/index.php?id=3852. Accessed 3 September 2011.

Tumber, Howard and Palmer, Jerry (2004), *Media at War: The Iraq Crisis*, London: Sage.

UNESCO Declaration 174/EX 46 (2006).

Walker, Joe (2011), Interview in *Wired Magazine*, July 29, 2011.

Westin, Alan (1974), 'You Start Off with a Bromide: Conversations with Film Maker Frederick Wiseman', *Civil Liberties Review*, 1: 2, p. 60.

Vicente, Ana (2008), 'Documentary Viewing Platforms', in Thomas Austin and Wilma de Jong (eds.), *Rethinking Documentary: New Perspectives, New Practices*, New York: McGraw Hill, pp. 271-7.

Vidal, Gore (2004), *Imperial America: Reflections on the United States of Amnesia*, New York: Nation Books.

Wall Street Journal Online, 28 April 2007, Interview with Alex Gibney.

Westen, Drew (2007), *The Political Brain: The Role of Emotions in Deciding the Fate of the Nation*, New York: Public Affairs.

Winston, Brian (1995), *Claiming the Real*, London: BFI.

Wolterstorff, Nicholas (1980), *Works and Worlds of Art*, Oxford: Clarendon Press.

Zerubavel, Eviatar (1997), *Social Mindscapes: An Invitation to Cognitive Sociology*, Cambridge Massachusetts: Harvard University Press.

Zoonen, Lisbet van (2005), *Entertaining the Citizen: When Politics and Popular Culture Converge*, Oxford: Rowman & Littlefield Publishers.

Index of names and titles

(All names and all film and TV titles)

½ Revolution (2011)
11th Hour, The (2007)
21 Days to Baghdad (2003)
24 (2001–2010)
60 Minutes (1968–)

Abbott, Jenifer
Abid, Kasim
About Baghdad (2004)
Achbar, Mark
Accidental President, The (2001)
Act of Killing, The (2012)
Afghan Star (2008)
Afghanistan – Never Mind the Taliban (2006)
Afghanistan – The Dark Ages (2001)
Afghanistan Unveiled (2005)
AFR (2007)
After Saddam (2003)
Age of Stupid, The (2009)
Agnew, Spiro
Agony of Vietnam (ABC, 1965)
Ahmad, Fenar
Ahmed, Zeena
Al-Adhadh, Riyadh
Al-Assad, Bashar
Albright, Madeleine
Al-Sadr, Mohammed
Alive Day Memories: Home From Iraq (2007)
Allende, Salvador
Alpert, Jon
Alvi, Suroosh
Ambassador, The (2011)
America at a Crossroad (Series, 2007–2009)

American Experience (1988–)
American Masters (1986–)
Anderson, Barbara
Anderson, Ben
Anderson, Benedict
Anderson, Joseph
Andet Europa, Det (2006)
Antonio, Emilio
Appadurai, Arjun
Apted, Michael
Arkin, William
Armadillo (2010)
Armstrong, Franny
Assange, Julian
Ascent of Money, The (2009)
Asylum Game, The (2003)
Attenborough, David
Auken, Sven
Austin, Thomas

Babel (2006)
Babylon i Brøndby (1996)
Baghdad ER (2006)
Baghdad High (2008)
Baghdad Hospital: Inside the Red Zone (2008)
Bakrawi, Janus Nabil
Banding File (series, 1985–91)
Barnouw, Eric
Bath, James
Battle for Basra, The (2003)
Battle for Bomb Alley, The (2011)
Battle for Europe (2005)
Battle for Haditha (2007)

Engaging with Reality